THE POWER OF PERSEVERANCE

THE POWER OF PERSEVERANCE

SIR MAHESH PATEL'S
Pioneering Journey

PAUL UPHAM

First published in India by HarperCollins *Publishers* India 2024
4th Floor, Tower A, Building No. 10, DLF Cyber City,
DLF Phase II, Gurugram, Haryana – 122002
www.harpercollins.co.in

2 4 6 8 10 9 7 5 3 1

Copyright © Paul Upham 2024
Inside photos courtesy of Sir Mahesh Patel

P-ISBN: 978-93-6569-217-4
E-ISBN: 978-93-6569-318-8

The views and opinions expressed in this book are the author's own and the facts are as reported by him, and the publishers are not in any way liable for the same.

Paul Upham asserts his moral right
to be identified as the author of this work.

All rights reserved. No part of this publication may be reproduced, stored in a retrieval system, or transmitted, in any form or by any means, electronic, mechanical, photocopying, recording or otherwise, without the prior permission of the publishers.

Typeset in 11.25/15 Sabon LT Std at
HarperCollins *Publishers* India

Printed and bound at
Thomson Press (India) Ltd

This book is produced from independently certified FSC® paper
to ensure responsible forest management.

*For my mother, Savitaba, and my wife, Usha,
the two people who had the most impact
on my life.*
—Sir Mahesh Patel, OBE

Contents

Introduction	1
Prologue : Queen Elizabeth II in Fiji, 1970	3
Chapter 1 : Gujarat	5
Chapter 2 : Fiji	9
Chapter 3 : New Zealand	19
Chapter 4 : Papua New Guinea	29
Chapter 5 : England	40
Chapter 6 : City Pharmacy	52
Chapter 7 : Australia	62
Chapter 8 : India	72
Chapter 9 : Sydney	85
Chapter 10 : Worldview	94
Chapter 11 : Order of the British Empire	103
Chapter 12 : Giving Back	113
Chapter 13 : Fires and Ashes	125
Chapter 14 : Knight Bachelor	140
Chapter 15 : Business Life	155
Chapter 16 : Mentor	168

Chapter 17 : Missteps	182
Chapter 18 : Where Are You From?	196
Chapter 19 : Passion and Perspective	205
Chapter 20 : Port Moresby, November 2022	218
Chapter 21 : Fate and Karma	257
Chapter 22 : Tomorrow	263
Chapter 23 : The Ganges	270
Epilogue	275
Acknowledgements	285
List of People Interviewed	287
Notes	289

Introduction

Sir Mahesh Patel, OBE, walks into a room, and immediately all eyes and ears focus on him—his passion and enthusiastic, childlike smile, his joyous love of life attract and energize everyone around him.

He assures me that we first met in 2008. Yet, to my embarrassment, I do not remember.

I was working in property management at the time. Sir Mahesh can describe our conversation in such detail that I know the meeting must have occurred. His command and recall of the personal details of those he encounters around the world are superior to most.

It was my good fortune to meet Sir Mahesh and his wife Lady Usha again in 2013, which I certainly do recall. Over time, a personal relationship was formed.

In late 2021, Sir Mahesh read my 2007 biography of world champion boxer Kostya Tszyu and a separate fictional feature film script that I was developing. He kindly entrusted me with the task of putting into words his amazing life story. I am honoured to do so.

In researching this book, it became apparent even those closest to him do not know the full Sir Mahesh Patel story. Of course, his many geographical relocations over the years have contributed to the misplacing of many pieces of the historical jigsaw.

I was determined to bring them all together and paint in words the life of Sir Mahesh Patel in full colour and, with his strong encouragement, record the imperfections as well.

This is a complete view of a husband, father, family member, businessman, philanthropist and friend. Now, you can read the inspiring story of Sir Mahesh Patel and marvel at his perseverance, his achievements and the many amazing things about him you did not know.

Prologue

Queen Elizabeth II in Fiji, 1970

It was a hot, sunny autumn morning on 5 March 1970, when the British royal yacht *Britannia* sailed into the port of Suva. Queen Elizabeth II was on a special tour of Fiji. This archipelago of 330 emerald islands set in the blue South Pacific Ocean had become a British Crown colony under Queen Victoria's rule on 10 October 1874. The royal visit was in preparation for a historic event: the granting of independence to its people and the formation of the Dominion of Fiji.

The Queen, resplendent in green dress, complementing hat and white gloves, stepped ashore and was presented with a bouquet of flowers by a young Fijian girl in local traditional dress.

The Queen, accompanied by Prince Philip, the Duke of Edinburgh, dressed in his white Royal Navy uniform, moved forward, and both waved to the thousands in attendance, who had waited patiently, hoping to see the reigning monarch in person. The couple were then officially welcomed and treated to a traditional Fijian tribal dance known as *Meke i wau*, which is performed only for high chiefs.

Later, thousands of Fijian school children lined the main streets waving British flags, as the Queen and her cavalcade of motor vehicles approached.

Eleven-year-old Maheshbhai Patel, with his beaming grin, cheered enthusiastically and waved, as the popular monarch slowly drove by.

As unlikely as it would seem for two individuals so far apart in status and geographical location, forty-two years later, in Buckingham Palace, Queen Elizabeth II and that same Fijian boy of Indian heritage would reminisce together and smile, talking about that warm Pacific day.

Chapter 1

Gujarat

Gujarat is the westernmost state in India and has 1,600 kilometres of beautiful coastline stretching along the Arabian Sea. It is the fifth-largest Indian state by area. The capital is Gandhinagar and its largest city is Ahmedabad. Gujarati is the state's official language. Gujarati food is primarily vegetarian.

The Gujarati people have a rich history of commercial activity, dating back centuries. Their trade with other civilizations, including Egypt and Bahrain, aided Gujarat's development immensely. They specialized in arranging shipping and trade across the Indian Ocean.

Tomé Pires, a Portuguese colonial administrator and diplomat who visited India in the early sixteenth century, wrote of the Gujarati traders: 'These [people] are [like] Italians in their knowledge of and dealings in merchandise ... They are diligent, quick men in trade.'

Two men who played significant roles in the civil rights of Indian people and their country's eventual independence, were born and raised in Gujarat.

Mohandas Karamchand Gandhi, known the world over as Mahatma Gandhi, is venerated for his non-violent struggle against British rule in India. Born in Porbandar in 1869, Gandhi was an Indian lawyer and anti-colonial nationalist who led the successful campaign for India's independence, won in 1947. Further, Gandhi held strong beliefs in the rights of women and urged 'women to fight for their own self-development'.

Vallabhbhai Patel was born in Nadiad in 1875. He was also known as Sardar Patel—'Sardar' means 'chief' in Hindi, Urdu, Bengali and Persian. He was an Indian lawyer who became an influential political leader. One of Mahatma Gandhi's earliest political allies, and a senior leader of the Indian National Congress, he played a prominent role in the country achieving independence. He was the first deputy prime minister and home minister of the newly independent India, from 1947 to 1950.

Both Gandhi and Patel are considered by many as the founding fathers of the Republic of India, highly respected for their personal sacrifices and unconditional community service.

Bhagwanbhai Ishwarbhai Patel and his wife Jiviben Patel lived in Mandala, a village in Dabhoi Taluka in the Vadodara district of Gujarat. Bhagwanbhai worked as a booking clerk at the local Mandala railway station.

Their second daughter, Savitaben Patel, was born on 31 May 1929. Her parents named her Savita upon seeing their child's amazing glowing complexion. 'Savita' means the sun; It can also mean a humanitarian and generous individual. 'Ben' means sister, and is used as an honorific as part of the name to denote respect. 'Bhai', meaning brother, is similarly attached to male names.

Savitaben lived with her five sisters, Shantaben, Kantaben, Kapilaben, Manjulaben and Jayaben, and one brother, Dahyabhai. Tragically, Dahyabhai died of smallpox at the age of eight.

Shortly after, when her sister Shantaben sadly died from a mystery illness, Savitaben became the oldest sibling of the family. She took on the role of big sister to her four younger sisters. She accepted the role passionately, promising her parents that she would always take care of her siblings.

Bhagwanbhai and Jiviben Patel held strong beliefs in religion and culture. They followed the tenets of the Swaminarayan faith with complete devotion. It is a branch of Hinduism, which was founded by the yogi and ascetic Shree Swaminarayan, at the end of the eighteenth century in Northern India.

The Swaminarayan followers adopt his teachings of practising high morals, love and compassion for all, irrespective of caste, creed, colour or gender. He encouraged charity towards those less fortunate and education for everyone, including lower castes and women, which was unheard of at the time.

At the age of seven, Savitaben was taken to their local temple and formally initiated into the Swaminarayan faith. The Swami (the then head of the sect) blessed her and, as was traditional, gave her a personal secret Swaminarayan mantra as a lifelong chant. She became a devout follower.

With the strong encouragement of her parents, Savitaben attended school and joined the Girl Guides movement. She was an avid reader. She believed these helped her maintain 'good mental and physical health'.

But life would change for Savitaben at the age of eleven. Her parents decided it was time for her to discontinue her schooling and prepare for marriage, as was the tradition at the time in the Patel community.

While disappointed by the decision, Savitaben accepted it as a dutiful daughter and prepared for her new training, working with her mother to manage the home in preparation for her betrothal.

Two years later in 1942, at the age of thirteen, Savitaben's marriage was arranged with Maganbhai Patel, son of Prabhudas Patel, from a respectable family in the Karkhadi village. The wedding was held over four days at Savitaben's home in Mandala.

After two years of getting to know each other, when Savitaben was fifteen, both families agreed that Savitaben and Maganbhai were now ready to live together in Karkhadi.

Prabhudas Patel had built a large home for his four school-educated sons and owned separate farming land. Maganbhai worked on the family farm with his brothers, managing the farm staff, the sale of the produce and the accounts.

At the age of seventeen, Savitaben became pregnant and, as was the tradition, she returned to her parents' home in Mandala for the birth of first daughter Taraben. Two years later, sister Kusumben arrived. The new parents rejoiced at the blessings they had received.

Sir Arthur Hamilton Gordon was appointed Governor of Fiji in June 1875 by the British. In 1878, Gordon decided to import indentured labourers from India, making use of a British scheme to assist their regional colonies. It was a substitute for slave labour, following the abolition of the trade in the early nineteenth century. The Indian workers, employed on five-year contracts, were paid and worked in the sugar cane fields in Fiji. The same scheme was used to send Indian workers to the Caribbean, South Africa, Mauritius, Sri Lanka, Malaysia and Myanmar, creating the many Indian diasporas around the world today.

While the indentured labour scheme was discontinued in the 1920s and many of the workers returned home to India, many remained in Fiji to earn a living, thus creating a pathway between India and Fiji.

Maganbhai Patel's brother Chhotabhai had settled in Fiji. He sponsored Maganbhai and Savitaben, who were granted a permit to live and work in Fiji. At the age of only twenty and now married for seven years, Maganbhai and Savitaben Patel, made the difficult life-changing decision to relocate to Fiji with daughters Taraben and Kusumben. In 1949, the young family boarded a train in Karkhadi and travelled via Vadodara and Bombay (now Mumbai) and then to Calcutta (now Kolkata).

After a two-week wait in Calcutta, the family boarded the *Orma*, which made regular trips ferrying passengers to and from Suva, the capital of Fiji. The voyage to their new home took twenty-eight days and nights.

Savitaben would say of the journey in later years when telling her life story to relatives: 'The sun had set in India and risen in Fiji.'

Chapter 2

Fiji

Maganbhai Patel and Savitaben, with daughters Taraben and Kusumben, arrived in Fiji in 1949. They moved in with Maganbhai's older brother Chhotabhai Patel and his wife Chancharben, who had arrived eight years earlier and had settled down in Ba, a town in the northwestern part of Viti Levu, the largest island of Fiji. (Incidentally, in Gujarati, 'ba' means 'respected lady' and is used as an honorific appended to senior women's names.) Chhotabhai had set up a grocery and general shop in the main street of Ba, with a two-storey house built of wood and tin just behind it. Maganbhai, Savitaben and their daughters moved into the lower storey.

Savitaben later recalled her initial impressions of Fiji. 'It was a green and fresh landscape everywhere and not as many people as there were in Mandala and Karkhadi.'

Chhotabhai asked Maganbhai to manage the business for him. Their new company name was C.P. Patel. They sold food grains, sugar, oil, onions, potatoes and fruits in one part of the store, and general merchandise in the other.

Maganbhai and Savitaben worked long hours to make the business an eventual success. But the early days were difficult. Maganbhai's father wrote to the couple, encouraging them to return to India if their life was unbearable. At one point, when their lives were extremely difficult, Maganbhai suggested to Savitaben that she return home to Karkhadi with their children and that he would follow in a few years. Savitaben refused, expressing her faith in God and that He 'would not deny us the fruits of our labour'.

In 1950, Savitaben became pregnant again. Their first son Pravin arrived and the family were overjoyed. In 1951, the second son Bhupen arrived. Following quickly in order were daughter Tarulata, son Bipin, son Jagdish, son Mahesh, and finally son Anil in 1964. Savitaben was thirty-five years of age when her ninth child, Anil, was born. Mahesh, the eighth child, was born at the Mission Hospital, two miles outside of Ba, in 1959.

The name Mahesh is a short version of a name of Sanskrit origin, Maheswara or Umamaheswara, meaning 'Great Lord'. It is a popular name for Hindu boys as it is one of the names of Shiva.

'To be honest, I never asked my parents why they chose Mahesh,' he recalls. 'They would have looked through an ancient book, and due to my horoscope, they would have looked for a name with the letter "ma".'

Mahesh's traditional Gujarati name is Maheshbhai, following the Gujarati tradition of adding 'bhai' and 'ben' to names.

'My name was Maheshbhai,' explained Mahesh. 'Then everyone thought "Bhai" was my middle name, so I thought, *I'm going to be called Mahesh Patel*.'

Mahesh Patel and his family have vivid memories of growing up in Fiji.

Mahesh Patel: 'Ba is inland. It is basically a sugar town. We had a railway track running right in the middle of town. As soon as a train stopped, we would pull out sugarcane and eat it. That was fun, a real country life: walking to school, going out to pick fruits from the trees, getting stung by bees, chasing off wild dogs. It was really a one-street town. Everybody knew everyone. We had aunties across the road and sometimes you would yell over the balcony, "Hey, shall we go to the movies tonight?" That's how close-knit we were.'

Mahesh Patel: 'We grew up in a large family with six boys and three girls. We had an uncle who had eight children. At any point in time, there would be fifteen to twenty people living in a three-bedroom house. Our front door was never locked. There was no key. Sometimes, because we used to sneak out, Mum and Dad would put a chair behind the door. When we would try and push the door, the chair would scrape on the floor tiles and screech. I remember when I was eight or nine, I went to a movie at one of the old traditional cinema halls and fell asleep. Nobody in my house noticed I was not home. There was no headcount. I woke up around midnight. It was dark and I started crying. I was banging on the door. A policeman passing by heard me. He got the theatre owner to let me out and took me to our house. I got into trouble with my parents.'

Anil Patel: 'Mahesh was a good brother. He always looked after me. As I was the youngest, he was the one I looked up to. With everybody else, the age gap was too big. It was a large family; everybody was doing their own thing. He was the brother I could relate to.

'Back in those days, I was quite skinny. He told me to drink raw eggs with milk. I wanted a watch. He said, "If you have that every day, I will give you a watch." He did. A small ladies' Seiko. I would have been eight or nine.'

Mahesh Patel: 'When my parents used to travel, they would take my youngest brother Anil along because he was too young to leave at home. I used to get left at my auntie's place. Daksesh Patel is my first cousin, one of many, but he's closest as we grew up together in Fiji. This is how close we were as family: I remember in Class 2, I put down Daksesh's mum's name as my mother's name ... I've got that health card somewhere at home. I spent so much time with my Aunty Manjulaben Patel when I was young, I wrote her name in place of my mother's in my school health card.'

Daksesh Patel: 'I consider Mahesh one of my closest cousins. He is five years older than me, and at that age, five years was a large gap. When I was a kid, I used to look at Mahesh as my elder brother because I did not have any brothers; I have two sisters.

'Mahesh felt like a brother and he still does. His father and my father and their forefathers came from the same village in Gujarat. There is a strong connection there. Then, our fathers end up marrying two sisters. So, we have connections on both our mothers' side and fathers' side. We are uniquely close.'

Anil Patel: 'Mum and Dad were strict vegetarians. It was the belief of the village back home. As we grew up, our parents told us the importance of being vegetarian and not eating meat. Being vegetarian made us part of the home village. "Our bodies are not made for it. The body can't take it," they said. Eating meat back in those days was taboo at home. The first time I ever tried fish was with Mahesh. I must have been twelve. We went on a picnic, and I ate fish and chips. A school trip or a picnic was a good opportunity to eat meat. When our parents were alive, we would not eat meat in front of them; not even cook it at home. When they were away, we did cook meat at home, but we would still use a different set of utensils. That is how strong the beliefs of my parents were.'

Taru Patel: 'Mahesh had a lot of friends his age and he used to love going for picnics to the river or the sea.'

Daksesh Patel: 'We would go out to a river and cook food. We used to swim in the river and in those days the water was so pristine, you could almost drink the water coming out of those waterfalls. We used to have lots of fun and play all sorts of games. That used to be our brotherhood and our bonding time. We got up to all sorts of mischief. We'd play, we'd swim and we'd eat.'

There is also a strong recollection amongst the family that Mahesh Patel had a sweet tooth as a child.

Anil Patel: 'On Sundays, when the shops closed after lunch, my parents would have a siesta. That's when the kitchen was free to be raided. Mahesh had a sweet tooth. He ended up getting a nickname we still call him—Penda, which is a type of sweet. But don't call him that!'

Bipin Patel: 'Mahesh was nicknamed Penda. He had a sweet tooth, and if there was a sweet item around, he wanted to eat it.'

Daksesh Patel: 'There was a famous sweet shop in Ba called Bhikhabhai. It was Mahesh's favourite destination to go and buy penda. He was the kid with his hands always in the lolly jar.'

But the most important component of the early life of Mahesh Patel and his family was the success of their grocery store. Mahesh's father Maganbhai worked endless hours to provide for his family.

Mahesh Patel: 'The Ba shop was a grocery and general store. Grocery was the main frame: imported rice, sugar, oil, all the lentils. Pots and pans. I have got a lot of memories working in the store. It was a general store, so it was labour-intensive work. We would open up the cases and stack the shelves. When I was too young to go to the shop, I still insisted I wanted to go. It was our livelihood and gave you things to do. When I was thirteen or fourteen, I remember my brother Pravin went to India to get married; I took leave from school for a whole week to work in the shop.'

Kusum Patel: 'My father was always working hard for all of us kids. He wanted us to get an education. He was always there for us. We would go and help him in the shop.'

Mahesh Patel looks back with regret that he didn't find a way to be more emotionally connected with his father Maganbhai and have a better relationship.

Mahesh Patel: 'We didn't really have any downtime with our dad, and I regret it to this day. Because he was always busy: get up, go to work, work till late. Typical migrant story you hear anywhere in the world. It wasn't a part of our culture to sit with our dad. He would give us five pence to go see a movie instead of loitering around while he was working. He was considerate. He had a lot of issues with my uncle and my cousins, running their business for them. Mum said he wanted to separate himself from their business. It resulted in one of our family's defining moments. He had asked mum to take all the kids and go back to India. She held her ground: "I'm not going unless you come with us." If it wasn't for Mum, we would not be sitting where we are today.'

There is a feeling among some of his siblings that Mahesh was the favourite child of his mother. This is disputed.

Bipin Patel: 'Mahesh was Mum's favourite. I would definitely say that. He was so dedicated. I don't think I did any of those things he would do. He would always sit down with Mum and give her a leg massage. I don't know why. But I do remember he was very close to our mum. That's the way it was until the day our mum passed.'

Kusum Patel: 'Our mother was a great person. Really outgoing. Very happy and always helping people. She was always there for anyone who needed help. Really generous. I remember Mahesh and Anil as little boys. They were always together, getting ready and going to school. Before school, they would help my mum to clean the temple and get the flowers. They were both very helpful.'

Taru Patel: 'We had a big family, and my mum used to get up early to make our lunches. I helped her and then when I started going to high school, Mahesh took over. We had a prayer room in the house which we decorated with flowers. We would clean the altar. One day, Mahesh started doing it. As soon as he had his shower, he would take Anil and they would go off and pick flowers and do all those things.'

Anil Patel: 'Everyone thought Mahesh was Mum's favourite. We used to call him "the favourite". Mum was a religious person. In the mornings she would do her prayers. She would go out and get some flowers from the garden from her friend's house. I would make excuses not to go, but Mahesh would go out and do it. Lighting up a diya (oil lamp) for prayers every morning—he would be the one doing it. So, he became the favourite. It was just something within him. Mum would give the opportunity to everybody, but he had the determination to do it.'

Kusum Patel: 'No, I wouldn't say that Mahesh was Mum's favourite. I think she loved us all equally. I think Anil is just teasing Mahesh and everyone else in the family—he is always like that. When I would ask my mum, she would say: "Look at my ten fingers, if you cut one off, it will hurt as much as if you cut off one of the other fingers." We were all the same to her. That is how she described it.'

It was perhaps jealousy that led to the vandalizing of Mahesh's school shorts one day. The perpetrator was unknown until now.

Anil Patel: 'Mahesh used to pick on me. I remember once he really annoyed me. I cannot remember what the occasion was, but it was in high school. It was something to do with uniforms.'

Mahesh Patel: 'My high school uniform was grey shorts and white shirt. I was always conscious of my appearance. Yes, I remember my shorts being ripped. I don't even know who it could have been.'

Anil Patel: 'He did annoy me. I cannot recall how. So, I went and ripped his pants. They were nicely ironed, so I carefully ripped and folded them up in a way he would not see the rip and put them on. He went to school wearing them and then *oops*! He was asking mum, "Who did this?" I was too scared to put my hand up.'

Mahesh Patel did not follow the exact same educational route as his older brothers, sisters and cousins, and he wasn't fond of doing school homework either, according to some of them.

Daksesh Patel: 'Mahesh was unique. We all went to a community school—it was a very Indian-orientated school. Then we went to high school, either Xavier College run by the Christian Brothers or A.D. Patel College, which was run by the Gujarati community. Mahesh went to the Methodist school. He was one of the very few from the Patel clan in Ba who did so. It was run by the Methodist Church. A lot of indigenous students go there. In those days, the Methodist school was ranked amongst the top five high schools. But it is not a school that everyone liked. It was in a bit of a rough area, surrounded by indigenous villages. Very nice people, but it is not an easy school. You got shaped up [roughed up] sometimes. I thought, *how the hell is Mahesh going to go to that school?* But he did it—he would always joke about things—he was a cheeky bugger. He was very sarcastic. He always plays a game and that habit never died.'

Bipin Patel: 'Mahesh was a good boy, but a very funny chap. We used him for excuses with our oldest brother Pravin to get away from studies. Every time in the afternoon or evening when Pravin would sit down with us to do revision or multiplication tables or some homework, within a minute, Mahesh couldn't hack it, and he would say, "I'm feeling sleepy". He would sing a little song, "I'm feeling sleepy, I'm feeling tired." Pravin would clip him on the ear, but sometimes we were let off. Mahesh did not want to do his homework or any studying. He hated all that. We were very young, but I still remember that.'

Pravin Patel: 'Mahesh was a talkative boy, but he was not pushy. I can remember when he was in Class 3 or 4, he was not getting good marks or good positions in his class, so I was teaching him spelling and maths. I was trying to teach him, but he was trying to get away from studying. He would say, "I'm feeling very hot, I'm sweating." He was always making those excuses. But I didn't back off. I can't remember if he improved his marks in school, but it must have helped—look at him now.'

Daksesh Patel: 'Mahesh used to be scared of his elder brother Pravin. He would get smacked because he was cheeky and misbehaved.'

Mahesh credits his brother Pravin for pushing him to do well in school and make the most of the opportunity for further education, something that Pravin did not get.

Mahesh Patel: 'My oldest brother Pravin, of all the brothers, was the most academically ahead. But he got pulled out of school when he was seventeen because Dad needed someone to help with the business. For a very long time, this inspired us to study because Pravin had sacrificed his education for us. That is something that stuck with us in our minds going forward. A lot of kids would be happy to leave school, but Pravin wanted to stay on because, academically, he was very talented.'

Pravin Patel: 'I remained in Fiji the whole time growing up. I went to school up to Senior at Cambridge in Fiji. I was forced to stay back and look after the siblings. I was forced to go into the business. I didn't want to do that, but eventually, I decided I would stay and work hard for the whole family.'

Mahesh Patel: 'I did try to study hard. It was a sense of obligation to my brother Pravin. He told us to stay at school. He explained, "You guys better not flop and mess around." That was always in the back of your mind: "You can't be wasting your time. It's hard-earned money." It wasn't cheap to go overseas and study. We did go off the rails once in a while, but in the back of your mind, it drove you.'

Mahesh's two oldest sisters had travelled back to India for arranged marriages. His older brothers had been sent for their high school years to India or New Zealand. His father wanted Mahesh to travel to India to go to university. But the defiant son would not hear of it. He wanted to complete his high school years in New Zealand.

Mahesh Patel: 'At that age, I had no vision for my future. I was just killing time; I was just hanging out doing something. We didn't have television or air conditioning at home. We just hung around at the store. That was excitement for us. But no, I don't think I had any visions of being a businessman or opening my own store. In those days, some of my siblings went to India because it was cheaper and because of our heritage—*be a doctor, engineer, or accountant*. I didn't want to be a doctor. I hated blood, and I didn't want to do injections. Doctor was the first thing I ruled out. Others, I didn't even think about.'

Maganbhai Patel looked at his son Mahesh sternly one day and asked, 'What are you going to study at college?' Without much thought, the fifteen-year-old simply plucked his future career out of the air. 'I'll become a pharmacist!' he said.

Chapter 3
New Zealand

Maganbhai and Savitaben Patel strongly believed that their children should go back to India to propel their lives forward.

'The original plan was for all of my brothers and sisters to go to university in India,' explains Mahesh Patel.

The Fijian university system was not fully developed in the 1970s and '80s. Fijians required lower marks than Indians for the Fiji university placements.

'It was a sensitive thing, then,' Mahesh notes.

His father and mother kept telling him, 'Go to India, become a doctor, or an engineer or an accountant.' Part of it was because of his parents' Indian heritage, but the cost factor was also considered. If Mahesh went to university in India, there were many relatives, extended family, and friends of relatives where he could stay cheaply.

His elder siblings Tara, Kusum, Bhupen and Taru had gone to India. But his older brothers closest in age, Bipin and Jagdish, had more recently gone to university in New Zealand, giving Mahesh an opening.

'I was fifteen,' he says. 'I did not really want to go to India. I did not know India. In Fiji, the most common places kids moved on to were Australia and New Zealand.'

As discussions progressed about him relocating to India, Mahesh wrote an application letter to Mount Albert Grammar School in

Auckland, New Zealand, unbeknownst to his parents. Fortunately, he was accepted.

The next problem then presented itself. It occurred to him one day: *'I don't have a passport!'*

One of the employees at his father's grocery store helped Mahesh obtain his first Fijian passport. 'His name was Abdul,' Mahesh recalled. 'I will never forget him. Abdul got the passport application form, helped me fill it out, and I sent it away.'

When he received his new Fijian passport, it was time to confront his parents.

'I want to go to New Zealand.'

'What are you going to do?'

Even at this late stage, Mahesh had not given any thought to what he wanted to study and what his career path would be. 'I had no idea,' he recalls. 'I just plucked something out of thin air.'

'I'll do pharmacy.'

'But you have no school to go to.'

'No, I got accepted. Here is the letter.'

'You don't have a passport.'

'Yes, I do have a passport. Here it is.'

'No. School in New Zealand will be too expensive.'

Mahesh Patel: 'My parents were not well-to-do financially, and it was not cheap going overseas. My father didn't quite agree with me wanting to go to New Zealand. My eldest brother Pravin, who was working in the family business, did not agree either, and I bawled my eyes out. I said, "No." I was stubborn. My mother supported me. She said, "If he wants to do that, you should let him go."'

Pravin Patel: 'I can't recall Mahesh ever saying what he wanted to do in life. I do recall my father and I discussing two of the brothers wanting to go to school in New Zealand.

'My father said we should send Mahesh to India. He came to me and said he wanted to go to New Zealand. I said, "No. You are going to India," and he started crying. I had to back off, and my father and mother said, "Alright, let him go to New Zealand."'

Bipin Patel: 'Become a pharmacist? No, I cannot remember that bit. In those days, not just our parents, but for all the parents in Fiji with Indian heritage, their first choice would be for their children to go to school in India.'

Anil Patel: 'I don't think we ever had that conversation on what Mahesh wanted to be and why he wanted to go to New Zealand. In his own mind, he probably wanted to be a pharmacist. But he never said it. He never said it in front of me and if he did, I cannot recall it.'

If it was a split-second decision to say 'Pharmacy', why did Mahesh say that when he could have come up with multiple other careers?

'I have no idea,' he replies, laughing. 'It was just something different. I knew what a pharmacist was. I had seen pharmacies. I just didn't want to be a doctor. I didn't think about accounting or engineering. Pharmacy just came to my mind because it was out of the box. It was something my parents never thought of.'

For anyone to travel and relocate overseas to a new country is daunting. To do so at the age of fifteen without his parents, must have been extremely difficult.

Mahesh Patel: 'If you ask me where did I get the courage, I don't know. When you are younger, you have no fear. In those days we were not well off at all. Before I went to New Zealand, my father pointed out I did not have the proper clothes. So, I had to borrow some of my older brothers'. I didn't have long trousers. We all wore shorts in Fiji all the time. I didn't have proper shoes. I had to borrow shoes, and I went with three pairs of trousers and a couple of shirts to New Zealand. Packed my bag and off I went.'

But before going to school in New Zealand, Mahesh had to negotiate the flight. He had never been on a plane before and was a vegetarian who did not eat meat.

Mahesh Patel: 'In those days we didn't know you could request vegetarian meals on the plane. I remember it was one of the Asian airlines flying to Auckland. I sat in the plane thinking, *This is pretty cool*, and was served with food. I said to myself, *I can't eat the meat*. I started eating the salad, and this is how naive we were—I looked at my salad and thought, *Right, I'm going to leave the grape till the last*. It was a bloody olive! This is how sheltered we were. We didn't even have a television. We grew up eating traditional Indian food. Grapes yes, but olives never, because that's not part of Indian cuisine. I thought it must be a dark grape.'

The country of New Zealand in the southwestern Pacific Ocean consists of two major landmasses known as the North Island and the South Island, along with over 700 smaller islands. New Zealand's capital city is Wellington, and its most populous city is Auckland, both located on the North Island.

Mahesh Patel travelled to Auckland in 1975 to complete his final three years of high school at Mount Albert Grammar School. It was never easy.

Mahesh Patel: 'There were days in New Zealand when I didn't go to school because I didn't have 10 cents for bus fare. You try and tell that to kids now and they can't comprehend it. The milk was 8 cents a pint and we used to shortchange the milkman to save that one cent. Because he never counted. We bought six bottles—there was no way he was going to count. That's how valuable every cent was to us.'

After completing Year 12 and graduating from Mount Albert Grammar School at the end of 1977, Mahesh Patel applied for the Diploma in Pharmacy course at the Central Institute of Technology in Wellington. But in a massive shock to his career plans, he was not accepted into the course.

'There were limited places at the pharmacy school in those days,' he explains. 'They allowed only three overseas students. Each year you had to apply, and it wasn't purely based on marks. It was aptitude and marks. Kids who got in that year were on a government scholarship from Tonga, Fiji and Papua New Guinea. I didn't get in. I said, *Okay, what am I going to do?*'

He instead applied for and was accepted into a Bachelor of Commerce degree at Auckland University in 1978. Mahesh selected Commerce as he had passed economics in high school, but he admits, 'I had no idea of accounting.'

Towards the end of the year, he reapplied again for the Diploma in Pharmacy in Wellington. He was called in for an interview with the Dean of the Pharmacy School.

Mahesh Patel: 'I was doing three additional chemistry papers as part of the commerce course in case I got accepted into pharmacy school. The maximum university papers allowed to be studied at a time was five or six, so I was doing three extra papers on top of that. When I met with the faculty head of the University of Auckland, he told me to drop them and focus on my bachelor of commerce. I told him I really wanted to do pharmacy. He warned me, if I failed any of these papers, he will not let me move on to the next stage. It was a risk, but I still did them. Two weeks before my final exams, I got accepted into pharmacy school. I could have said, *It doesn't matter now*, but I still sat all the exams to make sure I passed.'

It was during his time at the Central Institute of Technology in Wellington, from 1979 to 1982, where Mahesh Patel would form three of the closest friendships of his life, which remain in place till today.

Jiten Patel: 'Mahesh and I have known each other from our childhood, around Class 4 or 5 of primary school. During school holidays we used to go to his hometown Ba, where I learnt how to play cards in their grocery store. Mahesh was very quiet in his younger days, but naughty.

'We stopped meeting during school holidays after maybe Class 6 or 7. During our high school days in Fiji, we lost contact. We had never spoken about going overseas for schooling. It just was a coincidence that we ended up in the same high school in Auckland. Mahesh was very quiet and mostly kept to himself during our high school days.

We didn't reconnect after the gap since our primary school days. We hardly spoke to each other or socialized then.

'It so happened we both ended up in Auckland University. He was doing Commerce and I was doing Bachelor of Science. He was one year ahead of me and after one year in university, he went to Wellington to do the pharmacy course. Again, we never spoke about this either and by coincidence, I ended up going to pharmacy school, the following year in 1980. This is when we reconnected. We were flatmates in 1981 and 1982. Lots of memories were created then.'

Jagdish Patel: 'I am from Fiji and Mahesh is from Fiji, and we first met in New Zealand. Our families knew each other. There are a lot of Patels; we are not related. I did not know him personally in Fiji. I lived in Suva and never went to Ba for holidays. My parents knew his parents. I knew of the family, but I did not meet Mahesh. I first met Mahesh properly in New Zealand when we were high school students, though we went to different high schools in Auckland.

'I ended up living with the same group in the same flat. I am slightly older than Mahesh, but we were in the same year at school. I was boarding at the school and had to move out to live somewhere else. I had a friend there from Suva and he had some friends from Ba. I said, "I need a place to stay." He said, "You come and stay with me." He had a room. In that same five-bedroom apartment were the three brothers, Bipin, Jagdish and Mahesh.'

Vasant Bhuta: 'I had gone to Wellington, New Zealand, in 1976, to complete my education. My sister Ramila followed in 1979, to undertake her studies at the pharmacy school. Mahesh had moved from Auckland to Wellington in the same year to study pharmacy. Overseas students in New Zealand, let alone in Wellington, were not very common in those days. Overseas students from Fiji going to Wellington were even rarer. So, when Ramila told me that there was another person from Fiji at the pharmacy school, I was intrigued.

'I met Mahesh in early 1979, not really expecting much more than establishing an acquaintance with a common Fijian background. How wrong I was! We got along like a house on fire right from the outset. The distance between our two universities, around 45 minutes by train, was no hindrance as we would meet most weekends. This turned into parties on a more regular basis. In between the parties and studies and everything else that typical university students do, the seeds of a long and a deep friendship were sown.'

Jagdish Patel: 'Initially, when I first moved in, Mahesh was quiet because there were two elder siblings, so he didn't open up that much. I do remember, we were watching television one day and he was saying he wanted to watch something else and I said, "Don't you bloody change the channel." But he changed it, and I swung at him and literally hit him. He did nothing. He just brushed it aside. No apology, nothing. Everything was normal. That was when we started to become good friends.'

Mahesh Patel: 'I do remember the television dispute. Jagdish was short-fused in the early days. He would pick a fight. Jagdish is one of my four closest friends. He is also a great mentor of mine.'

Jagdish Patel: 'Mahesh was in Wellington and he was spending time with Vasant and Jiten, but we used to keep in touch. I was at Mahesh's twenty-first birthday in Wellington. He had a massive party in the university hall. We threw an orange and vodka cocktail all over him. He went and had a shower to wash it off and when he came out, he walked straight into the main entry door's glass panels, and it shattered. He bounced back off. He was cut a little bit from the broken glass. But then a delivery guy turned up and tried to push the door open with his hands, thinking the glass was still there and fell through. We all were drinking and having fun. Even today, I say to him, "Somebody invites you and you are ready to go." He just loves to party.'

In his second year of pharmacy school in 1980, Mahesh Patel failed his final exam, one of the few times in life he has ever failed at anything. It taught him a valuable lesson.

Mahesh Patel: 'I wasted a whole year. Jiten had his twenty-first birthday party. It was a big, long party. The next day I had my final exam, and it was a practical. In pharmacy, you have theory and you have practical. With practicals, you are making ampoules and capsules. I didn't get home until late that night. A few hours later, I had my practical test. My hands were shaking. I had been an 80-percent result student throughout the year. I stuffed up. I can't remember if I had a piece of particle in the ampoule or mucked up the dose of morphine in the ampoule. My tutor, she just failed me. I had to repeat a whole year for that.'

Jiten Patel: 'In 1980, I celebrated my twenty-first birthday and Mahesh was in his second year in pharmacy. Mahesh had his dispensing exam the next day after the party, which he failed, and to date he blames me for this. But look at where he is now. Then, in my second year of pharmacy, I failed the exact same exam! Both of us missed a year failing that one and only exam.'

Mahesh Patel: 'What a life changer it was that I spent an extra year at pharmacy school. In pharmacy that was the rule: fail one exam and you have to do the whole year again. I had to tell my family that I failed, but I didn't tell them I was partying. They were not impressed. Maybe I was a bit overconfident because I was always at 80 percent. But when you are twenty-one, you don't think of being angry with yourself; at least, I didn't. I was disappointed, then I thought, *What am I going to do? I'll just make use of the year.* That is why I did a couple of distance-education courses at Massey University, including a paper in commercial law. I had part-time work, so I did not have to rely solely on my parents for funding.'

Including the repeated year, Mahesh Patel spent four years in pharmacy school, graduating at the end of 1982. He then had to complete one year of internship as a pharmacist in New Zealand.

Another long-time friendship Mahesh made in New Zealand was with Magan Patel, who recalls, 'We first met in pharmacy school in Wellington and were flatmates. Mahesh came across as a simple, honest person. Easy-going, straightforward, no-nonsense.'

Mahesh Patel: 'With pharmacy, you need to do time in hospitals and in retail pharmacies. I was working in the suburb of Paraparaumu. It is a town in the southwestern part of North Island. I was working in a pharmacy that was in the top 1 per cent of all pharmacies. It was a big thing. Apart from my two bosses, I was the only male in the fourteen-member staff at the pharmacy. My bosses wanted me to stay on after the year, but I thought, *No, I want to go back to Fiji. I've had enough. After eight years in New Zealand. I'll go back.*

'Then halfway through the year, when the boss started pushing me for a decision, I said I probably want to go to Nauru. At that point in time, Nauru had all the phosphate mines. I heard everyone there drives a Mercedes and has lots of money. I was a twenty-four-year-old kid. A few weeks later, my boss came to me with a newspaper cutting, it was for a pharmacy manager required in Papua New Guinea. I sent a handwritten application and gave it no more thought. My boss said he would give me a reference. Then I went back to Fiji at the end of the year in December 1983.'

When Mahesh Patel returned home to Fiji, some of his family members already had other plans in place for him.

Mahesh Patel: 'During my time in New Zealand, I would travel back to Fiji during the Christmas holidays. I would work in the family store. I will never forget the day I came back at the end of 1983. My father was so proud. He told everyone, "My son's coming back." By then we owned a whole building. He told people, "My son is going to open a pharmacy there." But I told him, "Whoa, I'm not ready for that yet."

'My brother Bhupen was a doctor. In Fiji, pharmacists were really in short supply, almost every one of them owned their own stores. They could never take holidays, because there was no one to come in and take over. So, Bhupen had got five locum jobs lined up for me. I asked my brother, "Hang on, how did you commit on behalf of me?" I basically worked round the island and soon realized that it is not much fun when you own a pharmacy. You are stuck there.'

Mahesh Patel was having fun in Fiji working as a pharmacy locum and partying at night, but his life would soon pivot and change forever.

Mahesh Patel: 'In April 1984, my home phone rang. It was a man named Mr Foung in Papua New Guinea. He said I had applied for a job last year, was I still interested? I said yes. He replied, "I will come back to you." I got off the phone and said to myself, *What am I getting myself into*? I did not know where Papua New Guinea was. I did not even look it up when I applied. I just knew it was in the Pacific somewhere, maybe near Nauru or Tonga. But then I did not hear from him for a while. I thought, *Maybe he is not interested*.

'Later, I found out he'd had a long conversation with my former boss to whom I reported during my internship. He was a big fan and gave me a positive reference. In May, Mr Foung rang me back to say I'd got the job. At that time, Fiji pharmacists were getting paid 12,000 Fiji dollars. This new offer came in at 18,000 Fiji dollars (670,500 Indian rupees). This was good money. I told my family I was going to go. They all said, "Don't go, it's too dangerous a place." I replied, "I'll be fine." My mum said there were snakes and she heard it was very dangerous. "I'll come with you," she suggested. I replied, "Mum, if it's dangerous, why would I take you there?"

'I finally told them, "That's it, I'm going."'

Chapter 4

Papua New Guinea

Mahesh Patel returned from New Zealand to Fiji at the end of 1983. He had started working as a locum pharmacist when he was offered a contract position as a pharmacist to work in Papua New Guinea. It came as a complete surprise to most of his family that he would leave Fiji to work in another country. The family felt trepidation but was intrigued as well.

Papua New Guinea is a country in the southwestern Pacific, which comprises the eastern half of the island of New Guinea and its offshore islands in Melanesia. The capital of Port Moresby is located on the southeastern coast of the country. It is the world's third largest island country by area. From 1902, it was controlled by Australia as part of the British dominion. It became an independent sovereign nation in 1975.

Kusum Patel: 'For a child to go out to a different country like Papua New Guinea—our parents would not know how he was doing. My mother liked to cook and take care of the children. She was worried about Mahesh going there. But I thought it was a good opportunity for him to grow. I felt really happy about that. He would get to see another world.'

With the confidence of youth and perhaps a little naivety, Mahesh Patel left Fiji, headed to a new country for an appealing work opportunity and a new life. When he arrived in Port Moresby on 10 June 1984, Mahesh Patel had very little information about whom he was working for, where he would be working and even living. Prior to the internet and world wide web, everything was organized by letters and the telephone.

Mahesh Patel: 'I had 35 Australian dollars (1,946 Indian rupees) in my pocket when I arrived. I didn't know what my new boss looked like. I had no details at all. I just knew that I had a job in Port Moresby. I arrived in the middle of the afternoon. It was hot and sticky standing outside the airport. All I knew was my boss was of Chinese origin. I asked every Asian-looking man that came along, "Are you Mr Foung?" "No," they replied. All the passengers had gone and I was still standing there by myself. I asked myself, *What am I going to do?*'

Eventually, a man dressed casually in shorts and t-shirt walked up to him. 'Sorry I'm late,' said Ian Foung. 'I had to pick up some flowers for my father's passing anniversary. Would you mind if we make a little detour?' Mahesh Patel's first ever stop in Papua New Guinea was at the 9 Mile Cemetery. Sitting in the car waiting for his new employer, he thought, *What have I got myself into here?*

On his first night in Port Moresby, Mahesh stayed at a little rundown hotel in Boroko. He then moved to a two-bedroom apartment in Paga Hill, arranged by Mr Foung.

'My landlady Margaret Richardson,' says Mahesh, 'lived in the residence in front.'

Located high on a hill, the apartment, one of a block of four, had a great ocean view of the Coral Sea.

Mahesh arrived with just one suitcase. He found one teaspoon in the apartment. There weren't even any curtains in the loungeroom. He had to fit the apartment out as he could afford to, over time.

Mahesh Patel commenced work as a pharmacist at Chapman's Pharmacy at the intersection of Nita Street and Angau Drive in the Boroko shopping district. The business was originally owned and operated by pharmacist Bill Chapman, and later bought by the Foung family.

With his usual enthusiasm for life, Mahesh worked hard and quickly made many friends.

Mel Donald: 'My father was transferred to Papua New Guinea by his employer in 1972 and the rest of the family was moved to Port Moresby in 1980. I met Mahesh around two weeks after he arrived in Port Moresby. Mahesh was very friendly and helpful so he very easily became our go-to pharmacist whenever we needed any medical supplies. Living in Port Moresby in those early days also came with all sorts of challenges as the medical services in town were not great, hence having a pharmacist like Mahesh as a friend made a huge difference.'

Shefali Mehta: 'My husband Shailen and I were invited by two of our very good friends, Mr Ling James Seeto and his wife Mrs Anna Seeto, to their home for dinner. James was knighted by Queen Elizabeth II a few years later. Mahesh Patel was also invited to the same dinner to introduce him to us as wantoks [a Melanesian term for close comrades or community members]. Mahesh was working at the pharmacy owned by a friend of Mr Seeto and had arrived just a few days earlier. Mahesh is and was at that time a likeable bloke. He was an honest, genuine and hard-working young man, with a twinkle in his eyes to succeed in life.'

Dan Ansbaugh: 'In 1981, USA's Professional Air Traffic Controller's Organization (PATCO) went on strike for better working conditions. Within forty-eight hours, President Ronald Reagan fired 12,000 of us for striking. I sent out fourteen applications all over the world looking for employment. In June 1983, I was offered a position in Port Moresby, working at the Civil Aviation Training College and Jacksons International Airport. In 1984, while picking up my mail at the Boroko post office, I stopped by Chapman's Pharmacy which was located next door. Looking behind the counter, I noticed this very dapper-looking young fellow. Striking up a conversation, I was amazed Mahesh was from Fiji. Little did I know it would become a lifetime friendship. Mahesh was a real gentleman, and somebody I wanted to be friends with.'

Greg Wisbey: 'I travelled from Australia to Papua New Guinea to be the regional sales and marketing director for a large international company in 1984. Mahesh and I arrived in Port Moresby at about the same time. We were in allied areas. Ours was a business relationship to start, as the company I worked for was a major conglomerate with pharmacy supplies. Mahesh and I are in a similar age group. We were single guys and we were knocking around Port Moresby in the same social circles. We were mates. He had a moustache like a caterpillar on his top lip. I had a Mexican-style moustache. Because it is a tight community there and everyone knows each other, when someone new comes along, you welcome them in.'

Gareth Joseph: 'I met Mahesh when he first arrived in Papua New Guinea. We were both in our early twenties. I was working as a product manager for a company which sold office equipment. Mahesh and I developed a slow-burn friendship. It just graduated organically. Back then, there was not much to do in Port Moresby, other than go to the clubs. You were out and about. Eventually, a group of us would fly from Port Moresby to Hong Kong for trips. We bonded on many levels.'

One of the earliest tragic events in the life of Mahesh Patel was the passing of his father Maganbhai Patel, on 8 January 1985.

Mahesh Patel: 'It came as a bit of shock. My brothers rang me and I was obviously quite emotional about it. I told them, "Listen, you guys are not going to have the funeral until I get there." They held it back for one day. I was devastated. So much so, that after the funeral, I was planning not to go back to Papua New Guinea. I thought, *Let me fulfil my dad's dream and open my own pharmacy in Fiji*. Then I got a telephone call from my boss Mr Foung. He was desperate for pharmacists. He said, "Why don't you help me out and finish your contract." I thought I would do the honourable thing and finish up my contract till June 1987 and then come back to Fiji.'

Maganbhai Patel was cremated and part of his ashes were taken to the Ba River to be scattered there as per the families' Hindu culture and rituals. The remainder were taken to the Ganges River in India and immersed there by youngest son Anil Patel, in December 1985.

Attending the funeral of Maganbhai Patel and spending time with his mother and other family members brought back many fond memories of his father but also reinforced some regrets.

Mahesh Patel: 'I remember a couple of years before he passed away, when I came back from studies in New Zealand … Because he was a diabetic, Mum used to give him injections every day. Maybe he was a bit of a wuss like me: he didn't want to give himself the jab. He was Type-2 diabetic, but I think it must have been a lifestyle issue for him. They migrated in late 1949. In those days, they didn't eat well, they didn't exercise. It was just work, work, work. The amount of stress they had! He was a smoker. I tried smoking—typical back of the school toilets. But I never adapted to it. I didn't like it. Thank God for that. None of my brothers smoked.

'There is one moment I cherish with my father. Mum had to go to a wedding in another town. Normally, she would not go unless Dad went, because of the injections. They didn't have disposable syringes. It was the old ones where you had to boil and sterilize the syringe and needle—it was a big rigmarole. I volunteered to stay with Dad: "You go. I can do the jab." That evening, I sat and had a beer with him—a moment I still remember till this day. Never in my life did I think I would ever have a drink with my dad. It was just the two of us in the main sitting room. He asked me to go and get us a beer from the fridge. I was surprised he offered the beer to me. It was a moment in time. We did not chat much. We had never built that relationship of mateyness or friendship; it was always a very strict father–son relationship. But now he was accepting me as an adult. The first beer with my dad.

'Then in 1985, my father passed away. To date it is a huge, huge regret for me that I never got a chance to spend more time with my dad. This is why I impress upon my kids, and try to guide a lot of youngsters: every opportunity you get to spend time with your parents, take it, because you'll live to regret it later on. We got so busy in our own lives. Then we lost him when I was only twenty-five. He was not sick, but he had a lot of underlying health issues. He had diabetes. He had blood pressure. He had cholesterol issues. He had a heart attack and collapsed in the bathroom. Stress would have been a major part that contributed to it. He was sixty-three. It made us all think about the smoking and the diabetes.'

Back in Port Moresby, working at Chapman's Pharmacy, Mahesh Patel was dealing with the emotional loss of his father. But a sliding doors moment that would change his life forever occurred soon after.

The Steamships Trading Company, commonly known in Papua New Guinea as Steammies, is a diversified business entity trading in shipping, transport, property and commercial operations. Created in 1918, Steamships has played an important development role in investing in Papua New Guinea (or PNG, as the residents call it) and the Asia-Pacific region. John Swire & Sons (PNG) Limited is a majority shareholder.

In early 1986, Mahesh Patel received a telephone call from his employer Ian Foung, advising him that a group of men from Steamships would be visiting the pharmacy for an inspection.

Mahesh Patel: 'Some people from Steamships came in, had a look around and asked me some questions about the business. I rang my boss about a week later and asked, "What was all that about?" He said they want us to open a pharmacy inside a department store. I asked, "What do you think?" He replied, "Nah. It's not going to work. Not interested. It's a waste of time." I went home and thought about it. *That's a great idea. It's a one stop shop for everybody.* Then I thought, *Hang on, maybe I should approach them?* Because there were only three pharmacies in town. I approached Steamships to see if they were interested.

'They said, "Yes, give us a proposal." I didn't know anything about business proposals. I had some friends in an accounting firm and they put some papers together with me. I had a friend, a Malaysian guy, George. We were party mates who hung out together. George asked, "Why don't we go into business together?" I said, "Great. I need a big brother." We started working on a proposal. Then, unbeknownst to me, George went and lodged a foreign investment approval for the pharmacy. He had lodged an application because he had contacts there. But he did this without my approval and he put my name down as a shareholder.

'One of the directors of the National Investment Development Authority for Foreign Investment, told my boss what had been done in my name. I was still working at Chapman's Pharmacy. One day Mr Foung rang me and asked, "Can you stay back after work?" Two days before that he had pulled out all the supplier files, which were part of the intellectual property. I thought he must be updating them. He came to see me in the afternoon and said, "I'm really disappointed in you. You are setting up your own business." I replied, "No, I'm not." At that time, I did not know George had lodged the approval request form. Mr Foung then gave me my final pay cheque and my return ticket to Fiji. He took my car keys from me and told me to leave. It was a total miscommunication. I had done nothing wrong, but he would not listen to me.

'I could have used the plane ticket Mr Foung had given me to fly back to Fiji, but I was now determined. I was going to set up this new business of my own in Port Moresby. My landlady, Margaret Richardson, and I had become good friends. I told Margaret, "I haven't got a job." Margaret replied, "Just stay there, don't worry about the rent." She let me stay rent-free for a while. I did offer to pay it back, but she would not accept. I had other friends, Scott and Karen—they were from Gosford on the north coast of NSW. I used their car. Karen was a hairdresser. Scott was a builder. I used to drop Karen off at the hairdressers and then drive around. So, I had transport and a place to live sorted. They are the friendships one has built. I couldn't work as a pharmacist, though. There were only two other pharmacies in town and you needed a work permit, which I now did not have. I was just surviving on money that I had saved.

'I went to Steamships to meet their general manager, a Welsh guy, in charge at the time. He was sitting in this, huge room, typically Colonial. I went in nervously. He looked at the proposal—it was only two or three pages. He literally tore it in half and chucked it in the bin.

That was the arrogance they had. I was stunned. He said, "No, no, no. You are way off the mark—not interested." I asked, "Well, what are you looking for?" He said, "We want a percentage commission of your sales." I asked, "Do you mind if I go away and re-do it?" He said, "Yeah, why not." I went back and re-did the proposal. We would give them 10 per cent commission on sales. Because that covered the rent, the electricity and a whole bunch of things. I went back to another meeting with the general manager, who said, "This is close; we want 12.5 per cent." I said, "Okay." Steamships accepted my proposal and even provided a cash register so they could track the sales. That is when the new journey began.'

Mahesh Patel now had a golden ticket with Steamships to start his own business. But with no income and limited funds, he did not have the full financial backing needed to open the pharmacy. He needed help.

Mahesh Patel: 'In Port Moresby in those days, Thursday night used to be the disco night at the Yacht Club. I was there one Thursday night and one of my friends, Les Moore, asked, "What's wrong? You look a bit down." I told him what had happened. My deal with George did not work out. Les was the general manager of a building company, Bodiam Constructions. He said, "Give me the business plan. I'll send your proposal to my boss in Sydney, Alan Jarvis." A few days later he came back to me and said, "Yes, he's interested." Alan Jarvis was an entrepreneur. He and I had never met before. But we talked and agreed on a deal where we each put in 40,000 Papua New Guinea kina (867,000 Indian rupees) to start the business. I borrowed money from my family, which eventually my wife Usha and I repaid, in lieu, by paying for my younger brother Anil's education expenses in Australia, as my family did not want or expect the loan to be repaid.

'Alan Jarvis was a really good businessman. I learnt a lot from him. It surprised most people that we were partners together. We never had a shareholders' agreement. It was a gentlemen's handshake. He really was my mentor. He was a through and through businessman. I don't know why he accepted my proposal. I never asked him that, which is a pity.'

Caleb Jarvis: 'Why did my father Alan go into business with Mahesh? I think there was a timing element to it. At the time, Dad was a builder and a property developer. I think the answer is obvious, and Mahesh would know this, although he is being modest: that Mahesh is a talent, he is intelligent and very enthusiastic. At that early stage, they were both extremely ambitious. Papua New Guinea just presented so many opportunities. You had Mahesh being the superstar that he is, a visionary. You had Alan, who was very experienced, who had built well and had capital in his pocket, ready to go at that time. They were introduced at the right time at the right place.'

With their new partnership confirmed, Mahesh Patel and Alan Jarvis went about checking their business plan. They went back to Steamships and modified some parts of Mahesh's original proposal before signing a contract to open their first pharmacy in May 1987. It had been one year since Mahesh had left employment at Chapman's Pharmacy. Life seemed to be on the rise again. But unknown to him, there was a group working to block his new business venture before he could even begin.

Greg Wisbey: 'There was huge pushback at the time against Mahesh starting his own business. One of the guys from my company, higher up than me in the business, did his best to block Mahesh. Basically, the trading business in PNG [Papua New Guinea] is run by the PNG Chinese. The Chinese community there were all about family. There was a lot of tension about Mahesh and his new business. The company I was working for wouldn't normally get involved in personal attacks or anything like that. But the other pharmacies got together and told my company that they had to block this guy because he was going to open a pharmacy of his own. They were going to do everything they could, to have Mahesh booted out of the country.'

Mahesh Patel: 'On 28 May 1987, we opened the first City Pharmacy store at Garden City, Boroko. There were four staff members. The day before, I got a letter from the Papua New Guinea Labour Department with a deportation notice, saying I had to leave the country by 31 May 1987, because I have been working illegally. I did have a visa to stay in PNG, but I wasn't working because no one was paying me. Through my network of friends, I was put into contact with Rose Kekedo, the secretary for Labour. I rang and said, "Rose, I've got a deportation letter from you, what's the problem? I've not done anything wrong." She said, "What do you mean?" I said, "You've signed it." She replied, "You know what Mahesh, I get fifty letters, I just sign off. Don't worry, let me look into it." She made some enquiries and found my whole file had gone missing. Rose called me back and said, "You are not going anywhere. Stay put, I'll look into this." It was a scary time. I had been unemployed for one year. I thought someone was going to come and shoot me. I wasn't politically connected. They were refusing to give me my foreign investment approvals. I didn't understand PNG politics at all. Finally, it was sorted out and I was allowed to stay.'

Mahesh Patel enjoyed the challenge of running his own pharmacy. The hours were long but the business was succeeding. Later in 1987, he received an opportunity to expand.

Mahesh Patel: 'Initially, I did not think big at all. I was just thinking about getting my own pharmacy. I didn't have any serious thoughts beyond that, to be honest. I said, *Let's just open one store*, because that's the vision I had in Fiji, of opening my own store. In November 1987, Steamships said they had a spot available in another location. "Would you want to set up there?" I said, "Okay." We recruited a foreign-based pharmacist and opened our second store ten minutes' drive from Garden City.'

It was after the opening of the second City Pharmacy store in November 1987, inside the then Steamships flagship department store in downtown Port Moresby, that Mahesh Patel gave serious thought to significantly expanding his business with Alan Jarvis.

Mahesh Patel: 'That is when I started thinking, this is not a bad formula, because it was low capital expenditure, you are really only paying for the stock and staff. The fit-outs are all done. Now, Alan and I targeted any supermarket we could approach to get one of our pharmacies set up inside the store.'

Caleb Jarvis: 'Alan and Mahesh, they were very different people. If you looked at it as an outsider, you would question how it all worked. But it was one of the greatest business relationships I have ever witnessed. Dad came in with all his corporate experience, brought the structure, and was very good in the chairman's role. It was one thing to set up one store. I think the real risk came when they had to keep investing into the business to start growing it.'

The partnership with Alan Jarvis would flourish and go on to be both commercially and personally fruitful. But it was not the most important partnership of Mahesh Patel's life.

Chapter 5
England

Ushaben Patel was born in Mbale, Uganda, in 1959, to Manubhai Patel and Kamlaben Patel. Usha is the middle child of three sisters and two brothers. Her parents' families were from the villages of Dantali and Bodal in Gujarat, India. Her father was also born in Uganda in 1934. Usha's great grandfather was the first of the family to go to Uganda for work. 'It was to better our lives,' explains Usha. 'Life was so hard in India and a lot of people were going to Africa for work to improve their lives. My father and grandfather were both accountants. My father was educated in Africa. They did quite well in Uganda and travelled in and out of India.'

Her father's home was not too far from her mother's in Gujarat when they were young. They had an arranged marriage. They were betrothed when her mother was thirteen years of age and married when they were both in their twenties.

After two years living in Uganda and nine years in India ('Dantali was a very small village,' she recalls), Usha and her family emigrated to Kent in the United Kingdom when she was eleven. Her father went to England to obtain work and secure a new home for his family, while they waited in India to be called over. Because her father had worked in the British protectorate region in Uganda, the family automatically received British passports, which made their eventual move to the UK easier.

Usha has an older sister Yamini, an older brother Sunil, a younger sister Ragini and younger brother Rakesh.

'When Dad first went to London,' remembers Usha, 'it was tough for him. His job was not highly paid. There was a lot of discrimination. Dad was very intelligent. I felt he wasn't valued for all the work that he did. He didn't have any choice but to get on with it. Mum also had to work full time in a factory to supplement Dad's income. Both my parents were hard-working and never gave up and that is something I took to heart.'

The family lived in Chatham, a town located in North Kent, in southeast England. It was developed around Chatham Dockyard and several army barracks, together with nineteenth-century forts, which provided a defensive shield for the dockyard.

The Hindu religion was important to Usha's mother; to her father, more so in a quiet way. Usha went to the local Anglican church—the Church of England.

'I picked up the best of both worlds,' she says. 'I wouldn't say I'm a staunch Hindu or follow any religion particularly. I follow wise teachings—whatever they may be. Buddhism probably resonates more with me, to be honest, because it is more a way of life.'

Ragini Shah: 'I would describe my sister Usha as someone who is intelligent, courageous, kind, compassionate, generous and very grounded. Whatever difficulty life has thrown at her, she has dealt with dignity, love, wisdom and forgiveness. For all the good in her life, she has received it with love, gratitude and generosity.'

Being a foreign student whose first language was not English was difficult. Usha worked diligently at her studies to make the most of every opportunity for improvement she could find.

Usha Patel: 'I did not go to a very good school, because I did not speak any English at the time. As a child it doesn't bother you too much. I do remember standing in the playground when I was fourteen, thinking, *What am I going to do with my life?* I did register that I would study hard and not miss out on any opportunities. At the time, my English was not that proficient, so the school would not let me take my O Levels. But lucky for me, I had a teacher, Mr J. Davey, who really looked out for me. He put in a good word for me. I vowed that I would seize this chance and do well. I wasn't going to let myself or others down.'

When she was sixteen, Usha Patel decided what career path she wished to pursue after excelling in physics, chemistry and maths in her A Levels, the final school exams.

Usha Patel: 'Dad and Mum always emphasized on a good education, and because we saw my parents struggle, it added extra weight to it. My dad always wanted us to go to university and get qualifications and become something. I had the choice between becoming a pharmacist, optometrist or physiotherapist. I went for pharmacy as it interested me the most at the time.'

Starting her pharmacy course at the age of eighteen in 1978 at the Leicester Polytechnic, Usha Patel undertook three years of study and one year of intern training. After graduating in 1981 with a Bachelor in Pharmacy (Hons), she did her traineeship year in London and then worked in the city as a pharmacist. At the age of twenty-three, she made a move away from her family home in Chatham.

Usha Patel: 'My parents always wanted us to be independent. Girls and boys were always brought up differently, but they wanted us girls to be able to stand on our own two feet and be self-sufficient. I moved away from home after uni to Portsmouth and bought a house with my sister. I really grew up there because I had to do everything myself that goes with being an independent adult. I started work in a hospital, then various community pharmacies. I don't think I had any real aspirations or dreams at that stage. I was lucky enough to be able to afford to travel extensively once I started earning.'

Usha's life path would begin to change dramatically in 1985, though she would not realize it at the time.

In July 1986, Mahesh returned to Fiji for his brother Bipin's wedding. It was the first time in twenty-one years that all nine Patel brothers and sisters were together.

Mahesh Patel: 'My brother Bipin was getting married in Fiji. The year before, my dad had passed away. It was a bit of an emotional time. My mum was on her own and there was a lot of pressure on her. You are having celebrations and a wedding and her husband had just passed. She was the talk of the town—and it's a small town. Also, there was a bit of a class system. We come from Gujarat. My sister-in-law Sujla was from the Punjab region. Some people raised concerns about the regional and cultural differences. It was a bit archaic.

'We as a family said, stuff the society, it is our business. My mum was saying, "My husband is not here, and all this is happening," and the townspeople were saying that we shouldn't allow it. We, as a family, thought we should all turn up to the wedding. All nine brothers and sisters got together in Fiji, as moral support for my brother, my new sister-in-law, and my mum. Then the whole town turned up. There were 3,000 guests!'

After the wedding ceremony, his mother and sisters told Mahesh he was next in line and asked: 'When are you getting married?' Mahesh's automatic reply was, 'I don't know.' He had girlfriends in the past, but nothing serious warranting marriage.

Like so many others of Indian heritage at the time, arranged marriages had been a normal part of Patel family life. Mahesh was semi-open to the idea. He asked to view some photos of potential brides. 'I thought, they show you some pictures and you say, "I like her, I like her, I like that one," and I'd pick. I had no idea how it all worked,' he says, laughing.

But his sister Tarulata declared excitedly, 'I met this lady in India. She is a pharmacist. She's from London. Nice family. Nice girl.' Mahesh replied, 'OK, I'll check her out,' half-jokingly.

Usha Patel: 'I went to Gujarat with mum every year and she would visit a spiritual guru whom she had known since she was very young. I happened to be with mum there in 1985. My aunt Manju Masi lived in a city called Baroda and Mahesh's sister Tarulata lived in the same compound. She was married to a heart specialist. It was a gated community and she was living a few doors down. I was with my aunt one day and Tarulata happened to come along. She came up for a cup of tea. I was just chatting to her. We probably talked for a couple of hours.'

Tarulata Patel: 'I was living in India with my husband Rajendra. I knew Usha's aunt. Her aunt told me that Usha's father wanted her to marry someone outside of India. I had a lot of brothers, so when she talked to me about it, I thought Mahesh would be very good for her. Her aunt told me Usha's family were interested in an arranged marriage. My husband talked to Usha first and asked her what sort of husband she would like. She said she wanted someone intelligent. Mahesh was a pharmacist and she was also a pharmacist, so I thought they would match. I asked her aunt Manju for Usha's photo, so I could show it to Mahesh. I had a talk with Usha's mum and then Usha came along and talked to me as well. She was very kind. I was really very impressed. She is a calm and down-to-earth person.'

Usha Patel: 'I was open to an arranged marriage because that's how we were brought up. My aunt gave a photograph of me to Mahesh's sister. It was sent to Fiji. That photograph was our first introduction. Then I got sent his photograph as well. His sister called me to talk about the marriage. I was told he was a pharmacist. My mum was the one who liked his face. Because she can read faces. I said, "Where does he live? I don't want to go to Fiji." When I was told he was in Papua New Guinea, I said, "I don't want to go to Papua New Guinea." I did not even know where it was. I had to look at a world map.'

The two families, spread over England, India and Fiji, knew that plans for a newly arranged wedding were well advanced. The only person who seemed not to know what was going on at the time was the anointed groom, Mahesh Patel.

Back in Port Moresby in October 1986, Mahesh had just arrived home late after attending the local Thursday night disco. The phone rang, shattering the early morning silence. He was concerned: 'You think something's wrong.'

Usha Patel was on the phone, calling from London, and she was troubled. She had just realized the wedding plans were still underway and she was concerned about the speed with which the two families were planning the marriage. She decided to put a sudden stop to it.

'Our families are talking and saying that we are going to get married,' she said agitatedly. 'I'm not getting married. I've not met you. I don't know you. Nothing is going to happen.'

Mahesh listened carefully to this woman he had never met, feeling ambushed.

'Sorry, I didn't know this,' he replied meekly. 'Let me check and I'll get back to you.'

It was five in the morning, Fiji time, and knowing his mother would already be up attending to her morning chores, he called her on the telephone. The shock of the call from Usha now had him fully awake.

'Mum, what's going on?' he asked.

'You said you would be okay with it,' she replied.

'No, I said I'd check her out,' said Mahesh.

Later that same night, Mahesh called Usha in London to apologize, saying his sister and family, 'had jumped the gun', and this 'was a misunderstanding'. It was an unusual first meeting via telephone, but their conversations continued encouragingly over the next twelve months.

'I was unemployed at that time in 1986,' recalls Mahesh, 'I was trying to set up the new business. Usha was a pharmacist, so we started chatting on the phone regularly: "What do you do?" and so on. Over almost twelve months, we became pals on the phone. Chatting away.'

In November 1987, Usha Patel travelled to Papua New Guinea to meet Mahesh Patel for the first time in person. She stayed four weeks in Port Moresby and it was a genuine case of curiosity.

Usha Patel: 'I spoke to Mahesh on the telephone for about twelve months, because he seemed like a really nice person. For me, Papua New Guinea was people living in grass huts in remote areas. I was thinking, *What the hell is a person doing out there?* I thought, *I'll go and check this place out.* Because, normally, I'd never get to visit a country like Papua New Guinea in my lifetime. It was curiosity about a different country. He had talked about it a little bit and I was quite interested to see what he was doing out there. There was nothing formal at that stage between us. It was just two people talking and getting a feel for what was going on.'

Mahesh Patel: 'I was nervous. This girl is coming out from London and I have never met her. I called my mum and said, "I don't know how these things work." My mum came to PNG as well to meet her. Usha's father didn't want her to go and see a bloke he had never met. But her mum supported her.'

Usha Patel: 'Mahesh was in the process of starting his own business. Sometimes we would discuss pharmacy. We had multiple conversations on the phone. I'm not sure if he asked me [to visit], or if it was just curiosity, but if I was going to be with somebody, potentially, then I should go and check out the place, because what if I got married, went there and found I didn't like it? I did not want to be in that situation. I would rather pre-empt things, I'd rather do it on my terms.'

Ragini Shah: 'Usha was very brave to go to PNG. Though my parents, brothers and sisters were worried at first, we all respected her decision.'

Mahesh Patel: 'At that time, we only had one HiAce van that we used for transporting goods and my after-work commute. The day before she arrived, my driver had an accident and smashed the car. I drove to the airport with this beat up HiAce van to pick up my bride-to-be! She was looking at me as if wondering, *Where on earth have I landed myself?* It was crazy.'

Usha Patel: 'My flight was from London to Singapore and then from Singapore on the local airline Air New Guinea. I was a bit scared when I arrived. But I liked the place in a sense because it was open. It was the idea of working in a business from the foundation stage that really appealed to me because I knew I could make a contribution rather than just be there for the sake of it all.'

Mahesh Patel: 'Usha stayed a few weeks and I told her I wanted her to meet all my friends so she could see who I am. They were a mix of Papua New Guineans, typical Aussies, Pommies and Kiwis in party mode. They just loved her. She said, "Your friends are wild and they drink too much." I said, "I am showing you. I am not hiding anything."'

Shefali Mehta: 'Usha stayed with my husband and me when she first came to Papua New Guinea. She appeared to us at first impression a perfect match for Mahesh. Usha had all the positives that catered for Mahesh's success. She was simple, honest and hardworking, a vegetarian and teetotaller.'

Usha Patel: 'I asked his mum to come over from Fiji because I wanted to meet her and for her to meet me. Fiji was in some ways similar to Papua New Guinea. She liked it because it gave her peace; it was just she and I talking and nobody else, and she could just do her own thing around me.'

Greg Wisbey: 'I could tell Usha was a lovely person and came from a good family and her intentions were right. But I knew Mahesh very well. So when Usha came in, it was like, *How is this going to work? How is anyone going to be able to corral this guy?* It is like rounding up cats. When Usha first arrived, she was almost like the Madonna—an untouchable golden child and then there was Mahesh, the original party boy.'

Usha Patel: 'I spoke to Mahesh at length while I was visiting. I liked the fact there was honesty about the way he went about doing things. Even if people made mistakes, he was very forgiving. He was quite cool about a lot of things that people would get upset about. He wouldn't sweat the small stuff. He was very easy-going. I don't think in that way he has changed that much at all. A good sense of humour. That was important.'

The trip went well for both parties. Usha Patel saw the business and the life Mahesh Patel was building. She met his friends, some of his family and, importantly for her, his mother Savitaben. But most importantly, she met Mahesh Patel the man and got a sense of who he really was, albeit over a short introduction period.

Mahesh was attracted to Usha, but more importantly, he enjoyed a new friendship and appreciated her enthusiasm for the new country he was passionate about. As a qualified pharmacist, she could be directly involved.

Usha Patel: 'I went back to London and we both decided it would be okay to go ahead with the marriage. I probably had already decided at the end of the four weeks. It all happened very quickly. Mum was okay with it, but Dad was still unsure. Then, once it was all decided, we went shopping for clothes.'

Mahesh Patel: 'Usha spent a few weeks with me and then went back home to London. Then obviously the pressure came from her family saying, "What are you guys doing?" I said, "Alright, we like each other; we don't know each other that well, but let's get married."'

Usha Patel: 'My father respected my wishes, but was concerned that I would be going to the other side of the world. He said, "What if things go wrong for you? Whom are you going to fall back on if you're so far away?" Mum was different, because she herself had been in an arranged marriage and she went to Africa by herself on a five-week boat trip in those days. Then she brought us back, all four from Africa to India, all by herself. My mum is a warrior in her own right. My experience was nothing compared to what she must have gone through. It was decided we would have a small ceremony in Papua New Guinea. We didn't have any choice. Mainly because the business was just starting. My mum and brother Sunil came over for the wedding. My dad couldn't make it then.'

Four months after they had first met in person, the marriage of Mahesh Patel and Usha Patel was held on 20 February 1988, on the balcony of the old-style federation house where the groom was living. There were thirty people in attendance, including five immediate family members.

Mahesh Patel: 'I couldn't afford a big wedding and I didn't want to put pressure on my family. Usha's mum Kamlaben and brother Sunil came. My mum, my brother Anil and my uncle Vinod Patel came.'

Anil Patel: 'Usha was brave to come out to Papua New Guinea. Of all the places, going from England ... from London to an unknown developing country. You have to be nuts, right?'

Mahesh Patel: 'I said that we need to have some sort of a traditional Indian ceremony out of respect for our mothers. But there were no Indian priests in Papua New Guinea. A friend of mine was the Malaysian High Commissioner. He said his son was training to be a priest and he could perform the ceremony, Indian style. I got the biggest surprise when he arrived and he was only sixteen years old! We also had a civil celebrant there to make the marriage legal under Papua New Guinean law. We were all sitting there on the balcony of my house, where we had set up everything, including Indian god idols. There was a little bit of an Indian ceremony to keep our mums happy. We got married and did all the signing of the paperwork.'

Usha Patel: 'Indian weddings tend to be stressful, financially costly and lengthy affairs. I always wanted a simple wedding, whereby the stress would be limited as much as possible for everyone involved, especially for both our mothers. They were happy with the wedding and everything went well.'

The wedding party then relocated to the Travelodge Hotel for a larger group dinner.

Mahesh Patel: 'There was only one major hotel. The Travelodge. We had the dinner and reception there. Out of respect for my mum, we said, "We'll keep it all vegetarian." Because the Malaysian High Commissioner knew the managers there, it was the first time they allowed anyone to come into the kitchen to supervise the cooking. Mum was very fussy about eggs and meat products.'

Halfway through the reception, the then Governor General of Papua New Guinea, Sir Kingsford Dibela, arrived unexpectedly.

Mahesh Patel: 'Sir Kingsford was a friend of mine, being the patron of the Red Cross, and I was thinking he would not attend, being too busy with his official duties. I had met him socially and mentioned I was getting married. I did not think he would show up. He turned up with his entourage and we made room.'

The Patels' wedding was held on a Saturday. The celebrations carried on into Sunday. On Monday, they were both back at work. Mahesh and Usha were now each managing their two City Pharmacy stores.

Mahesh Patel: 'We had a blast that night. A very simple reception. We got a few photos out of that. This was on a Saturday. Usha reminds me of this. On Monday, we were back at work.'

Usha Patel: 'I got married on a Saturday and on Monday, I started working in our second store. I didn't have time to think about anything. We just worked seven days a week.'

Greg Wisbey: 'When Usha first arrived, I was really surprised. Because she was a very quiet lady and she was gobsmacked by PNG. At the time, there were struggles and problems in Port Moresby. But Usha has been the best thing for Mahesh. If he didn't have Usha, he would not have had the success he has now. No way. She compliments him perfectly and makes him a better person.'

Gareth Joseph: 'Mahesh getting married? No, that never surprised me. Nothing Mahesh does ever surprises me. He will be doing something in PNG one moment and the next moment he is in India at the foothills of the mountains of Kashmir, taking his mother to a marketplace. He is mercurial and he has the Midas touch. So, when it came to getting married and finding someone who supported him, it was no different.'

Dr Bhupendra Patel: 'Usha is the ideal wife for Mahesh. Contrary to western society, Hindu women live by certain codes of conduct, in their behaviour at home and in society, which is difficult in this age and time. Not everyone can abide by this. Usha does.'

Tarulata Patel: 'Yes, it seems I was the connection in the Mahesh and Usha story. Her aunt came into my life and that is how I came to know Usha. I met her mum and dad as well in India. They are very kind. Her mum is the same as Usha—very kind nature and talks very softly. I am very proud of both Mahesh and Usha, and that I was able to help.'

Usha Patel: 'You meet the people you are meant to meet and be where you are meant to be. Papua New Guinea was the place I was meant to be in. Higher forces orchestrated it all, as on my own volition, I would never have ended up there.'

Though the marriage ceremony went smoothly, there was a lot of hard work to be done in the immediate future and quite a few ups and downs for the couple to navigate over the course of the ensuing years.

Chapter 6

City Pharmacy

Mahesh and Usha Patel's honeymoon was short. Approximately thirty-six hours, in fact. After getting married on Saturday, 20 February 1988, they were both at work on Monday morning, managing their respective City Pharmacy stores.

'At the beginning,' recalls Usha Patel, 'I was there seven days a week. Just doing all the jobs that needed to be done.'

One year later in 1989, they were finally able to travel to England to visit Usha's parents at the family home in Chatham, Kent.

Mahesh Patel: 'We didn't have relief pharmacists. That hampered our travelling. Then in 1989, we found some managers to employ and took off to London. That was the first time that I met Usha's father and the rest of their family. It was all very normal when we arrived. I was the new son-in-law. I was trying to impress them and they were trying to impress me.

'I did make an embarrassing mess of myself. My father-in-law Manubhai was an accountant by profession and a lot of his clients were Indian migrants and Sikhs. They loved their Scotch. I came from Papua New Guinea where we didn't drink much Scotch. We drank beer in the tropics. I was the guest, newly married, and they kept pouring me drinks while I chatted away. I had never tried Scotch before. I enjoyed it at first, but then I overdid it. I didn't realize I'd had too much. I came home and threw up at my in-laws' place that night. The lights go on. Usha's worried. I have passed out. The next morning, I get up quietly, very sheepishly. I hear the clank in the kitchen and I am thinking, *How am I going to face my mother-in-law?* But they were more concerned for me than angry, and wanted to check if I was okay.'

Usha Patel: 'I was afraid of him choking on his own vomit. That's how bad he was. I couldn't lift him up. My sister Ragini had to help me roll him onto his side. I was more concerned about my mum and dad getting worried, thinking, *Who the hell has our daughter married?*'

Ragini Shah: 'I first met Mahesh when he came to the UK after Usha and he were married. I particularly remember his sense of humour. He was a very driven and focused individual who knew what he wanted from life. He was very funny; a fun-loving, family-oriented person who was always up for a good laugh. He was also always very disciplined and organized.'

In July 1989, Usha Patel became pregnant for the first time. As well as making allowances for leave coverage at their respective pharmacies, the happy couple had to decide where their new child would be born.

Mahesh Patel: 'Usha wanted to go to London for the birth of Nikhil, because her mum was there. I also gave Usha the option to go to Cairns in Australia. She said, "I have no family there. I will be by myself. I'd rather go to where Mum is." It was a long haul to go to London in those days. It wasn't that comfortable for her, being heavily pregnant.'

Mahesh and Usha were blessed with two sons. Nikhil Patel arrived in April 1990 and Ajay Patel in January 1992, both born in London. Usha travelled back to the UK by herself weeks in advance. Mahesh arrived in London just in time before Nikhil was born.

For Ajay's birth, Usha again travelled back to London, but also had Nikhil with her this time. But when their second son arrived, for the first time since they were married, Mahesh was not where his wife had expected him to be.

Mahesh Patel: 'When Nikhil was born, I arrived just in time. Then, when Ajay was born, I missed it. I messed up my flight. He was earlier than expected. Then Usha had to stay the minimum time to get the vaccination jabs for them, it was six to eight weeks. She brought Nikhil back to PNG by herself on the plane. When Ajay was born—and she still reminds me—she brought both of the boys back by herself. That was tough going for her.'

Usha Patel: 'I don't know how, but when I was carrying Ajay, I managed to go to London by myself on that thirty-hour flight with Nikhil. Then I brought the boys back home by myself. On the plane, Nikhil had one seat, and I was holding the bassinet with Ajay. Whenever I see an upset baby on a plane now, I always say a quiet prayer for the baby and the mum. I send them healing energies, because I think, *I've been there and I know what that feels like*.'

It may not have registered with Usha at the time, but this pattern of Mahesh's other commitments taking precedence over important family events would become a major problem the family of four would have to deal with.

Usha Patel: 'Mahesh missed Ajay's birth. He was at the Hong Kong Rugby Sevens and he didn't believe me when I told him it was time. When he did arrive, he stayed for two weeks and then went back to Port Moresby. I stayed in London to wait for Ajay's vaccinations. I probably did think, *bloody Mahesh*, at the time. I was really frustrated more than anything. Luckily my family were there to help me.'

Mahesh Patel: 'The overall feeling about becoming a father was one of delight. When we got married, I always wanted kids. My vision was to kick the ball around in the park with them. That was always the intention. If I look back, I missed out on that opportunity with my dad. We were always going in and out of school and then travelling to New Zealand, so I had no time with him. My goals at twenty-five or twenty-six were to get married, have children and live happily ever after.'

Usha Patel: 'I felt a huge responsibility being a parent. I felt in the dark. You are just trying to do what your parents did for you. We do learn that sense of duty from our parents.'

A further complication for Usha was that Nikhil was born with a defect in his right leg, something that would impact the entire family in the years to come.

Usha Patel: 'Nikhil was born with some of his toes touching his knee. His leg was bent at the ankle, which had affected his growth plate [a cartilaginous area responsible for new bone growth in children]. My sister Yamini, who lives in America, arranged for Nikhil to be seen by an orthopaedic surgeon. We went regularly to refit special moulds that would help bring his foot down, and to learn the physiotherapy techniques that I kept up in PNG. He would need some serious operations as he got older.'

By the beginning of 1992, there were four City Pharmacy stores in the business. The first was in Garden City, Boroko, and the second a ten minutes' drive away, inside the then Steamships flagship department store in downtown Port Moresby. A third and fourth store were then opened inside the Burns Philp store in Boroko and in Anderson's Foodland in Koki.

With much hard work from both Mahesh and Usha, and through the guidance of Alan Jarvis's business expertise, the City Pharmacy chain was flourishing and ready for further expansion.

Usha Patel: 'Initially, there was no bigger business vision for me. I thought we'd just be in Port Moresby with our four stores and we'd be quite happy. Mahesh obviously had bigger plans. Or at least they evolved over time, bit by bit, where he could enlarge it to his vision.'

Greg Wisbey: 'That concept of Steamships pharmacies in the stores and the way Mahesh carried that forward and arranged the contracts with Steamships was really clever. Because of the local security situation, it was a bit of an issue sometimes for people to go shopping. Your wife doesn't necessarily want to make a trip just to visit a pharmacy when she can park securely at Steamships, go inside and find everything under one roof. So, when Mahesh got Alan Jarvis with him, it was a perfect storm. Because with those two, you had Alan's skillset and his financial know-how and then the vision, passion, work ethic and everything else that Mahesh brought. That's why it worked.'

Robyn Jarvis: 'My husband, Alan, and Mahesh were an impressive two-act team. Never a contract between them, not one piece of paper. Mahesh sometimes looked bored in board meetings, but Alan was pedantic with the routine of business. I sympathized with Mahesh as we, also, were subjected to the formal way of doing things. Mahesh may not agree, but the impression was that Alan was the wise, old man and Mahesh, always on a plane, the explorer and reporter.'

Mahesh Patel and Alan Jarvis ambitiously moved beyond Port Moresby and, in 1992, opened five new City Pharmacy stores in regional Papua New Guinea.

Mahesh Patel: 'They were all in different provinces: Lae, Madang, Mount Hagen, Goroka and Manus Island. That was no mean task. At that time, we employed Neville Barrett, who was an integral part of this roll-out. I said, "We are going to build these new stores. We need one finished each month in five locations."'

Neville Barrett: 'I moved from New Zealand to work in Sydney and I hated it. I then found a little advert in the newspaper. They were looking for a retail guy in Papua New Guinea. I didn't even know where Papua New Guinea was. I was interviewed by Alan Jarvis. I spoke to Mahesh on the phone before flying up. We were told by others there were crocodiles going down the main street in Port Moresby and you would get malaria. Mahesh said it was not true. He said, "It's a city, don't worry about it." Well, he lied to me. I got to Papua New Guinea, and there was this little building which was basically the airport. Some people were hanging off the barbed-wire fence around the hut, looking at me. You get off the plane and it is just so hot and I'm thinking, *My God, what have I done?*'

Usha Patel: 'Neville is a real character and a lovely guy. Those were the good old days. That time for me was special. Neville was a good guy, and good for the company as well. People loved him. He is the sort of person you want to have in your business.'

Robyn Jarvis: 'Not long after Alan and Mahesh settled into their partnership, I was astounded at the fast pace of growth. Eventually, twenty-seven pharmacies opened, creeping offshore into the islands further afield, and, at one point, there was even an ambition to take over a pharmacy chain in Australia. After a lifetime of construction, it became clear that the future in PNG lay in letting Mahesh go for it, and Alan closed down the PNG arm of Bodiam Constructions.'

Neville Barrett: 'Mahesh would say I helped with the growth of the business and I probably did to a degree. To be fair, Mahesh was the driving influence. There was me at the front, there was Mahesh in the middle and there was Bob Patel out the back, running the distribution centre. We just improved little things. I brought some influences out from Australia. I had a retail background. We improved the look of the stores. We had a direction, but Mahesh drove it. He said, "This is where I want to be," and we had to interpret that. Between the three of us, we pulled it off rather well.'

Mahesh Patel and Neville Barrett had an unforgettable return to Port Moresby after one of their regional trips in 1993.

Neville Barrett: 'We went to Lae to visit a pharmacy there. Store visits by Mahesh were not good for the likes of me, because he would see something wrong at 1,000 metres. The team and I worked hard on this store to make it really good but it wasn't. It looked the part, but there were fundamental things wrong with it. Mahesh was not happy! We got off the plane in Port Moresby and it was raining. He got held up at gun point and they stole his car. What else could go wrong?'

Mahesh Patel: 'It was at the old domestic airport in Port Moresby. When we went for short trips to regional areas, we left our cars in the carpark. We returned after a trip and, as I got in my car, the central locking opened all the doors. One guy jumped into the front passenger seat and pointed a gun at me, while others jumped into the back seat. I was ordered to get out of the car, which I did quickly, and they drove off. I hurriedly looked for Neville, who had gone to his car, a ute [utility coupe], and without thinking, directed him to follow the guys who had taken my car. We sped off and caught up with them and they turned into a side road. They then turned around and began coming at us! We got scared and drove into the nearest police station yard. The stupidity was that because we had a ute, we thought we could ram into my sedan they had stolen, forgetting they had a gun. It was really a foolish move on my part.'

Prior to their regional expansion, a large fire destroyed one of the four City Pharmacy stores.

Neville Barrett: 'Our main store with the biggest turnover burnt to the ground at Boroko. Everyone is running around saying, "This is bad, this is bad." I'll never forget, I said to Mahesh, "We've got a warehouse full of stock, let's get trestle tables. We'll go outside the burnt area and have a fire sale." It was a major success. We were doing just as good a turnover selling goods off trestle tables. Mahesh loved it. He said, "That's bloody brilliant." We got all these flyers made: *Fire Sale!* We had vans pouring in from the warehouse with stock to keep up. We had to keep the turnover going. We had bills to pay.'

Mahesh Patel: 'It was all very straightforward with the insurance claim. We didn't own the building. We just lost the stock inside, which insurance paid for quickly. We had a little pharmacy inside the Burns Philip supermarket. But it was our store with the biggest turnover, so as far as the whole business went, it was critical at that point in time.

We were in that growth phase. We didn't have that big warehouse and company infrastructure then. Yes, we did sell stock on trestle tables immediately afterward, and we had a laugh about that.'

Neville Barrett: 'What is Mahesh like working under pressure? You can see a certain amount of concern. There is absolutely no stress whatsoever. Then you can see the cogs in his brain working out how we are going to get out of this.'

The first evidence of Mahesh Patel's community spirit and willingness to give back on a large scale became apparent to those around him very early as he created City Pharmacy Limited (CPL) in Port Moresby.

Mahesh Patel: 'From 1989 to 1994, I was chairman of the Red Cross fundraising committee. I just got asked. The Red Cross need continual fundraising, and their biggest programme was the Miss Papua New Guinea talent contest. We were just starting our business, and we sponsored a girl one year. We thought it was a good idea to market our company.

'Then the committee, which was full of ladies who had been doing it for years and years, said, "Why don't you join the committee?" I said, "Okay. I'm sure there are a lot of improvements we can make." When I came in for my first meeting, they said, "We want you to be Chairman. You can be the neutral guy." The Miss PNG contest was the biggest single fundraiser for the Red Cross and extremely high profile.'

Mahesh Patel: 'We had the first live television broadcast for the Miss Papua New Guinea talent contest. There is always this suspicion about fundraising, so the first thing I did as Chair was approach one of the big four accounting firms and ask them to audit our books. I needed to show transparency. At Red Cross, the funds are limited, so I used to get my head of finance go there every Monday for half a day to check the books. Then, I could confidently go and tap on the doors of CEOs and ask, "Will you donate funds, will you sponsor a girl?" Eventually, after five years, I dropped off the Committee because it required a lot of time commitment.'

Mahesh Patel further extended his community service to include working on the team for the Pacific Games. It is similar in format to the Commonwealth Games, but restricted to South Pacific nations.

Mahesh Patel: 'The first Pacific Games I was involved in was in 1991 when Papua New Guinea hosted them. The government had asked for volunteers. The protocol side of things for the official guests was being coordinated by my friends Monica Harris and her husband Dr Bruce Harris—lovely couple, Americans. I knew Bruce through softball. He said, "Why don't you volunteer?" So, I turned up and asked, "What do I need to do?" They said, "You are in charge of the Protocol Committee." I asked, "What does that mean?" The Chair replied, "The Department of Foreign Affairs will come and teach you." What it meant was that I would be liaising with every dignitary who arrived, and then I had to coordinate all the medal presentations. Oh, and he adds, "You need to find 150 or so volunteers." I had this role for six months, and I did not go into my work office. I used to get home at two or three in the morning. Bob Patel, a close family friend of ours moved from Fiji to help with the running of the business.'

In the early 1990s as the City Pharmacy business grew, Mahesh Patel was the company CEO and Alan Jarvis the chairman. Mahesh and others have strong memories about those early days when it was smaller and more personal.

Mahesh Patel: 'When we were growing our business and had about sixty or eighty staff, every Christmas, Usha and I used to write individual gift cards and wrap gifts. For all of them. We would bring home all the Christmas cards and wrapping paper, write and fold. In the card would be a cash bonus and we would give them either a box of chocolates or a Christmas cake. I was reading an article about the importance of not losing touch with the people you are working with. In the digital world, people are forgetting about the human touch. That's when I thought, *Wow, we used to do that*. But when you become bigger, you cannot do it. We give them cash bonuses and gifts now, but it is not the same as a handwritten Christmas card and gift. It also came up in our market research within our own staff—their biggest want was about them getting recognition. It's not all about money. It's also about being acknowledged. So, we started a staff recognition programme.'

Tracey Gotele: 'I started working for CPL at Boroko in 1990, when there were four CPL stores. I started as a cashier and then went on to serving customers. That was my first ever job, and I loved my work as a cashier. Then, I learned about the products. To do customer service in the store, you have to learn about the products, so I began to equip myself with knowledge about those items and customer service. When Mahesh was CEO, we would go to him with our requests, and he was always so accommodating. He would just say, "Approved, done". And the problem would be solved there and then.'

The expansion of the City Pharmacy business and the increased financial returns allowed Mahesh and Usha Patel to reassess their long-term future and realize a goal Mahesh had set for himself years earlier.

'The vision was always to work your butt off for ten years,' he explains, 'and then make it big enough so you can actually get away and do your own thing.'

In December 1994, the family moved to Sydney, Australia, for their children's education, while maintaining a home in Port Moresby.

Chapter 7

Australia

Mahesh and Usha Patel and their two young sons, Nikhil and Ajay, moved from Port Moresby to Sydney, Australia, in December 1994. There were two primary reasons for the move. The Patel's wanted to ensure their sons had the best possible schooling, while ensuring Nikhil's medical treatment was a priority. Mahesh's business partner Alan Jarvis influenced their decision to choose Sydney—it was where he also resided with his family. Alan's wife Robyn Jarvis helped them find a home to purchase.

Mahesh Patel: 'I've seen a lot of expatriates living in PNG going troppo [an Aussie term for going a bit crazy because of the tropical heat and humidity]—you start going to the pubs too often and drinking too much beer; you have a different lifestyle. I didn't want to do that. Also, I wanted the kids to have an education at the highest level.

'If I had the chance again, I would have kept them there in Port Moresby for a few more years. But my business partner Alan, who lived in Sydney, influenced us. That's how we ended up in Sydney at the end of 1994, when the kids were ready for school. Alan said Sydney was the best place to live. In hindsight, both Usha and I think maybe Brisbane might have been better, because of the closer proximity to

Papua New Guinea and the warmer climate. We had been to Sydney before, but never had thought about living here.'

Robyn Jarvis: 'Mahesh was determined to fit in, even if he approached this unconsciously. I remember being questioned closely such as, *Where do you live? What car do you drive? Where do your children go to school?* He may not remember this, but these questions were fired at me at one of our earliest get togethers. Mahesh followed up on all these questions and made them real. He is able to ask questions, but, more importantly, if he thinks they provide answers to his unconscious ambition, he acts on them.'

Usha Patel: 'Ajay was three when we came to Sydney to live, and Nikhil was nearly five. We decided to come to Sydney to enrol them in school. I had never lived in Australia before, but had been for visits. I had friends in Papua New Guinea, and it was a great place to bring up young kids. Every Sunday we would be out on a boat. To be honest, I didn't want to leave Papua New Guinea, because it was my first real home. I was quite happy there. I had to re-do my pharmacy qualifications to work in Sydney. I worked as a locum pharmacist afterwards. Because Mahesh was in and out a lot, one parent had to be full-time at home. So, as usual, I worked around him.'

Nikhil Patel: 'I have fond memories of living in Papua New Guinea. I think it is why I still feel a connection, although I've lived in other countries. In the early days in Sydney, I remember meeting our extended family. Finding out we had cousins was the best discovery. I also recall my sixth birthday at a park near our childhood home and playing soccer with Dad. We had a very active lifestyle growing up from beaches to mountains, and everything in between.'

The new home meant a constant cycle of travel between Sydney, Port Moresby and Asia for Mahesh, which continues to this day. With him absent, travelling to Papua New Guinea for long periods of time, Usha was forced to bear the brunt of raising two young children alone and found it very difficult.

Usha Patel: 'I struggled a lot at the beginning and it wasn't easy for the boys either. Then after a while it became part of the norm. It was just something we got used to. But it wasn't a very good place to be. It would not have been my choice; it was never my choice. All the success, I have to say, has come at a cost. If I had my time again, I would have preferred if he could have stayed with us and been there more for us. I am not a very materialistic person—that I need this, that and the other. I would absolutely have preferred his time. The family, for me, was absolutely the first and foremost priority above everything else. Above the success. Because I feel, without your family, life is meaningless. I know where Mahesh was coming from, but at the same time, it was a big learning curve for both of us.'

Mahesh Patel: 'I was away a lot. I would come in on Friday, go to schoolboys' soccer on Saturday. Then on the Sunday or Monday, I'd be off on the plane to another place. It was all thrilling and exciting then, but looking back at it, I was just an idiot.'

Usha Patel: 'At times I got very angry, yeah. Could the travel have split up our marriage? Not the travel alone; it was a very complicated situation. I also had the boys to consider. Marriages can be challenging at the best of times. The long separations did not help. At the time, Nikhil needed a lot of my help, and not being there for Ajay was not easy.'

The separation anxiety was amplified by Nikhil's serious medical issue with his right leg. It would require major surgery as he got older, which was another reason behind the family's decision to move to Sydney. Born with a defective growth plate in his right foot, this affected his ankle and the overall growth of his right leg. The required corrective surgery and recovery was not easy on Nikhil or his mother.

Usha Patel: 'That operation needed to be done before Nikhil turned ten. The operation required was called the Ilizarov Method. An Ilizarov frame—an external metallic orthopaedic fixation device—was used to lengthen his right lower leg. The bone in his right leg was deliberately broken. The frame was applied to the outside of the lower right leg and some pins were inserted and connected through the upper and lower parts of the bone inside the limb. Then four times a day, I turned the pins a quarter of a millimetre, which created a one-millimetre gap a day, which filled up with new bone. After nine months of this, the maximum safest length was achieved.'

But that was not the end.

Nikhil Patel: 'Simply, it was an inevitable part of life. A part of my growing up. I don't have deep memories of the experience, after multiple hospital stays, I forget exact details. I had a unique opportunity to connect with other children I wouldn't have normally met at school or at the park. These new friendships helped me gain valuable perspective, that positivity was my choice no matter the environment surrounding me. With focus and perseverance, I could overcome any challenge.'

Usha Patel: 'Nikhil loved playing sports and all that stopped because of the long recovery. Nikhil asked me one day, "Where is your God now?" And that really broke me. I thought, *What do I say to a ten-year-old child?* When you see suffering of any kind, you do question where is God. After nine months, the frame came off, and Nikhil was still in and out of hospital with more operations due to complications with nerves and muscles.

'When he was around fourteen years old, he was running in the rain when he slipped and fell, and the new bone snapped. I'm shaking even now, thinking about this. His doctor was over 30 kilometres away, in the western suburbs of Sydney, and no city ambulance would take us there. I had to drive there myself with him in the back seat with ice on his leg. He was in absolute agony with no painkillers to help. The hospital put him on morphine straightaway. Nikhil went through another long arduous operation whereby a similar frame was used to keep the snapped bone in place to heal. After six months, the second frame was taken off. For the next couple of years, Nikhil was in and out of hospital with more operations due to complications.'

Ajay Patel: 'Looking back, I remember the day that Nikhil broke his leg, after his major surgery. He was just running out of the heavy rain. I wish I could have understood better in the moment that he was going through something really tough and I should have been at his hospital bedside making stupid jokes the whole time. Instead, I felt like a kid who didn't know how to cope. I have regrets, but I think the situation had a resounding impact on my life going forward. Now, anytime I see someone in need, I never hesitate to offer a hand. Those quiet times in the hospital felt heavy, filled with a sense of dread, and I kept thinking, "This must be really bad," but I didn't know what was happening. I just wanted things to go back to normal. Back to playing soccer in the hallways.'

Usha Patel: 'Ajay was only a kid then. Because we were on our own a lot, Ajay used to say, "Mum, can you please spend a little bit of your time with me in the evening or read something to me?" I used to read him these stories he found soothing. I probably didn't give him as much time as I should have because Nikhil took up a lot of my attention. That's when I felt Mahesh should have been there more for us. There was a time when I had planned to leave and move back to the UK, but the universe had other plans for us. I will always be grateful to my sisters Yamini and Ragini for coming out to Australia from the US to help look after Ajay while I stayed overnight with Nikhil in the hospital over long periods of time. Also, my thanks to Robyn and Alan Jarvis, who very kindly invited us to their beautiful farm in Tasmania for a break, which was very much appreciated.'

Robyn Jarvis: 'The boys were born, and I hope we were a small help and support when Nikhil needed ongoing medical assistance, as neither of them had family in PNG or Australia. Usha's spirituality is enviable and beautiful. Her calmness in dealing with Nikhil's physical ongoing treatments was very impressive.'

Usha Patel: 'I was forced to go on a spiritual quest to find answers during a particularly traumatic time in my early forties, which brought me down to my knees. Spiritually speaking, I did get my answers, but to follow, accept and practise what I had gleaned was another matter altogether. Since then, it's been an ongoing process of continuing a practice that has helped me forgive myself and others. At the same time, I have gained more peace and acceptance without judgement. I have also learnt to enjoy all the good in my life with gratitude and love. Moreover, I mentally acknowledged that all my challenges can be my teachers, if I so choose, and serve as opportunities to grow and forgive from a totally different perspective. But for the grace of a higher power or God, I could never have learnt this on my own.

'I am not particularly religious, but I had taught the boys the importance of daily prayers. Prayer is a reminder to ourselves that we are helpless without God's support. No effort is complete without prayer, without a definite recognition that the best human endeavour is of no effect if it does not have God's blessings behind it. Prayer is a call to humility. It is a call to self-purification, to inward search. On that inward journey, each one of us has to discover what works best for us as one size does not fit all. On that, I hope I had conveyed enough to the boys to be respectful and honour all the different paths that lead to one destination.'

In 1995, Mahesh and Usha Patel purchased a pharmacy business in Mascot, Sydney. Usha managed the business, and this, coupled with Mahesh's absences overseas, pushed her to reach out to others for support, particularly among school connections for sons Nikhil and Ajay. A phone call to Andrew and Edwina Petrie resulted in a close ongoing friendship.

Andrew Petrie: 'Usha looked up the school attendance list and found my wife Edwina's name. My son Tom was in the same class as Nikhil. Usha rang up and said she was on her own, so we went and met her, and that's how the friendship started. Then, when Mahesh came back from one of his many trips to PNG, we met. Soon after that, they had a party at their place and we were there with a whole lot of other people.'

One of Mahesh Patel's overseas travels was to Singapore in 1996, to attend a business executive training course. It was here he met another attendee, Udhay, who became a close friend and business mentor.

Udhay: 'Because I come from a corporate background, I'd say Mahesh is what I call a "first principles" kind of guy. He understands the essence of things and he has strong views on retail and a deep understanding of the pharmaceutical industry. Very approachable, friendly and smart—not in some sort of abstract corporate sense—but in a hands-on way: being able to build something, operate and run something. Very quick to get to the core issues. He doesn't waste a lot of time, but he does it in a very nice way. It is not off-putting or overbearing in any way at all. It is very gentle—soft edges. Those are the traits we have built on.'

Also in 1996, there was an addition to the management team at City Pharmacy, with the appointment of someone close to both Mahesh Patel and Alan Jarvis. Caleb Jarvis graduated from university in 1992 with a Bachelor of Arts degree, and a double major in economics and philosophy. He spent time managing several digital mobile phone businesses and had experience in retail in South Australia. The opportunity to join City Pharmacy arose in 1996. After working his way through the company, Caleb was appointed Group General Manager and Executive Director for City Pharmacy Group of companies in 1999 at the age of 28.

Caleb Jarvis: 'I worked really closely with Mahesh and Alan, running the business for them. It was a great experience. I look back now and wonder how I did it. At twenty-eight or twenty-nine, it was really challenging. I had some good leadership and management experience from my other retail jobs. I think, at the time, we had about seventy-five expatriate managers and hundreds of local staff as well. It was a difficult time in Papua New Guinea. In 1997, we had the Sandline political scandal crisis. Interest rates at that point were running at about 23 per cent. A really challenging economy. We had very high levels of inventory, some big loans with big interest rate repayments, and all the while, Mahesh and Alan, while sympathetic, were hell-bent on growing the business and were pretty demanding. They were travelling in and out of the country. So, it was pretty much left on my plate.

'I remember, probably around 1999 or 2000, Mahesh told me, "My vision for the business is that we will be turning over 400 million kina in ten years." I thought, *He is cracking insane*. That was tenfold of where we were at the time. I just went, *There is no way*. But through the property sales, through the acquisitions, and through the partnering with some of the bigger superannuation firms, he achieved it. There weren't too many people that really understood his ambition. It was just phenomenal. I was in the inner workings of the business. But I must admit, at the ripe old age of twenty-nine, I could not see it. Not only could I not envisage it, I couldn't work out in my mind how to get there. But Mahesh never wavered. He had this vision and he was going to achieve it at any cost. He did it, and credit to Mahesh.'

An important part of the success of City Pharmacy was obtaining quality products at prices which would allow favourable profits. This meant constant trips around Asia by Mahesh Patel and his buying team to find reliable suppliers, which is still ongoing.

Caleb Jarvis: 'Mahesh has got a network that spans the globe. He knows how to get stuff done. That is why he is such a good businessman. We would have some great trips sourcing product from all over the planet, and a lot of it came from Asia. I had these terrific experiences and opportunities with Mahesh and often alongside the retail managers Neville Barrett and Bob Patel. Behind Mahesh's success is a team of truly amazing people who have contributed to his and Alan's achievements; they went above and beyond. While Mahesh has got the celebrity status, a lot of people worked very hard over decades to help everybody reach this level and I think that's got to be said as well.'

Neville Barrett: 'Travelling with Mahesh? Magnificent. Loved every minute of it. We would be in some stinking hot market in India and then we would have to get on a plane at midnight to get to Thailand. We would arrive in Thailand at 6 a.m. and be in the market at 6.30 a.m. If you didn't sleep on the plane, tough luck.'

Caleb Jarvis: 'We worked hand-in-hand with some really good buying agents based in Hong Kong, Ramesh and Kishin Mahtani. We had to go into New Delhi to buy a lot of product and we were looking at getting pharmaceuticals manufactured, so there was lots of business to be done there. Travelling in India can be chaos. The English Oxford factory was sold to India, so they all drove around in these old Ambassadors. You would have two hundred cars driving into a roundabout, all at the same time, and every single person beeping their horn. In the back seat were Kishin, Ramesh and Mahesh. They sat me in the front and had me drive them around New Delhi in the Ambassador. We were just laughing at the traffic and I was on the horn the whole time.'

Ramesh Mahtani: 'I met Mahesh in Port Moresby nearly forty years ago. I used to do trading business with Steamships and I met him at his first pharmacy. He was very friendly and smart and I instantly wanted to do business with him. Mahesh was interested in some of my products and so we started working with each other. Whatever he wanted, I sourced for him. We worked as a great team and went on so many trips that I have lost count of how many times we went to China, Thailand and India. More recently we even went to Dubai. Mahesh gets along with anybody irrespective of their age or the colour of their skin. He has a very friendly nature and is willing to listen and help. He is extremely generous.

'Mahesh has always had a great sense of humour. One happy incident that comes to mind is our first buying trip to Thailand. After we had completed our business, on our last night, we went out for a lovely Italian dinner. Maybe we drank a bit too much. It was way past midnight when we left the restaurant. Mahesh saw this elephant on the side of the road. He insisted we get on and go for a ride. The man driving the elephant refused as he was not licensed to do so at night. Mahesh offered him so much money that he consented. There we were at 2 a.m., riding on an elephant and singing away. Next morning, Mahesh was as sober as a judge while I had a king-sized headache!'

The other component of Mahesh Patel's numerous overseas trips was to source new business opportunities and potential expansion points for the City Pharmacy empire. As his business continued to expand in the mid to late 1990s, it opened up new geographical possibilities for Mahesh Patel in the Pacific. Then, in 1999, he would take a step up into what he considered to be the big league of business—back in his ancestral homeland.

Chapter 8

India

Mahesh Patel has a complicated relationship with his family's ancestral home of India. His father Maganbhai Patel and mother Savitaben Patel were born in Gujarat and emigrated to Fiji in 1949. He may have looked Indian in appearance, but Mahesh considered himself Fijian.

While his two oldest sisters, Taraben and Kusumben, had travelled from Fiji back to India, their birth homeland, to live and marry, Mahesh never visited the country until prompted to for work reasons in his early thirties.

'I think the first time I went to India was in 1991 or 1992,' he recalls. 'It wasn't for family; it was a business trip. We won a contract to supply medicines and I thought I'd better go and check if this factory actually existed. I was really scared going there. I had heard all the stories about getting mugged and hassled, and getting duped into different things. I was quite nervous.'

Instead of family connections prompting new business opportunities, it was the other way around for Mahesh. When he finally visited India, it opened the door to other ancestral connections for him.

'It was expensive in the early days to travel,' he explains. 'When we were at school, we couldn't afford to travel. I graduated, and then I was busy working. It was only after I started my own business I thought,

Alright, let me go over to India. Since then, we have gone quite often for business and now for other more important reasons.'

In 1995, Mahesh took his mother Savitaben back to visit her home village of Mandala. It was then he first realized how very different his life could have been.

Mahesh Patel: 'We went to where my parents were from, very much later in life. It was a small village. They traditionally came from a farming background, tobacco farmers.

'Interestingly when I went to my mum's village, looking around, the first thing I did was put my arm around her and say, "Thank God you went to Fiji." I don't know how our lives would have been if my parents had not taken the plunge to go to Fiji. I would never have ended up in Papua New Guinea. It was a life-changing journey for us all.'

The genesis of Mahesh going to live and do business in India eventually came from three different drivers.

Mahesh Patel: 'There was a big long route as to how I ended up in India. There is an offshoot to that story. Our plan then was, if we are going to do business in the Pacific, do we look at Fiji where I was born? Do we look at Tonga? Do we look at Samoa? I ventured out to these places, but the amount of effort required to do business was huge against predicted sales. We started in Micronesia.'

The Federated States of Micronesia is a country spread across the western Pacific Ocean comprising more than 600 islands. Pohnpei State is one of the four states of the Federated States of Micronesia. Guam is an important neighbouring island state.

Mahesh Patel: 'We started a pharmacy business in Micronesia in 1995. Only because I got a call from the then prime minister of Papua New Guinea to have breakfast with him in Port Moresby; the President of Micronesia was in town and they wanted pharmacies and primary health care there. The population of Pohnpei is 40,000. You have got three or four islands under the American trust. We thought,

That's exciting; let's venture out. The prime minister then started the first direct flights from Port Moresby to Guam. I was on the first one and I was on the last one. It didn't last long—the traffic wasn't there. Alan Jarvis and I used to travel up to Pohnpei. To get up to Guam, you take a right turn and the third stop is yours. The seventh stop is Hawaii. It was just an island hop.'

Greg Wisbey: 'Everywhere we travelled, Mahesh and I would look to see if there was some new business opportunity that we could identify. For many years, I worked as an island trading consultant and became a specialist on Micronesia. I flew into that region every couple of months or so. I'd do a circuit that would take me from Australia, up through the Philippines, then east towards the Caroline Islands, Palau, Yap, Guam, Saipan, Chuuk (Truk Lagoon), Pohnpei, Kosrae, and on to Majuro in the Marshall Islands. Then finally on to Hawaii and back home to Australia. It was in those areas that I saw opportunities.'

Mahesh Patel: 'There were so many journeys made. We were looking at Pacific-wide expansion at that stage. In Indonesia, we almost got started. Then in Vietnam, we had some options to start but pulled out. Greg and I did a trip to Burma. In Myanmar, we almost got started in the hospitality business there, but it didn't work out. Then, in 1996, when I went to India for my niece's wedding, that's when I thought, *What about India?*'

That family wedding may have been the second awakening he needed, but another event in 1996 may also have changed the earlier mindset of Mahesh Patel with regard to doing business in India. It was perhaps the third and final inspiration needed.

A business conference in Singapore, titled 'India: Uncaged Tiger', was an opportunity for executives outside the country to gain insights into India's burgeoning corporate scene. It was held from 19 to 21 June and was billed as the first global Indian entrepreneurs' conference.

Daksesh Patel: 'Mahesh was always ambitious. I told him I was going to this conference in Singapore. It was a very high-profile conference and was attended by the who's who of business leaders of Indian origin. They presented a lot of papers and spoke about their vision and their desires and how we can propel business. It was a great place to do a lot of networking. At the same time, it was a good place to learn and get motivated. I asked Mahesh to come and he quickly accepted. There were Indians attending from all around the world. At the conference the theme was: *Why is India lagging behind China? Why can't India do something that China can do?* There were a lot of motherhood statements.

'There were also ambitious viewpoints. I got excited just by listening to them. I was working in Fiji at the time. Mahesh said to me, "I think we should go to India," and I said, "Okay." Then he said, "Don't talk about it. Do something about it. Let's pack up and go. What's stopping us from going now?" I was shocked. *What are you talking about man?* It's not that simple. It's a bloody jungle out there. From that day, he just got into that zone and he just went. I am certain Mahesh was inspired to move to India after attending that conference. That was Mahesh's turning point to go to India.'

In the second half of 1996, Mahesh Patel started a formal investigation into setting up a new pharmacy business in India. But cautious of such a huge new market, he had to be sure it would work by finding the right connections.

Mahesh Patel: 'I spoke to a few people during my visit to India and they were excited about the idea of the modern-day drug store concept. At that time, they had the old behind-the-counter set-up, where you go in, give your prescription or enquire about medicines and beauty products, and they serve you from behind a counter. It wasn't self-service. But as we were coming from such a small place, Australia, Fiji and PNG into India, I knew we must do some market research. I had a cousin living in India, Natin Patel, and he introduced me to a gentleman who had just come from London. He had a market research background and understood what I wanted to open. He helped me.'

While researching in India in 1997, Mahesh Patel met Antoinette Amputch and found she had a similar geographical ancestry. She was born in Suva, Fiji. Like Mahesh, her father's parents were originally from India. A university-graduated chartered accountant, Antoinette was working in the insurance industry in India in a liaison capacity, where she didn't write local business. She had also previously worked in Australia and Papua New Guinea, but had never met Mahesh there. They would later reconnect in Port Moresby and strengthen their friendship while also forming an important business relationship.

Antoinette Amputch: 'Mahesh was easy-going. He just joined in. We had both been in Papua New Guinea, so we had that in common. It was more the friendship. What you saw was what it was; if he didn't like something, he would say so. It was very even-keeled. It didn't matter if you were female or male. He just melded in, and we kept social life and business separate.'

During his pre-move investigation, Mahesh Patel found a local joint venture partner for a chain of new pharmacies in India. By 1999, he was ready to make a major move by relocating his family from Sydney.

Mahesh speaks Hindi and Gujarati and gives himself a score of five out of ten in both languages. Usha Patel speaks Gujarati fluently and is also able to read and write the language. She also speaks a little Hindi.

'The Indian language I picked up because we did that at school in Fiji,' explained Mahesh. 'But as soon as you speak, people will know you're not from there. It's the roll of the tongue.'

With their language ability, there was some comfort level for the couple that they would be able to manage in their new surroundings.

Mahesh Patel: 'I think I gave Usha and the kids about one week's notice, that we were moving to India to start a new business. The boys were excited and started researching which school they were going to. From my perspective, it was good that Nikhil and Ajay were going to learn Indian culture and see a different side of life. It was a bit of a grounding for them.'

Usha Patel: 'I wanted Nikhil and Ajay to go and take in the culture. I think that was my major decider. I really wanted them to have some experience of India. We were fortunate they were not in formative classes. Nikhil was around eight and Ajay around six. The timing was right. So, I said, "Fine, it will be good for them for a couple of years."'

Nikhil Patel: 'It was strange as it felt like we moved overnight. Initially, it was a culture shock. Although our life in India was different, my experience was great. I made lifelong friends, was immersed in our culture and felt a sense of "home."'

Ajay Patel: 'I remember moving to India. It was both exciting and a bit scary. I remember waking up in the dark to catch the plane. I felt like I was an ancient explorer on an adventure looking for new insights, with the exception that I was comfortably warm, thoroughly fed and completely dry. Once we got to India and settled in our beautiful house, it had, seemingly infinite levels—four storeys—very different building styles to Australia and there were monkeys swinging on the branches of the trees just outside my window, which was always a plus for a young boy growing up in an urban environment. Living in India was such a different experience, compared to where we had grown up all our lives, and it gave us a better understanding that, for a lot of people, life is a struggle.'

Mahesh Patel: 'When we first went to New Delhi, we stayed in an apartment. The kids were excited to go to school. The next morning about 6 a.m., the power goes out. We're used to that in Papua New Guinea. Then we realize the water pump is electric. Because there is no twenty-four-hour running water in the taps. The very first day we had an electricity cut and a water cut. I said, "Welcome to India." In Papua New Guinea, there were a couple of instances, where we had to pump water out of the swimming pool to bathe the kids to send them to school, on occasions of water shortages in the early 1990s. In that way, we were somewhat prepared. But it was a new grounding for the kids.'

Mahesh Patel: 'The traffic jams on the road can be bad. Just dealing with poverty is challenging even when you are generous. Everyone has a driver and I remember in the early days Usha would pull over and the street beggars would come along and I would say, "No, don't give it to them," but she, with the goodness of her heart, would start giving them ten-rupee notes. After the first few times, I said, "You can't do it." So, she started to carry a bag of fruits—okay, they are hungry, we'll give them food. So, one day, she put the window down and gave this guy an apple. He threw it back at her. I said, "Right, that's your lesson."'

Regarding the new pharmacy business venture, the most important thing Mahesh Patel did to make it happen was to commit to living and working in India. The first store opened in New Delhi in 2000 and expanded to a total of five pilot stores in the city within 14 months.

Mahesh Patel: 'I found a joint venture partner. We needed somebody locally to work with us. When I gave him the business plan, he didn't even look at it. He asked me, "Who is going to run it?" I said, "Me, I'm moving here." He said, "Right, done deal," and we shook hands. The idea was I had mapped out another 140 stores nationwide.'

While the five stores themselves were successful, government restrictions meant that multi-brand outlets were not approved for foreign investment, so Mahesh and his foreign investors in the business were unable to provide any further capital to support expansion.

Mahesh Patel: 'Foreign investment in multi-brand retail has not opened up in India till date. It is just a government regulation. Walmart tried. Carrefour tried. It's Indian owned, unless it is a single brand. I was part of the business chamber. I was sort of the poster child: Indian, but with a foreign accent. We did a group presentation to a parliamentary committee in India. They said, "You can do the talking." I thought, *My Hindi is really bad*. Luckily, it was a young minister who understood what I was saying. About job creation. About modern retailing. He looked at me and said, "You know, Mr Patel, all your points are very valid. But we've got a vote bank of sixty million corner store operators.

If we allow you guys, foreign investors, to come in, they would all vote against us." We had to sell the business and eventually found a buyer. We got a 35 per cent return on our investment, which wasn't too bad. But that wasn't the end game; it was something we had just started to build.

'I remember when Australian businessman Kerry Packer tried to enter the Indian television market and he lost millions of dollars. From the outside, there was a negative perception of India. But my belief was, if you are doing business in India, go and live there. Because it changes your perspective. Some foreigners have had bad experiences in India. But there are a lot of in-India success stories as well.'

After two years away, in 2001, Mahesh, Usha, Nikhil and Ajay Patel returned to Sydney, and decided to spend more time in Papua New Guinea, with a new-found perspective of their Indian ancestral home and life in general.

Mahesh Patel: 'Just learning the value of water. Nikhil and Ajay used to freak out when they came back to Sydney. When people were hosing down streets, they would say, "Why are they wasting water?" I think they enjoyed their time in India. Nikhil is still in touch with a schoolmate whom he went to school with in India. They are still good friends. It was a pretty good experience for us all.'

Nikhil Patel: 'I was shy when we went to India. My oldest mate, Sikandar, approached me on the playground and invited me to his birthday. We're still friends today and are both based in the US. Our time in India was short, although it was meaningful and life-changing.'

Ajay Patel: 'Living in different places as a child had both positives and negatives. I couldn't be completely neutral to the experiences. Upon arrival in India, suddenly, my classmates were a diverse mix of voices and cultures, and my own PNG/Aussie accent was accepted without any judgement. I found it fascinating to be around so many people from various backgrounds. But I also struggled. Returning to my ancestral home, I think we all felt a bit out of place. Integrating two different cultures was challenging but it gave me the opportunity to explore the ideas of culture, place, and family. Throughout it all, I always saw my classmates as just people, each with their own stories. The experience shaped my understanding of the world and myself, teaching me to embrace change and find connections in unexpected ways.'

Nikhil Patel: "I definitely have an emotional connection to India. I enjoyed my time there and didn't want to go back to Sydney so soon. I had built a good group of friends and moving frequently had its challenges.'

From his Sydney base, Mahesh Patel continued his business trips to Papua New Guinea and spent considerable time in India, searching for new opportunities where he could invest his pharmacy chain sale profits.

Mahesh Patel: 'I stayed back for a while because I built such a network of people in a short time. I had a little bit of money to re-invest in India. I spoke to a lot of people from different families and like my original business in Papua New Guinea, it happened very quickly.'

A landlord first introduced Mahesh to family members of Mira Kulkarni and her son Samrath Bedi. They met and continued to see each other in social settings. At the time, Mira was developing her range of Ayurvedic skincare products. It was a startup business needing capital investment and business experience guidance.

Mahesh Patel: 'When I first went to New Delhi, my landlord introduced me to a family member for advertising and marketing matters. Through him, I got introduced to Mira and Sam and we built a friendship. Sam was in his twenties and I hung around with him. I would take him out for Friday night drinks at the Australian High Commission social club, where they served Australian beer and steaks brought in from Australia. Sam loved this and we still go there. It was at one of these times we were having drinks in a pub at the Hyatt Hotel that Sam popped the question. He said, "Why don't you think about investing in my mum's business?" I said, "Okay, let's talk about it tomorrow." This was in 2002.'

Samrath Bedi: 'Well done, Mahesh. I'm surprised he remembers it so vividly. Because he recalls it as it actually was. We did become friends through a common relative. We did hang out, like he said, at the High Commission, so he is absolutely right. The first time I brought the subject up was at the bar in the Hyatt Hotel in Delhi—it was called Djinns. It was where he had mentioned he had sold his pharmacy stores and said, "I've got money in India. I'd love to work here." Actually, I said it jokingly: "You've got money, and you've got experience opening retail stores. Why don't you invest in us?" But he then followed it up with me. He sent me a message: "Are you serious? Send me a business plan." So, I scampered around looking for a business plan. I had no idea what a business plan entailed. I spoke to my mother Mira, and I went to my stepfather Raju, who helped me write the business plan. That's how we got Mahesh into the business.'

Mira Kulkarni: 'Mahesh was exiting his pharmaceutical business in India at the time. We were looking for someone to invest in our new venture, and Mahesh seemed to fit in. My initial impression of Mahesh was that he was someone who had built his business from a grassroots level and had worked hard to make it successful.'

Samrath Bedi: 'Why did we go into business with Mahesh? It was a mix of his personality, my gut instinct and whatever deliverable knowledge that I could see. I saw that he understood retail and he had set up stores in India, that he knew what a brand entailed. He told me about his history in Papua New Guinea and Australia. He had the business experience and the money to invest, and I really liked him. I thought, *Why not give it a shot?*'

Mira Kulkarni: 'Actually it was probably destined! I did not have either the experience or the knowledge to know whether Mahesh was the right partner. I just went with my intuition, which was generally right.'

Mahesh Patel: 'Because it is a single brand and manufactures everything in India, you are allowed foreign investment. Mira made concoctions in her garage, in her kitchen. She gave it out to people to try. When I did my market research, albeit for a day, I asked a couple of people who use the product. They said, "It's fantastic." I decided, if the product is good, the financials don't matter.'

Samrath Bedi: 'We were two absolute greenhorns in the business world. I had no experience in business, and neither did my mother. We always looked at the positive side. We never looked at the bad situations which could have arisen by taking a wrong partner or by getting in a situation that could have been turbulent. We never looked at it like that. We Looked at it this way: *We've got nothing*. Things could have gone very badly wrong. There was absolutely no due diligence. There was nothing more than how we knew him socially and a handshake. Literally, that's what it was.'

The company started by Mira Kulkarni and Samrath Bedi was Mountain Valley Springs India Private Limited. As their first investor, Mahesh Patel joined in February 2002. The company created, developed and manufactured the luxury Ayurveda brand, Forest Essentials.

Mira Kulkarni: 'Mahesh brought a skill set that was diametrically opposite to the way I envisioned the stores. He came from the more mass set of rules that were considered the right way to set up a retail store. The number of products on the shelves, the navigation and so on. However, because we differed on many points, I think eventually we were able to bring the best of both viewpoints when it came to the Forest Essentials store format.'

Samrath Bedi: 'Mahesh brought in a certain discipline. He brought a structured way of thinking. Mahesh is logical in his approach—in terms of how we would set up our board meetings, how we would set up certain business practices, how he would look at the future. He was helpful in starting us on that path of just basic business 101, literally.

How he would think logically to what the future would hold. How he would start to invest in the future. A lot of the basis ideologies of business in the beginning.'

Forest Essentials is now an Indian multimillion-dollar success story, with 175 stores in India, the United Kingdom and Dubai as of June 2024. The company opened their first international outlet in Covent Garden, London, in November 2022. Eight more stores are confirmed for the Middle East. As further evidence to their rising megastar business status, cosmetics giant Estée Lauder now owns a significant minority of the company.

Mahesh Patel: 'Mira Kulkarni is an amazing creator of products. Samrath is running the business. They have both been extremely successful. It is probably one of the biggest homegrown brands which has come out in that category. They have received huge accolades and are massively followed. The company is doing extremely well. In the early days, when we were setting up the first retail stores, I was involved. But after that, Mira and Sam have been running the show, and I cannot praise them enough.'

While business success is always a key indicator, more importantly, the relationship which they have built as friends has become family-like.

Samrath Bedi: 'My wife Karishma came into my life a little later, in 2008. Mahesh and Usha are as much family to me as my own mother is. Mahesh is like a mix of a semi-father and semi-brother. I treat him as both. Usha, of course, is just the loveliest person on earth. Yes, more than Mahesh's good fortune, I think that we had good fortune in getting to meet them.'

Karishma Bedi: 'I first met Mahesh during my wedding celebration in India in March 2008. He had a very earthy yet distinguished air about him. He looked thoughtful and was initially somewhat reserved, but you knew when you spoke to him that he really listened, that he read between the lines and knew all the things you wanted to say but didn't articulate. Spending time in his company made one feel seen and heard. In time, this relationship was strengthened with my affection for both Mahesh and Usha, and theirs for me. They both have been like a silent pillar of support to me over the years and, in time, have come to adopt me like a god daughter.'

Mahesh Patel: 'We have built a close relationship with Mira, Sam and Karishma. Sam and Karishma's children call us grandma and grandpa. Because we built such a relationship, there was never a flicker of doubt about integrity or questioning anything. Even though we were minor shareholders and it was their business, we never saw it as "us and them"; it has become *our* business.'

Samrath Bedi: 'Mahesh is straightforward. He is generous to a fault. He is not a confrontationist—he doesn't like confrontations. He is someone for whom I could even use the word, *gentle*, in a "gentleman" way. He is a hardened businessman; no doubt about it. But he is a gentle, kind and generous person.'

Karishma Bedi: 'You cannot box Mahesh. He is a force. He is patient when listening to personal woes, pragmatic while discussing work. Worldly, while speaking about people and communities, and even spiritual now, thanks to Usha. He is curious, and I think discovery in life matters to him. He will offer perspectives that most others will not see or will fear. He will make you think of your best case and worst case, be the devil's advocate and push you—subtly and sometimes not so subtly—until you are doing the best that you can in every situation. He is never tired. He is thoughtful, indulgent, loving, caring and kind and knows not just how to move ahead himself, but also take his community and his people forward with him.'

While the success of Mahesh Patel in India would go on to further shape both his business and personal life in an extremely positive way, there was a price to be paid. His long absences away from his wife and sons in Sydney were creating a rift, which would ultimately result in significant regrets.

Chapter 9

Sydney

Mahesh Patel, Usha Patel and their sons Nikhil and Ajay returned to Sydney, Australia, at the end of 2000. After two exciting years away in India experiencing a new culture and way of life, they found themselves back in familiar surroundings at the family home, which had been leased out during their absence.

While their parents fell back into their own usual routine, with Mahesh resuming his regular business trips overseas, Nikhil and Ajay found it more difficult to adjust.

Ajay Patel: 'When we came back to Sydney, settling in was a little bit rough for a few years. Australia is idyllic in so many ways. Most people don't see what the planet is like for others and how they endure and live. I think the moves from Papua New Guinea to Australia and then to India and back to Australia again, really did shape the way I made decisions through my life. It was more the assimilating back in Sydney, which was difficult. It was literally the same people we were going back to school with—we just hadn't spoken to them in two years. Social groups changed. Friends' groups changed. It took a little while to settle back in. It happened eventually. I think Nikhil struggled a bit more than I did.'

Nikhil Patel: 'Moving back to Sydney was a challenge because I had become so comfortable and accustomed to the way of life in India. The culture, and also just being in the majority. Growing up in the Western world, we are all immigrants in a sense. But in this case, while we were immigrants, we weren't really immigrants. It's a bit difficult to describe, but in India, I just had that feeling of being in the majority. It was different.'

Despite having to readjust themselves to life back in Australia, Nikhil and Ajay Patel do have happy memories of their time living again in Sydney, though some were more memorable than others.

Ajay Patel: 'A lot of my memories are around sports and being outdoors, but I do remember having to sneak around Mum and Dad to go to the beach. In hindsight, it was a very dumb thing to do ... I have fond memories of going to the movies with Dad. The best few were definitely *Star Wars*, and when Dad snuck us into the theatre to see *Ali G*, quoting that film in school at that age was priceless. *Lion King* and the entire Hamlet arc hit us both really hard, but was a really great way for a kid to mature, with understanding around life, death and legacy. Sports also played a big role in our lives. Dad was competitive, almost always very present at our weekly games, kicking the ball around. Telling us how to kick the ball correctly, up to a point where we would say, "No, no, Dad. This is how we do it now." He was certainly impactful on how we played sports and how we still enjoy sports, especially soccer and rugby. We had a lot of park time together.'

Nikhil Patel: 'There was a park across the road from where we lived, and we would always go and play soccer. Dad used to play a lot with us. He is the one who got us into it. I started playing when I was around four and Ajay was three. In the early years, it was more relaxed, and then, as we got older, it became competitive. We would just have a kick around and do some passing drills. I played basketball as well. We had a hoop at the back of the house. Go out after dinner or on Sundays and shoot hoops. We also liked getting out on boat trips in

Papua New Guinea or in Sydney. Be out on the water all day and then come home to a good meal.'

Ajay Patel: 'With Mum, we would do what we called adventure walks. There were a few parks near us in Sydney and you can cross all the way through from one to another and so on. We would just basically get lost and then try and find our way home. That was a lot of fun. I used to enjoy those walks. I think we used to do that more when our dog Rex was there. We would go for these walks when Dad was away, just to get out of the house.'

Mahesh Patel: 'When we returned to live in Sydney from India, we got our first family dog, Rex. Nikhil was eleven. There was a breeder we found in Windsor Downs in western Sydney, about sixty kilometres away from where we were living. She was very serious about it all and had a questionnaire to be answered on the phone. I let the kids handle it. She didn't realize she had interviewed Nikhil and not me until we went to pick up the dog!'

Ajay Patel: 'We rode our bikes around the local area a lot. Dad used to take us bike riding too. I remember getting a scar. I got run over by another cyclist. I would have been aged eleven or twelve. Dad was there. It was this small little road in Double Bay—a no-through road. I think we were crossing, and I hadn't put my bike into gear and was still fuddling about. This cyclist was coming through, and I got in his way. A hundred per cent, it was my fault. I remember I got clobbered. Grazed up my whole leg. Still got some old scars from it. There was a bit of blood; a good many tears. I think I took a couple of days off from school.'

Mahesh Patel: 'Yes, I clearly remember Ajay's bike accident. I freaked out! Seeing the blood on his knees. I was angry at the adult cyclist who was riding so fast in a side lane and secondly upset, seeing my son on the road. He was crying but not as panicky as I was.'

Back in Papua New Guinea, there were two major changes at City Pharmacy in 2001. Both involving the chief executive officer.

Caleb Jarvis: 'I worked in Papua New Guinea a bit over five years. My wife Ellie, my girlfriend at the time, had moved up a year after I started and lived there with me for about four years. So, I had been there for five. At that point, the change was driven by our personal objectives. We wanted to start a family but felt it would be difficult for us to do it in PNG, and it was time for us to look at moving back to Australia. We had a board meeting and I told Mahesh and Alan at the end, look, the time has come. I started the process of listing the company on the PNG stock exchange. For compliance, we had to rewrite the company's constitution, going from a private company to a public company. That process took about two years to finally get it listed, but we got there in the end.'

City Pharmacy's growth as a private company had continued unabated, but Mahesh Patel's business partner Alan Jarvis was concerned about the personal liability exposure it meant for both of them and suggested they become a publicly listed company on the Port Moresby Stock Exchange.

Mahesh Patel: 'To be honest, initially, I didn't really know what becoming a public company meant. But it appealed to Alan, who was eighteen years older than me. When you were a private company, the bank would always ask for a personal guarantee from the shareholders. At that point in time, we said, "Let's do it." At least we will get respect from the banks. We will be publicly listed, audited and have transparency. Everything bundles in. It paid off, because it was a compliance listing. We didn't raise any money from the market to start, but when we needed funds three years later to buy the supermarket chain, that's when the superannuation funds came in handy.'

City Pharmacy became a public company in 2002.

Mahesh Patel: 'Alan and I still controlled a lot of the shares. We gave some shares to our staff. We lent them the money and let them pay it back. It was a soft loan, interest-free. I was looking at the share registry recently, and one of our staff now, Tracey Gotele, who purchased shares, was a teenager back then, and she still works for us. Becoming a public company was probably the best thing that happened.'

Now trading as City Pharmacy Limited, the companies' growth continued. But it was a chance meeting in 2005 that led to an even greater expansion, which would eventually lift the company towards becoming one of the country's biggest.

The Stop & Shop supermarket chain, owned by the Steamships Trading Company, was up for sale, and the deadline for tender submissions was closing fast. While it was a sale which could potentially impact the City Pharmacy stores located inside the supermarkets, Mahesh Patel was unaware of the opportunity to buy.

Mahesh Patel: 'I ran into John Dunlop when I was travelling from Fiji to Los Angeles on a Sunday. John had retired and was a director for Steamships. He asked me, "Have you put a bid in for Stop & Shop?" I didn't know it was for sale. He said the tender closed the following day, a Monday. I was flying off to Los Angeles. I rang my CEO and told him to put in a non-binding offer to Steamships. When I landed in Los Angeles, I rang John and asked, "How much should we bid?" We had not looked at the financials or done any research. John came back after doing some quick research and said, "I think something in the 20 million kina plus range is the right number. So, while I was in Los Angeles, I got our CEO to write a letter, making a non-binding offer for 20 million kina (433 million rupees). Steamships called back and said, "Okay, you guys have got it." I then had to ring the bank manager and ask, "Will you give us the money?" The bank said if the numbers stack up, they would loan the money and the deal went ahead. We were a much smaller operation back then. This step took us away from just being a pharmacy company into something much bigger.'

The acquisition of the Stop & Shop supermarket chain in 2005 started a ripple effect of financial success and further company expansion over future years.

Now known as the CPL Group of Companies, in 2007 they partnered with Post PNG to co-locate some City Pharmacy retail outlets. In 2009, they acquired the Hardware Haus stores chain from Steamships Trading Company. In 2011, they launched their chain of Boncafé coffee shops. In 2012, they opened Paradise Cinema in Port Moresby, Papua New Guinea's first multiplex cinema. In 2013, they acquired Sydney-based pharmaceutical wholesaler Cost Save Pty Ltd. In 2014, they opened a new concept shopping complex, Waigani Central, in Port Moresby, featuring a do-it-yourself hardware concept store, the largest-ever Stop & Shop supermarket, and a second Paradise Cinema complex.

In 2015, CPL moved into fashion retailing (in partnership with Jack's of Fiji), with the opening of two 'Jack's of PNG' stores in Port Moresby. The same year, they opened two Prouds Duty Free stores (in partnership with Motibhai & Co.).

Today, the CPL Group is Papua New Guinea's largest retail and wholesale organization, employing thousands of people. All of this began with one man running a small pharmacy with his wife, a man who had a vision for something much, much bigger.

Mahesh Patel: 'The most important thing about expansion is having the right management. But unless you are bigger, you cannot employ proper management. You can get pharmacists to manage the drug stores, but then as you get bigger as a company, you need a marketing manager, you need an HR department, you need an IT department and an operations guy. I was still managing all these people, but I needed to replace myself. That's when I knew, for the company to hire somebody of calibre and quality, it has to be big enough for us to afford the right person. That was the vision behind it. To get big enough to employ really talented people.'

One of those highly talented people employed during the companies' public company expansion was Ravi Singh. Born in India to a career bureaucrat mother and veterinary doctor father, he obtained an honours degree in Zoology at Delhi University. He then undertook an entry exam for a management degree and qualified 42nd out of a field of 35,000 students. Two years later, he graduated with a master's degree in business management.

Ravi Singh: 'After my master's graduation, there were several campus placement offers. I chose an upcoming fashion retail firm and worked with them for three years. Then I moved on to another leading fashion and grocery retail business in India and worked with them for six months. I then received an opportunity to work in Papua New Guinea. My boss from my first job was then working at City Pharmacy Limited. He offered me a data analyst job and I joined on 19 May 2003. From there, I consistently grew in the company and had the role of retail operations manager, general manager buying, and then finally the acting CEO role on 29 July 2008. I was confirmed as the company CEO on 1 July 2009.

'I first met Mahesh Patel on a hot Monday afternoon sometime in July 2003, when he came to the Waigani office. My first interactions with Mahesh were limited as he was the founder of the company and I had a few bosses between me and him. What I remember distinctly was that there was a kind of buzz when he was around. An energy as everyone in the office wanted to be on their best behaviour. There was a board meeting on that visit and though I had nothing to do with the meeting, it all seemed very busy in the office. There always was and is to this date, a positive energy that's infectious when Mahesh is around.

'Mahesh always believed in making the seemingly impossible a reality. On one of his trips to Mount Hagen, he met up with some farmers. At the time, getting PNG-grown fresh vegetables into Port Moresby was a struggle. The farmers in Hagen said, "We can grow what you want, we just want a market." Mahesh made a bold commitment to the farmers that he would provide them the market they needed and thus set in motion the setting up of a completely new fresh-produce supply chain in extremely difficult conditions. We started by doing charter flights four days a week to get the vegetables from Hagen. Then we set up a fresh produce depot behind the Waigani showroom. We got the first potato washer in the country and started sorting out the tonnes of vegetables we were getting from Hagen.

'We were doing something which had never been done before in PNG, but Mahesh was single-minded about this and committed to making it a reality. After a lot of ups and downs, we were able to set up a very good fresh produce depot, which now supports thousands of farmers. It started with a commitment from Mahesh: "I will give you the market that you want." If that is not inspirational from a business perspective, I don't know what is.'

Sir Michael Thomas Somare was the first prime minister of Papua New Guinea after independence and is widely referred to as the 'father of the nation'. His daughter, Betha Somare, is another who has fond memories of Mahesh Patel's efforts to help the farmers of Papua New Guinea.

Betha Somare: 'I have known Mahesh now for over twenty years. It was through a mutual friend, Graham Osborne, who introduced us. I instantly embraced Mahesh as a friend who is thoughtful, a deep thinker and philanthropist, who loves life. He is generous and fun to be with and candid when the need arises. I had the privilege of being asked to speak at the twenty-fifth anniversary of Mahesh being in PNG, at a dinner at the Lamana Hotel. I see his success as also PNG's success, as he has shown it is possible to do business in PNG. He seems fearless about the changes that a developing country is going through and continues to explore ways to partner with local entrepreneurs.

'Mahesh chartered planes to look for opportunities around PNG and I was fortunate enough to travel with him on trips, which also included his son Nikhil. We made stops in Hagen, Goroka and some other remote locations. This is how Mahesh made contacts to buy vegetables out of the Highlands. On another trip with Usha, we came across Bernadette and Bernard, who were making virgin coconut oil. Today, the oil also sells in Stop & Shops and City Pharmacies around the country.'

Mahesh Patel has always valued the importance of farmers and local producers, and has gone out of his way to help them where he could.

After the acquisition of the Stop & Shop supermarkets, one day he had a chance meeting with a small farmer.

Mahesh Patel: 'He wanted to borrow 3,000 kina (70,000 Indian rupees). He obviously got knocked back by the bank. It must be fate because I just happened to be walking down the back dock of the supermarket. He asked one of my staff if he could speak to me. He said he was going to buy an irrigation system to enhance his farm. I said to my staff, "Give him 3,000 kina. If he runs off, we're not going to go broke. But what you do each week when he delivers, you hold back some kina to pay off the debt. We're not into charging interest." The way I see it and my logic is, why should we not do it? He was a guy who was supplying us about fifty kilos of paw paw per week. Today, he supplies us 500 kilos per week, enough for virtually all the supermarkets.'

Chapter 10
Worldview

In the perception of many who know him, Mahesh Patel is a citizen of the world, constantly travelling the globe. Financial success and the drive to seek new experiences have afforded him the opportunity to see a wide range of geographical regions. A recent count of nations he has visited totalled over sixty-five.

Robyn Jarvis: 'People say the world is your oyster, but the Patels' treat the planet like a small city. Needed in London, Delhi, Mexico, London, etcetera. *Yes, we will be there. When?* Mahesh appeared to live on planes. Always on the move, even today. Most of these trips were business orientated, but many were for family gatherings. As an observer, I was and am impressed at the closeness of their family. Mahesh, Usha, Nikhil and Ajay are all there for each other, no matter how far apart they are in miles.'

One of Mahesh Patel's earliest views of the world outside of Fiji came via an English football team and one of their players, who was born in Northern Ireland.

Mahesh Patel: 'When I was growing up in Fiji, we didn't have television at home. Cinema was the main visual medium and that was only when we got the chance. We had magazines and comics. Soccer was the big sport in Fiji then for us. I don't know how or why, but I became aware of George Best, one of the great players. I started following his team, Manchester United. There was a coupon in a magazine in 1969, where you could order a poster of the Manchester United team. It cost one British pound. I would have been nine or ten years old. We used to get twenty pence a week as pocket money and I started saving. I went to the post office, this little boy looking up at the postmaster. I told him I needed a money order for the poster and he said I also needed return postage. The poster was one pound and the return postage was one pound. I continued saving my pocket money and waited another five weeks. I saved another one pound, went back and eventually got the poster. We didn't have personal rooms back then. We had a three-storey building, and on the top floor was the general living room. I stuck it up on the wall there. Later, in one of the floods or cyclones, I lost that poster. I wish I still had it. Ever since then I have been a Manchester United fan, and my boys have followed.'

Nikhil Patel: 'I have to follow-up with my dad's George Best poster story when I tell people I am a Manchester United fan, so they don't think I'm just one of these fair-weather fans. I've been a fan from day one. I remember waking up in the early hours of the morning in PNG to watch games. We would go and sit on the couch and fall asleep on Dad. He got us their 1999 Champions League jersey. I still have it at home in Sydney.'

Mahesh Patel: 'I did get to go to some Manchester United football games. Most of them have been in the cold. You have to wrap up. I love it there in London. In 2015, we went to the Rugby World Cup Final there. That was great. I love big crowds at sporting events. I've been to lots of F1 races. We went to the race in Germany, just before COVID-19. That is the home ground for Mercedes, which is my team. Sir Lewis Hamilton is phenomenal. I have his autograph on some of his helmets and photos. The time I was meant to meet him in Germany, he was unwell and didn't race. I might run into him one day in a flight lounge. A lot claim to be celebrities, but not many are true icons. Sir Lewis Hamilton is an icon.

'I've seen a lot of celebrities over the years. Usain Bolt was in Japan in the airline lounge. I am sitting there on my own, and he walks in. He's got the baseball cap on. Baggy pants. I didn't recognize him. Because he was tall, I thought he must be a US basketballer. I had just seen his documentary a couple of months earlier and I recognized his best friend, who is his manager. That's when I said, *Ah, that's Usain Bolt.* He happens to come and sit right across from me. And I was asking myself, *Should I, should I?* Then a Japanese man came along and asked for a photo for his son, so I said, *Right, if he's done it, so can I.*'

'Muhammad Ali would have been nice to meet. I went to his museum and it was just phenomenal; in Louisville, Kentucky. I went for the horse race, the Kentucky Derby.

'When I went to South Africa, I visited the Nelson Mandela Museum. I also met the South African rugby team captain Francois Pienaar, on whom the movie *Invictus* was made. This was at the 2011 Rugby World Cup in New Zealand. There was a captains' lunch. He was so humble; awed everybody. That's a true leader. Amazing character. He spoke about his first meeting with President Mandela. I've got a great shot with Pienaar, and one with them all together. Nick Farr-Jones and Phil Kearns were there too. It was one of these corporate junkets; I loved it.'

When considering Mahesh Patel's willingness to travel and see the world, evidence suggests that his mother Savitaben was a huge influence on him. During a trip to India in 1999 with him, his wife Usha, and sons Nikhil and Ajay, Savitaben's determination to live life and experience new places was fully demonstrated.

Mahesh Patel: 'I think I had more of my mother's genes than my dad's. That's where all my energy comes from. We lived in a three-storey home in Fiji and she refused to move from there. That was her home. I told her, "Mum, you're getting old, you have two flights of stairs to climb." One day we installed an electric lift chair on the stairwell. She was so vain she would never use it. She would walk up slowly.

'I remember we were in Kashmir. We went to a temple. She was very religious and she wanted to visit every temple around. "Mum, they are all the same," I said. At this, she said, "I want to go." I said, "Mum, you won't be able to climb the stairs." The kids ran up and down and counted the stairs, and there were 100 steps. They said, "No, Grandma can't go." She said, "Okay, I'll stay down near the car and do my prayers and pay my respects." I said, "Okay, that's fine." Then she says, "Maybe I'll climb ten steps." Her knees were gammy. She climbed ten steps using her left knee. Changed sides, then ten more with her right knee. Before we know it, she has walked all the way to the top.

'We were in India once, on the Ganges River. Really fast, streaming water. There was a small patch and Mum insisted she would go down to the riverbank just to soak her feet. To splash some water on herself and come back up. I was saying, "Mum, if you slip, if you don't hold onto the rocks, you will be washed a mile away." But she was okay, and she was in her eighties then. That's one thing we have missed out on, not understanding our parents better.'

Usha Patel: 'For Savitaben, with any natural body of water, just to dunk her feet in was a religious act. In Singapore, when we took her to the beach, she just wanted to put her feet in the water. Same in Papua New Guinea.'

In 2010, Mahesh Patel took his family to the FIFA World Cup in South Africa. While he is a huge football fan himself, it was his mother Savitaben, who prompted the visit.

Mahesh Patel: 'Mum travelled the world. She loved travelling. I think it was in 2007 or 2008 when I was in Fiji with her, she said to me, "Your father took me everywhere but I have not been to Africa." I checked the upcoming sporting events and the 2010 World Cup in South Africa was on. I said, "Right, Mum, we are going to Africa." I took her along and we took her on safaris. We didn't take her to watch the soccer matches because of the large crowds. But she'd watch on television in the hotel room and when we came back, she knew the scores. She returned, and all her friends were saying Mum was ecstatic about the trip, and telling them story after story.'

Nikhil Patel: 'Dad, my Grandma and I, also visited Kenya to see my cousins in Nairobi and the migrations in the Masai. Dad doesn't know this, but that trip was special as we got to share it with Grandma, but also as it was our first time experiencing Africa. It gave me a slight insight of possible similarities of where Mum grew up, which we were always curious about, after hearing stories from our Grandad. It felt somewhat full circle, connecting our global roots.'

Ajay Patel: 'We went on a safari to see the African wild dogs. We got up early in the morning. It is as cold as anything. We try and drink as much hot tea and coffee as we can, before we get onto the vehicle. We are driving through the dark and we see these African wild dogs. They are on the extreme level in the endangered species list. We end up following them for most of the morning. At the end, Grandma Ba asked, "Why are we waking up early, spending hours in this freezing car to watch dogs? You come back to Fiji and you can do the same thing from my balcony!"'

People from around the world may not know much about Papua New Guinea, but one World War II battle ground located within the country has become well known: the Kokoda Track.

The Kokoda Track campaign was part of the Pacific War of World War II, fought between the invading Japanese and the defending Australian and Papuan land forces, between July and November 1942.

Approximately 96 kilometres in length, the Kokoda Track is usually undertaken single file in most parts and is only accessible by foot. While it can be walked in both directions, the Kokoda Track travels from Owers Corner in Central Province, east of Port Moresby, to the village of Kokoda in Oro Province. It reaches a height of 2,490 metres as it passes the peak of Mount Bellamy, going through difficult jungle terrain in isolated areas.

A physically demanding trek, walking the Kokoda Track usually takes between four and twelve days.

Mahesh Patel, his wife Usha Patel, and their sons Nikhil and Ajay Patel undertook the challenge of the Kokoda Track trek in 2008. Joining them were the boys' Sydney-based cousins, Ravish, Tanuj, Ashish, Mishaal and Sameer. Family friend Antoinette Amputch was also in the group.

Mahesh Patel: 'I had wanted to do the Kokoda Trek, more as a physical challenge than anything else, for a long time. I thought, as my kids get older, it would be nice to do it with the family. In 2008, I started planning this with Pam, the tour operator and a friend of ours. I did not want to do this with a whole bunch of strangers. I floated the idea to my family and also to friends in Fiji. We ended up with sixteen people in total.'

Antoinette Amputch: 'To me, it was the curiosity. I did not have anyone close to me who had been in the war or anything like that. I just wanted to go and see what people were talking about.'

Mahesh Patel: 'It was challenging, and if it weren't for my family and friends and the motto of Kokoda being about mateship and camaraderie, I would have given up halfway through. It was very, very difficult, both physically and emotionally.'

Ajay Patel: 'It was rough, but what got us through was talking. Just the constant banter that we had between us all. Whenever you get tired, you just start talking about nothing. Something stupid. I don't even remember what we were talking about. It would distract you and keep you moving, keep you going.'

Antoinette Amputch: 'A funny memory. I was having trouble using the toilet holes with the smell. Usha took out two Dettol wipes and stuck them in her nose and said, "It's easy." That's Usha. Mentally, she is super tough.'

Usha Patel: 'This is what I am most proud of about Nikhil. Even with his leg issues, he wanted to do the Kokoda trek. He didn't want to be left out. We were all training and he wasn't training—you know, teenagers. I was worried about him making it. He was giving me a hard time. I said, "Nikhil, I've had enough of this now. You can stay back here for a week and we will make arrangements, somebody will look after you, and I'll go with Ajay and your dad." But he didn't want to miss out. I said, "If you come, I don't want to hear a peep of complaint out of you." God bless him, he didn't complain once. Nikhil finished. I had tears in my eyes; I was so proud. Thinking back on it, I don't know how he got through it.'

Nikhil Patel: 'Initially, I was doubtful If I could complete such an arduous trek. But knowing that historically, it was about brotherhood and togetherness, I pushed myself mentally to get through it, and I was glad I took up the challenge. There were moments when I just wanted to stop. When I have a goal in mind, so long as that goal is there and I know there is a break after that, I can push myself to that point. If there is a marker in my mind, I can get there. That is the attitude that I have.'

Ajay Patel: 'It was a lot of fun. I don't know how Mum and Dad did it at fifty. That blows me away. Especially Mum. Because she has never been an outdoors-type person. I was really proud to see her do it and Nikhil as well.'

Usha Patel: 'Kudos to Nikhil, he walked the Kokoda Track. I can't believe he did it. I know he was scared. I was scared, because I didn't do enough training either. I was hoping for something to happen at the last minute so it would be cancelled. At the end, we all cried, and I cried for him. For me, I was able to say to him, *You did this, you can do anything*.'

Mahesh Patel: 'When we arrived back in Port Moresby, while the group were taking photos, huge emotions poured out. Both Usha and I were bawling our eyes out. Tears flowing and body shaking. Till this day, I do not know what came over me. But apart from relief that we finished the trail, the emotions—and I still get teary-eyed recalling the moment—and the deep connection to the people and the country of Papua New Guinea poured out. Also, the fact that Nikhil, with the issues with his leg, overcame all the challenges of the tough and rugged trail. That was an extremely proud moment for Usha and me.'

Family holidays have always been important to the Patel family. The longest trip Mahesh, Usha, Nikhil and Ajay ever took was over five weeks and two continents, starting in July 2012.

Mahesh Patel: 'This was a massive trip. Usha wanted to do Machu Picchu. Ajay wanted to do the Amazon. Nikhil wanted to be in Brazil for New Year's—Rio specifically. We went to Argentina, Brazil, Peru and Chile. We had to zigzag. We went to the Amazon, Machu Picchu and the Inca Trail. It was an amazing trip. We covered quite a lot. Then, after all of that, we ended up in Antarctica. We did a cruise. It was a small boat, sixty-four passengers only. Antarctica was just phenomenal. A lot of the crew were scientists and researchers. We did three expeditions per day. We were there for one week. We had a dip in the ocean as well. The ocean was one degree. The wind chill was minus eleven. It was warmer in the water. You can't stay in the water too long or you will end up getting hypothermia. That was incredible.'

Nikhil Patel: 'We went through so many different types of environments. There was a river in Brazil where there are pink dolphins, native to South America. Then we stopped off by boat. There was a little animal sanctuary where they had snakes and monkeys. It was a protection area for them. That was cool. This monkey really liked me, and there is this photo of Ajay with a python around him. I didn't want the python. I said, "I'll stick with the monkey." He wouldn't let go. He kept on climbing up and sitting on my shoulder. He was trying to get my glasses.'

Ajay Patel: 'I remember the snake. But I thought it was a baby sloth that didn't want to let go of Nikhil. It had little claws hanging from its fingers. That was quite cute.'

Nikhil Patel: 'A sanctuary caretaker stepped waist-high into a pit of murky water. He began digging around and finally picked up this giant python. Mum told us stories when she'd walk to school and encounter a giant snake. She's always been calm with animals and taught us the same. I recall when I was five or six years old, there was a large furry spider in the corner of her room for a week. I'd run past every time. Mum just said, "Don't worry, it will go when it decides to."'

Ajay Patel: 'Some of the places we stayed in were those eco lodges, and it was quite amazing on the river, seeing the small South American towns. It has very similar vibes to Papua New Guinea. On the rivers there, you can see the village community using old fishing trap techniques that date back a few thousand years.'

Nikhil Patel: 'Antarctica was a unique place to experience. I saw similarities to PNG: a pristine paradise and untouched nature. It was definitely an adventure; We stopped at an old whaling station. A black sand beach in a horseshoe cove where Dad, Ajay and I went for a swim. A quick dip for as long as you can last in below-zero temperatures. Saving grace was the shot of vodka and towel waiting for us onshore. A core memory for me, and one of many moments revealing Mum and Dad's forever youthful sense of adventure!'

Ajay Patel: 'We took a plane and landed on one of the islets and took the boat and sailed on. We saw a leopard seal up close, as large as your couch. It was huge. That was beautiful. Going to a Post Office in Antarctica was a strange experience and the very fact that it exists. Later, I found out that it was there for all the scientists. It was cool to post our postcards out to our family and friends from there. Swimming in Antarctica was brutal and insanely cold, but you feel it as a burning heat. The trip was exhilarating and surreal. I am grateful to be able to experience that kind of remoteness. So serene and peaceful.'

Chapter 11
Order of the British Empire

George Frederick Ernest Albert, known as George V, was King of the United Kingdom and the then British Dominions and Emperor of India from 6 May 1910 until his death on 20 January 1936.

In 1917, King George V established a new award—the Most Excellent Order of the British Empire. The OBE, as it is more commonly referred to, recognizes distinguished service to the arts and sciences, public services outside the civil service, and work with charitable and welfare organizations of all kinds.

The King recognized the need for a new award of honour which could be more widely given in recognition of the large numbers of people in the British Isles and other parts of the Empire who were helping the war effort, both as combatants and as civilians on the home front.

For the first time, women were included in an order of chivalry, and it was decided that the Order should also include foreigners who had helped the British war effort.

From 1918 onwards, there were Military and Civil Divisions, as George V also intended that after the war the Order should be used to reward services to the State in a much wider sense.

Recommendations for appointments to the Order of the British Empire were originally made on the nomination of the United Kingdom, the self-governing Dominions of the Empire (later known as the Commonwealth), and the Viceroy of India.

Nominations continue today from Commonwealth countries that participate in recommending British honours, including Papua New Guinea.

From the earliest days of running his first pharmacy in Port Moresby as an owner-operator, people have always asked Mahesh Patel for community assistance. He has been willing to help where he could—something which perhaps comes from his parents and the community mindset they had taught him.

'Somebody comes to me with a proposal,' he explains. 'They want to start this village programme. *Okay, that's a good idea. That's a healthy lifestyle. Let's do this.*'

As the City Pharmacy business grew, expanded, and became more successful, the opportunities to help more and more people arose in varying ways.

A few years ago, a tall young woman visited Mahesh at the CPL head office in Port Moresby.

'She thanked me because we had been supporting their netball team as sponsors since she was six years of age,' enthuses Mahesh. 'Today, she is in the national team. Why did we do it? I don't know. I think it was because it was the right thing to do. But when you hear stories like that, you think, *Wow, you have made a huge difference.*'

As time went on, Mahesh focussed more and more on targeting healthcare and support for Papua New Guinea women in his charity efforts, including supplies of healthcare products and education programs in remote village areas.

Then, in 2007, the CPL Group launched the first women's empowerment programme in Papua New Guinea, the Pride of PNG Awards for Women, honouring ordinary Papua New Guinean women doing extraordinary things.

All this commitment and service to the Papua New Guinea community did not go unnoticed.

Sir Dadi Toka travelled to London to receive his knighthood from His Royal Highness (then) Prince Charles on 29 October 2010. He was recognized for his services to the Motu Koita community and the city of Port Moresby, and for his significant contribution to sport, particularly rugby league.

'Sir Dadi was the one who instigated the OBE for me,' reveals Mahesh, remembering a conversation they once had.

'You are doing so much work. You should be rewarded in some way,' Sir Dadi had told him.

'Sir Dadi, if recognition comes, it's fine. But I'm not going to go searching for it,' Mahesh had replied.

Each Commonwealth country has an awards council to receive nominations, investigate and vet their worthiness, and make final recommendations to Buckingham Palace. The monarchy then conducts its own screening to confirm the merits of those being recommended, to make sure there will be no disrepute to the royalty.

Although born in Fiji, as a then permanent resident of Papua New Guinea, Mahesh Patel qualified for awards from the British monarchy.

An official announcement was issued on 16 June 2012 from St James's Palace, the most senior royal palace in London.

The Queen has been graciously pleased, on the occasion of the Celebration of Her Majesty's Birthday, and on the advice of Her Majesty's Papua New Guinea Ministers, to give orders for the following promotions in, and appointments to, the Most Excellent Order of the British Empire: . . . Mahesh Patel. For services to healthcare, commerce and sports.

Mahesh Patel received the exciting news via Port Moresby media, as part of the Queen's Birthday long-weekend celebrations.

'It was announced in the newspaper,' he recalls. 'I had no idea what an OBE really was.'

Upon investigating what the award meant, Mahesh then had to decide how he would receive it.

'You can receive the award from the local governor-general,' he explains, 'or you can elect to receive it in person. Because it's expensive to fly to the UK, a lot of people don't do it. I had friends who told me I'd be stupid not to go to England to receive it. So, I said, "Sure, I'll go to Buckingham Palace."'

Mahesh Patel, wife Usha, and sons Nikhil and Ajay travelled to London for the investiture ceremony. It was held at Buckingham Palace on Wednesday, 21 November 2012.

Mahesh Patel: 'The boys were thrilled to be going. We were staying in a hotel just near the Palace. Literally, you could walk there. I hired a morning suit. I wanted to hire a car to drive us to the Palace, but it had to be a British car. I rang the hotel concierge and told them I was getting an award from the Queen. That is a big thing in the UK. The concierge was trying to find a Jaguar, but said they could only secure a brand-new Range Rover. I said, "That's even better." We'd been told we had to arrive early, well before the ceremony. It was held in the morning. The funny thing was, when we arrived at the Buckingham Palace front gates, the chauffeur pulled up and said he was not permitted to drive in. "We have a car pass," I said, showing it to him. He looked at it and was so happy. He did a live video call with his friends, telling them he's driving into the palace grounds. He was more excited than we were.

'We drive in through the main entry gates, where they check your passes and your passports. There is a long queue of cars, of course. Not coming from a fancy background, we didn't know all the pomp and ceremony. I told the driver, "Just drop us off here. It's fine." He said, "No way. I have to pull up right in front of the entry door to drop you off." He wanted to keep the car pass. I said, "Of course, it's no use to us. We'll just walk back to the hotel afterwards."

'You walk into the main entry and they identify you. All our phones were put into storage. They then show you where the guests are to be seated. The guests go one way to the audience room and I am led into another room. I get taken the back way, along a big long corridor. It's amazing, really. Then we go through the briefing. You are told that as soon as the Queen puts her hand out, it's time to go. There were 100 awardees. The girls were the most nervous in the group. They have to do the curtsy. Right leg, left leg. Everybody is practising. The ceremony is then held in ranking order. The knighthoods go first.'

Queen Elizabeth II: 'Investitures are traditional. I am always absolutely fascinated by the people who come, all the things that they have done.'

Queued up for his turn, one of the palace staff escorted Mahesh to his waiting spot before his name was called. As he waited to be received by Her Majesty, for a few seconds, he recalled the first time he had ever seen her in person, so many years ago in Fiji.

Mahesh Patel: 'We were all standing on the side of the road, waiting. For us, it was just a fun day out. I don't think it made much of an impact on us, seeing the Queen, leading up to Fijian independence, at eleven years of age. The whole school was there. It was a weekday, and the fun part was not going to classes. We were lined up on the streets, and the Queen drives past. We were given these little British flags to wave. At that time, never ever would I have thought that I would be meeting the Queen at Buckingham Palace one day.'

As he waited in the large ceremony room where so many other outstanding and world-famous recipients had stood before him, Mahesh admits, 'I was so nervous. It was mind-boggling, and not many people get a chance to do this.'

But as is his character, his thoughts were also of others.

'The kids were super excited,' he says. 'But the sad thing was, I wish my mum and dad were there to see me. Usha's mum and dad did not attend due to guest-number restrictions.'

Dressed in a black morning suit with long tails, grey trousers, white vest and resplendent red tie, Mahesh Patel was finally announced. He walked forward anxiously toward Her Majesty Queen Elizabeth II, in a lemon dress, wearing stunning white pearls and black shoes.

Mahesh Patel: 'When I met the Queen, I told her that the last time I saw her was in 1970, when I was eleven. She asked me if I was still living in Papua New Guinea. I then rattled off all the times I had seen her in person. I told her my wife Usha was from Kent in London. Also, that I had seen Prince Charles in Papua New Guinea a few months earlier during the Queen's Sixtieth Jubilee. I talked on, and she asked another question. It was quite an occasion, actually.

'The whole process took less than one hour. It is pretty regimented. You queue up. Just before they call your name, someone guides you out. Then they announce your name, and you walk through to a certain point where the Queen is. She asks you questions and pins the award on you. As you walk out, staff give you the award case. You then meet up with your guests, and we go out into the palace yard. That's the photo we have got of the four of us all together.

'Typically, we are star spotting. *Is there anybody else that we know?* And there happens to be Kate Winslet, the film star. She received a CBE for services to drama. She was with her family like most people. So, we didn't want to be an idiot and say, "Can we take a selfie?" I got Nikhil to take a photo. I said, "Don't focus on me; take a picture with Kate in the background."'

Mahesh Patel was overwhelmed by the positive reactions from family, friends, work colleagues, and associates to the news, as photos of him with Queen Elizabeth were published and shared.

Nikhil Patel: 'The OBE was exciting, and well deserved. Potentially awarded a tad late as Dad had altruistic impact upon people and society over the decades prior. Regarding my presence at the OBE ceremony, it's tough to describe the feeling, there are many. Overall, a great sense of pride. It all felt a bit surreal, especially thinking about where Dad started. He truly exemplifies that one can start anywhere and achieve anything; stay focused, stay disciplined and dream big; nothing is impossible.'

Ajay Patel: 'Dad deserved both his OBE and his knighthood. The impact both Mum and Dad have had on Papua New Guinea is undeniable. Being able to go to Buckingham Palace and being in siting distance of the Queen was special. When I think back to the memories of how we had to get dressed up in our suits. We went with Dad when he was going to get fitted for his morning suit. It was absolutely amazing. I was so excited for him.'

Kusum Patel: 'I felt very proud of Mahesh. I thought our parents are watching over him, and they must be feeling really proud too. It was giving us all family pride.'

Pravin Patel: 'We really felt very proud when Mahesh received his OBE and met the Queen. We wished both our parents were around to see it. We knew he was doing a lot of charity work, but we were surprised to see him awarded in this way.'

Taru Patel: 'I was so proud of Mahesh and I sent a message to all my friends and my husband's friends as well, telling them: look at my brother and his wife. I talk about them a lot to my friends. Mahesh was so proud of Usha as well, and then they sat down and said, *What are we going to do now?* They still carried on working, doing more charity work.'

Anil Patel: 'To receive an OBE is a big achievement. That is through your hard work, and that hard work is just not within your own family. It is in public and the services that you do. I was very proud and we made sure that all of Fiji knew about it. We got in touch with the local news editors, and they gave him a profile story and published it. We were very proud of Mahesh. But we didn't want to show off. There are two things: there is being proud, and then there is showing off. And never ever has Mahesh shown off.'

Ajay Patel: 'That is where the value of it is—the acknowledgement. It is life experiences and what they teach. To be able to sit back and think about what they imparted to me. Those were really exciting times. It was just nice to see him proud of getting acknowledged. Also, seeing Dad nervous—that was probably one of the best memories. You never see him sweating or uncomfortable. I have seen him like that a few times. He doesn't mince his words often. Those were actually really cool moments because they were human moments for him and for us to experience with him. I loved the pomp of it, and I know he loved it. For him to be able to go and get the morning suit, and me making sure he looks alright. That was special.'

Daksesh Patel: 'There was an immense amount of pride only because I think he deserved it. He was ahead of many others who got it. Notwithstanding that, I do have a huge crush on and recognition for the Royal Family. I'm a believer. I am a monarchist. I'm not a republican guy. If this is the recognition that gets Mahesh recognized by others, he deserves it.'

Amit Patel: 'We were all very proud, obviously. To have that kind of OBE title brought into the family is just incredible. Just by association, it is an amazing thing to have and an incredible accomplishment for all his work over the years.'

Mira Kulkarni: 'When Mahesh received his OBE, there was a feeling of immense pride in our entire family. It was also something that justified his ambition to succeed.'

Samrath Bedi: 'When I first heard about Mahesh receiving the OBE, there was immense pride. Because in the goodness of Mahesh, there is a lot that he does for others, whether it is through generosity, or his charity, or just wanting to give back. The award is a culmination of all his work. I was so happy to see him being recognized, because he downplays it. He never says, "Look, I've done so much, and look at who I am, and look at all this that I have given." He just does what he has to do. That's the nice part. I can't tell you how proud Karishma and I were of the fact he was being awarded. It was something that made us all very, very happy.'

Mel Donald: 'Mahesh has contributed a great deal to PNG in many ways personally and through his businesses. He definitely deserved the recognition and acknowledgement of the OBE award from the Queen.'

Andrew Petrie: 'Frankly, Mahesh had been so successful and committed to his charity work, I wasn't really surprised. He was spending a lot of money on educating children. He employed as many locals as he could. He had all these education programmes running. When you run things as he did and gave back so much to the community, it is not surprising he received his OBE. I don't know who else in PNG could receive it before him.'

Back at his apartment, Mahesh Patel has framed photos of his investiture with Queen Elizabeth II, hanging proudly in the entry hallway, just near a toy British bulldog door stop in the colours of the Union Jack.

Mahesh Patel: 'Looking at the photos, it is giving me goosebumps now. I was in Buckingham Palace and had never thought of doing that. We were lucky enough then to have the four of us there. Usha looks so happy in the photos. I think I felt a big satisfaction for myself for being recognized. I thought, *This is great*. I was also very proud that my family would be very proud.'

To conclude the memorable trip to London, there was another unexpected surprise for Mahesh Patel, OBE.

Mahesh Patel: 'We stayed a few days. Usha's parents live in Kent. It is one hour by train from London. I did my favourite thing: went and watched a Manchester United football match. We had special upgraded members' passes we bought on line. There was a big hall there for the members and they were announcing birthdays over the loudspeaker. People were having drinks and food before the game. Ajay went up to the emcee and told him, "My father Mahesh Patel, over there, just got awarded an OBE by the Queen." The event host immediately announced it and there was pin-drop silence. Everybody was looking around, asking, "Who is this guy?" The pride the British have for the Queen is phenomenal. Then, for the game itself, it was my very first match at Old Trafford. Lucky, we won that day. We played Liverpool, and we won in the ninetieth minute. That was a great finish.'

Chapter 12

Giving Back

From his earliest days working and living in Papua New Guinea, people have been asking Mahesh Patel for help. He has always been generous in his responses and willingly tried to assist as many as his means would allow.

'We have been part of the community from day one,' he says. 'We have helped with the schools and the communities. Any opportunity we get within our means, we are doing it.'

But, of course, the more help he gave, the more the requests for assistance flooded in.

'We would literally get twenty letters a day,' recalls Caleb Jarvis, 'requesting sponsorship and support. We had a percentage of the profits that we would always invest back into community sponsorship, be it netball or soccer or the local school, or whatever it was.'

But as City Pharmacy expanded further, the charity assistance programme became a bigger part of their business model and needed a new approach.

'As we went along, it went out of control,' says Mahesh. 'Because we would get requests from all sorts of people. *Support this, support that.*'

Perhaps further inspired by his Most Excellent Order of the British Empire award from Queen Elizabeth II in 2012, Mahesh restructured his charity work.

'One day I said to myself, *Let's create a formulized way of giving*,' he says. 'Because we couldn't manage. As we get bigger and bigger, the projects are going to get bigger.'

In January 2013, the CPL Foundation was created. One of the now CPL Group's core values is: 'We care—for our community, customers and people'.

'It's now about doing some really big programmes that make an impact,' explains Mahesh.

The CPL Foundation has four major areas of interest, focusing primarily on women and girls: (1) the economic empowerment of women, (2) education, (3) income generation for women and youth, and (4) health.

One of the first things Mahesh did with the Foundation was to ensure transparency and confidence in what was being achieved, as he had done during his time with the Red Cross. 'I engaged the big four accounting firms who were auditing CPL,' he says. 'I asked them to audit the Foundation's accounts, pro bono, so I can show people, *This is it*. It will not be like a lot of the aid agencies where people are questioning where the money goes.'

A major influence on the direction of the CPL Foundation and Mahesh Patel personally, has come from Stephanie Copus-Campbell, AM (Member of the Order of Australia). Considered to be an expert on Papua New Guinea and the greater Pacific region, Campbell has been committed to delivering sustainable impact through innovation and community-led development.

From 2009 to 2011, she was the head of the Australian government's aid programme with PNG. She has also served as head of Australia's bilateral aid programmes for Suva in Fiji, and was head of the Fiji and Tuvalu and Pacific regional programmes. During her early career with the Australian government, she worked on development cooperation with China, and on environment and infrastructure policy. She has also worked with CARE Australia in an executive leadership role and as a lecturer with Deakin University in international relations.

Stephanie holds a Master of Philosophy degree from Cambridge University (UK) and a bachelor's degree in political science from the

University of California, where she graduated summa cum laude (with highest honours). She is also undertaking a Master of Social Work through the University of Melbourne.

In 2021, Stephanie was made a Member of the Order of Australia (AM) for her contribution to social development in Papua New Guinea.

Stephanie is married to General Angus John Campbell, AO, DSC, former Chief of the Australian Defence Force.

The paths of Mahesh Patel and Stephanie Copus-Campbell first crossed in 2010. What could have been an uncomfortable situation resulted in a friendship and partnership which has greatly benefited some of the neediest people in Papua New Guinea.

Mahesh Patel: 'Stephanie and I were at a conference about how good AusAID was doing. We were on the same panel. She was head of Australian Aid Programme, AusAID, then. My speech was about how *bad* AusAID was: they couldn't deliver drugs out into the remote areas; they didn't do this and they couldn't do that. As I'm talking, I'm getting a cold sweat down my spine: *What am I going to say when I speak to her?* She had spoken first and I went on second. She had spoken of what good work AusAID had done. I was saying if you do the same thing again and expect different results, that is the definition of stupidity. The Australian High Commissioner was sitting in the front and Stephanie was at the back of the panel. I was asking myself, *What the hell am I doing here?*'

Stephanie Copus-Campbell: 'I clearly remember it. We were on a panel together at an Australia–PNG Business Council meeting. I was the head of the Australian development programme at that time. I was speaking about all the good things I did. Mahesh basically put forward all this research to say that aid was not really meeting its intended consequences. I thought, *This is annoying.* Then I thought, *Wow, I'm pretty impressed with his guy. I better get to know him.* I think Mahesh is a better friend than enemy.'

Mahesh Patel: 'As soon as I sat down after giving my speech, Stephanie walked over, shook my hand and said, "Great stuff. Let's catch up for dinner." She told me, "We don't engage enough with the private sector. We need to work together." We struck up a friendship immediately.'

Stephanie Copus-Campbell: 'Afterwards, I went up to him and said, I'm pretty impressed with your presentation, even though it kind of debunked everything I was saying. We hit it off from there. We became good colleagues and started sharing information and our thoughts. Then, when I left AusAid and went into philanthropy, he asked me to come and set up his CPL Foundation. From there, we have been pretty close colleagues.'

The CPL Foundation receives most of its funding directly from the CPL Group of Companies. Over 500,000 kina (11 million rupees) cash is allocated each year and is mandated by the CPL board. On top of that, the CPL Group of Companies also allocates paid staff and support services directly for use in dedicated CPL Foundation projects and events.

'The Foundation doesn't pay for any staffing or infrastructure cost,' explains Mahesh. 'That is paid for by CPL. If you use transportation, if you use logistics, if we do food donations, that is all paid for by the CPL Group of Companies. We are actually giving much, much more than the actual cash contribution. This ensures the money goes directly to the recipients where it is most needed. The Foundation money is purely for giving.'

The CPL Foundation board comprises Mahesh Patel, Stephanie Copus-Campbell, lawyer Eunice Parua, and Robert Guba Aisi, OBE, a veteran in legal and diplomatic work, who was Papua New Guinea's ambassador to the United Nations from 2002 to 2015.

Mahesh's youngest son Ajay Patel also now spends most of his own working hours on CPL Foundation projects.

'I have put Ajay in there,' says Mahesh, 'as I am hopeful he is going to take charge of the Foundation work programme in the years to come. He is doing the work I used to do with the bush tours, talking to farmers and is passionate about helping people.'

Ajay Patel moved some of his work focus from CPL Group of Companies to CPL Foundation in 2022.

'There are two main Foundation projects we were working on,' says Ajay. 'The Pride of PNG Awards and a family planning project we are doing with Stephanie Copus-Campbell. I think we will still do a fair few smaller projects. That is honestly what I enjoy, because you can have smaller impacts more consistently. But with the planned projects, where a lot more money is spent, we are looking at achieving some critical outcomes.'

Ajay Patel has an engineering mind, where he likes to make things work. He revels in the many good things he has found when working in Papua New Guinea.

'The primal nature that you get here,' he says. 'You can go driving and you will see forests which haven't been touched or haven't been carved. You can drive two hours and travel 3,000 years into the past. That is one of the positives. Another is the impact an individual can have in a society like this, especially in my position. If we were in a completely developed society, a lot of things are already in place and they are done by people who are very good at what they do. Whereas here, you have got a lot of gaps in a lot of different places, which means that in a way they need a jack of all trades to fill them.'

The flagship programme for the CPL Foundation is the Pride of PNG Women Awards for women's empowerment. Created by Mahesh Patel in 2007, current Papua New Guinea Governor General Sir Bob Dadae is the patron.

'We identify women from all across the country,' says Mahesh, 'and pick their projects from five or six different categories. We then support their project for life, whatever they are doing. I remember the very first awards we did in 2007. I took all the applications home. At 8 o'clock, I said, *I'll just flick through some and then go to bed.* At 2 in the morning, I was still reading those applications. I had tears rolling down my eyes. Sorcery-related stuff, gender-based violence, brave and courageous leaders in the community. It was just horrible [situations], and also inspirational to see the work that women do. We pick five or six awardees each year and take the projects all the way through, with any help they need and continue to support them.'

Supporting the women of Papua New Guinea and their projects, which ultimately help wider communities, are a clear focus for the CPL Foundation.

Asked to explain where his strong consideration for women comes from, Mahesh Patel thinks before answering.

'I suppose it's always been there,' he replies. 'It could be my upbringing by my mum, who was very selfless. I can't pinpoint a particular thing. Usha, also, has been such an inspirational support in this whole journey!'

In March 2015, the CPL Group launched a new Women in Leadership training programme. The objective was to develop aspiring female employees from all CPL business units to be future leaders in the organization.

'Empowerment programmes that invest in female employees pay off in multiple ways,' says then-CEO, Ravi Singh. 'Not only do they build the capacity of the organization by equipping women employees with the knowledge, tools and confidence they need to succeed in the workplace, these programmes give women the skills to take on leadership roles at home and in their communities. Enabling the success of our women employees will be crucial to our company's future and expansion plans.'

It was another step by CPL, using their business leverage to lead the way to effect change and signal to others in Papua New Guinea the intentions of the company, in step with the goals of the CPL Foundation.

Mahesh Patel: 'We have got objectives. It must be women and community-related. It must be sustainable. The new thing we are doing is measuring the impact and what the return on investment is. If we have two alternative projects to consider, whom do we support? Because we have limited funds. Where do we make the biggest impact?'

Stephanie Copus-Campbell: 'Mahesh is someone who wants to help everyone. I think he finds it hard—when someone pitches a good idea, he struggles to say "no". Where I felt I could help him with the Foundation, and then subsequently as we have grown, was this: while there can be things you do just because you want to do them, what you really want to do is have an impact. If you do a little bit of everything and not much of anything, you are not going to see that impact. You might be helping lots of people on a smaller scale, but if you want to grow and see results from your efforts, you need to focus your strategy and leverage more people.'

Finding the right projects for the CPL Foundation to support is a never-ending exercise. Mahesh Patel has seen a wide range over the years, with varying levels of success, both for the CPL Foundation and for projects he has supported personally.

Mahesh Patel: 'We don't give cash handouts. If a farmer comes along and wants a loan, we ask, "What are you buying?" If it is for an irrigation pump, we tell them to get a quotation, and we pay the supplying company directly. We just find projects to try and alleviate the poverty. Getting involved as well, rather than just giving a cheque.

'We have done so many different things, both big and small. There is Lucas, the blind farmer—we have supported his marketing and transport. This guy can climb a coconut tree, pick coconuts and bring them down. When he hears my voice, he comes up to thank me. When you hear stories like that, it is very rewarding.

'There were these ladies in Bougainville who wanted to send baskets of their produce. The freight was going to kill it. I rang the shipping company and said, "We spend 3 million kina (65 million rupees) with you guys. When the container comes back, it comes in empty. Why are you charging these women 10 kina (217 rupees) a kilo? They then said, "Okay, we'll do it for no cost." It's a community thing. It's not for me; I'm not going to make a profit out of it. All of a sudden, because of our intervention, that regular shipment has started. They are now bringing produce to market free of charge.

'We had eight trainers, mostly women, from Canberra and Melbourne, and we are running a cyber security training course for girls aged six to eleven. Also, hopefully, teaching them how to code, if there is interest. We have a pathway to the University of Queensland cyber security department to offer an eight-stage programme in cyber security. It has taken three years of planning to arrange that.

'Dubai hosted the World Expo in 2021. The staff operating the Papua New Guinean Pavilion wanted Papua New Guinean crops like taro, yams and others sent across. They wrote to us, asking for help. DHL was going to charge us 10,000 kina (216,700 rupees) to ship produce worth 2,000 kina (43,300 rupees). Air Niugini Limited, our national airline, should have paid for it, as it was in the national interest. They were just delaying a decision and time was running out. So, I just signed off on it. This is the sort of stuff we get dragged into. Why are we paying to send produce to Dubai? I tell the politicians all the time, I'm the biggest advocate for Papua New Guinea.

'Through Forest Essentials, I did a couple of trips to Nepal with the Estée Lauder CSR [corporate social responsibility] team. We visited some villages. We got this project idea of making paper from grass and marketing it as gift wrapping for one of their brands. It was a particular type of grass you can mulch without any mechanization and make paper out of it. I thought, *We can do this in PNG*.

'I had the guys from Nepal come over to identify the grass. It grows wild here. I sent some grass samples to Nepal. The first time I sent it, customs officials were baffled, "Why are you sending this useless grass?" We started the project in PNG for producing gift wrapping. We did these remote village trips and even chartered an aircraft to get to some of the villages. The village people thought we were politicians because that is the only time they usually see outsiders. That's how remote they were. No electricity. No running water. The Nepalese were very helpful in telling me what PNG could do. This is how all our agricultural projects started.

'In another region we went to in 2010, a woman came and cried on my shoulder. She said, "We grow pineapples. We sell a little bit in the market, and the rest goes to feed our pigs. There are still leftovers and we just throw them away. Please help us find a market." This is when we said, "Let's focus on local produce."

'I went to the Dadaab refugee camp in Kenya with Care Australia in 2012. I said, "You guys are not marketing yourselves. All you are showing is these stereotypical images of starving kids." The most important thing they were doing was providing free fresh water to 400,000 people in the camp. Care Australia funds it. I said, "I didn't know that. Why aren't you guys marketing this?" Because they are all based in cities, they are not thinking from that perspective. And when

I looked at the sewing machine classes they were running, I rang the agents of Singer, the sewing machine company. They said, "You tell us where and we'll supply 100 free machines." We were not leveraging our networks. I use that to the max now. Nothing for me. I just ask, "Can you guys do that?"

'Ajay rings me and asks, "Can you do this? Can you do that?" I say, "Okay." I've got no shame. All people can say is "no". A lot times people want to help, but don't know how to. With giving, there is always this mistrust, is it going to get misused? I never ask anybody for cash. But when the schools have functions, I ring the local beverage company and ask, "Can you give us fifty cartons of water or juice?" Coca-Cola just dropped off 100 cases of orange juice for an orphanage.

'CPL has 3,000 staff. If we teach our staff about waste management and not throwing rubbish away harmfully, we can make a difference. There is no cultural issue. In Fiji and Papua New Guinea, the people keep their villages very clean and pristine, because the church is there. They want to keep the environment very clean. But when they come to the city, they finish a can of soft drink and just chuck it on the street.

'We need education that says, "You need to practise cleanliness at home." If we can get our 3,000 staff practising that, they become advocates for the whole community. That's the power of the private sector, which the government agencies cannot do. I've got all the ideas. I've got the vision. But somebody now needs to drive it.'

American media icon and philanthropist Oprah Winfrey was rightly applauded in 2002, when she founded the Oprah Winfrey Leadership Academy for Girls in South Africa. The long-running daytime talk show host wanted to help girls who were growing up like her, 'economically disadvantaged, but not poor in mind or spirit.'

While Mahesh Patel has a highly impressive record of charity work in Papua New Guinea, few know that he also financially supports a school and orphanage in Myanmar.

Greg Wisbey: 'In 2015, one of my contacts mentioned an orphanage located in a place called Hlaingtharyar Township, the poorest suburb of Yangon, in Myanmar. It is a school run by monks. It is run under the government schooling system but they really get nothing extra from anyone. Mahesh said, "Let's go and have a look at it." We went and it is very humbling to see this place. There were 800 kids going to that school. They feed them one meal per day. They also have forty orphans who live in the school. They are kids who don't have any family in the villages they come from. They are cared for by these monks.'

Mahesh Patel: 'We were exploring opportunities in Myanmar. Over a couple of trips, I said, "Whatever we do, we want to be involved as part of the community." What can we do? The monks there, traditionally, would never ask for help. I'm saying, "I don't know what to give and what is enough or not enough." We sat there for half an hour and they wouldn't say what help they needed. I said, "Alright, let's go for a walk around the monastery." We started looking around, and they said, "These are the girls' rooms but we don't have girls' toilets here." I have seen some of these issues before in India and PNG. We got a quote from the local builders. It was around 30,000 USD (2.5 million rupees). I said, "Okay, let's do it."'

After careful consideration, Mahesh Patel decided not to go into business in Myanmar, but he kept in touch with the country via the school and some of the locals he had met. When the pandemic started in 2020, he did think, 'Maybe I was destined to be involved and help them more?'

With COVID-19 sweeping the globe, the government department overseeing the employment of the teachers at the school suddenly cut off their funding. There are eighteen regular teachers who work twelve-hour shifts.

When he was advised of the problem, Greg called Mahesh and reported, 'The kids are not going to school.'

Mahesh Patel responded in his usual way, with decisive action. From his and Usha's personal funds, he now pays 30,000 AUD (1.7 million rupees) per year, which funds all the teachers' wages and meals for the children.

An obvious question is why? Why do Mahesh and Usha Patel support the Aung School and Orphanage when they have never even lived in

Myanmar? Mahesh, in his travels, could simply have moved on from the country when he decided not to pursue setting up a business there.

Ajay Patel: 'Dad has worked really hard, and he has been successful. No, not everyone is like this. I think it is also to do with the way my parents grew up. To some degree, both their families did struggle. I am thankful for the bravery of our grandparents, without whose courage and foresight we would not have reached this point. The CPL Foundation was established to bring help to the communities in a more holistic way.'

Nikhil Patel: 'Dad and Mum have always taught us to give back, although they have a different perspective in how to accomplish that. It's a much more hands-on approach, a compassionate, heartfelt approach. It started off in an unguided fashion, helping people they came across, although Dad being Dad, he brought structure to the approach and then foundation. Mum, as always, was and is the compass and barometer.'

Body-building and film icon, Arnold Schwarzenegger, who was also the governor of California from 2003 to 2011, said, 'As I've grown up, got older, maybe wiser, I think your life is judged not by how much you have taken but by how much you give back.'
Sentiments that Mahesh Patel has demonstrated even when he was much younger.
'This lady wrote to me recently on LinkedIn,' he reveals. 'She said she grows mushrooms in the Eastern Highlands, but she needs a market. I told her to talk to our supply chain team. Let's see how we can do it. They have to produce in quantity, but if we can help her, we will.'
Even something as small as recruiting a new member to the CPL Foundation team is important.
'Up till now,' he explains, 'it's been really voluntary and all my staff have been contributing. One of my drivers said to me, "Boss, I'd really like to join the Foundation." Today he sent me an application. I went to HR and said, "That's the passion I want." So, when a job comes up, I want him to do it.'

Asked if he can ever see a time when he will cease his work with the CPL Foundation or at least dial it back a few notches, Mahesh shakes his head.

'I think I would struggle,' he concedes. 'It's like you are driving at 100 kilometres per hour and now you have come to a 50 zone. I'm getting there. But as soon as I go out to Papua New Guinea, it's *bang*, speeding up again. People will come with a proposal—a business proposal or a community service proposal. I just say, "Why should we say no?" My staff reminds me, "Boss, this is not part of our objectives." I say, "No, they are doing a good job, why should we say no?" We can afford to do it. It's going to impact lives. Let's do it.'

It seems Usha Patel has a mindset like her husband's.

'As we have become more successful,' she says, 'the question is, how much is "enough"? We have always had this philosophy that we would put back into society from which we took. Mother Teresa said that what we are doing might just be a drop in the ocean, but the ocean would be less because of that missing drop.'

Mahesh Patel loves his life and wants to continue his charity works in Papua New Guinea and other countries for many years to come. Why change what is such a rewarding part of his life? There is no end in sight.

In 2025, the CPL Foundation is preparing to launch a major HPV testing (for cervical cancer) programme through wellness clinics and City Pharmacy outlets, as three to five women die every day because of this.

'Our public hospitals are resource-poor,' says Mahesh. 'The private sector is unstoppable. This service will be available for a very small fee. I hope to be doing this for the next ten years' time and even longer. I think my passion will always be for projects that help communities, especially women. Because PNG is where I really grew up.'

Chapter 13

Fires and Ashes

Mahesh Patel was riding high on life in 2009. The CPL Group continued to grow. The public company acquired the Hardware Haus chain of stores from Steamships Trading Company to further diversify their business interests. The now twenty-three-year business partnership with Alan Jarvis, which had started on a gentlemen's handshake, was stronger than ever. Mahesh and his wife Usha's speculative investment in Forest Essentials in India was turning into another masterstroke, as the fledgling company started by Mira Kulkarni made great strides, expanding its range of Ayurvedic cosmetics, skincare and bodycare. Mahesh even held a 'twenty-five years in Papua New Guinea' party at the Lamana Hotel in June 2009, celebrating his arrival in the country. Life could not have been sweeter. But unbeknownst to Mahesh and those around him, a heart-breaking tragedy was approaching.

Alan Jarvis was an experienced and enthusiastic road cyclist. Extremely fit for a man of sixty-seven years, he enjoyed the company of a group who would take long bicycle tours together. On Saturday mornings they would regularly cycle the 160 kilometres from Sydney to Wollongong and back. Alan and his cycling enthusiasts were on a yearly biking tour in the Pyrenees mountains and Italy.

In June 2009, Mahesh Patel was woken by a telephone call at 2 a.m. from Alan's wife, Robyn. A distraught Robyn gave Mahesh the tragic news that Alan had an accident at Lake Como and had passed away in Milan.

The still half-asleep Mahesh, at home in Sydney, tried to process what he was being told.

'My throat dried and I just froze,' recalls Mahesh. 'I could not believe what Robyn was saying.'

The climb up the mountain above Lake Como in Bellagio was strenuous but the group met for a celebratory coffee and photos with their support group. On the steep descent, Alan veered off the road and careered over the cliff. As it was the weekend, paramedics, helicopters and mountaineers were all on standby and quickly swung into action.

Unfortunately, despite the efforts of the outstanding and professional teams, Alan Jarvis died in a Milan hospital that afternoon on 21 June 2009.

Mahesh, in the meantime, jumped into action. He and the Jarvis's daughter, Holly, flew to join her brother Caleb and their mother Robyn.

'A devastated Holly and I flew to London later that day,' says Mahesh.

Alan was cremated in Sussex and a funeral held in Bodiam in the United Kingdom. It was the village where Alan was born and attended junior school. Another service was later held in Sydney, for family and friends who were not in England.

'I was asked to say a few words at the church in Vaucluse, Sydney,' says Mahesh. 'I broke down and started to cry. It was such a shock to lose Alan. He was my business partner, but, more importantly, he was my mentor and friend. Initially, I was lost without him. But I knew how important it was to support Robyn, Caleb and Holly. Losing Alan would have been so difficult for Robyn. But she is such a tough lady. Usha and I have great love and admiration for her and her children.'

'For anyone lucky enough to be part of Mahesh and Usha's family,' says Robyn, 'as we were and are, they are always there for you. When Alan died in Europe, it was Usha's parents who stepped forward and even offered their home to us as we were away from ours. These gestures will never be forgotten.'

Mahesh had been planning an extravagant party for his fiftieth birthday in November 2009. But his entire mindset changed upon the passing of Alan Jarvis.

'We were all so shaken up,' said Mahesh. 'I said, *no, we can't have a party*. I didn't feel like I could celebrate, even five months later.'

Mahesh called Robyn and told her he did not want to go ahead with it.

'I just did not feel comfortable,' he says, getting emotional, recalling it years later. 'Robyn being so kind, as always, immediately tried to talk me out of it.'

'No, Mahesh,' she said. 'Alan would have liked you to have the party. Please go ahead.'

'Until I received Robyn's blessing,' says Mahesh, 'I could not consider holding the party. But she gave it and we held the party. She even attended, which meant so much to Usha and me.'

The birthday celebration was held in the restaurant at the lavish Centre Point Tower in Sydney, overlooking the city.

'Because of the size of the restaurant, we had to restrict the numbers to 110 people,' explains Mahesh. 'My mum was there. My brothers were there. Mira, Samarth and Karishma came from India. Ramesh and Kishin, and and their wives travelled from Hong Kong.'

While the party proceeded and the celebration was enjoyed, thoughts of Alan Jarvis were always at the front of Mahesh's mind.

'The last time I saw Alan in Sydney,' recalls Mahesh, 'he was on the verge of retirement. He said to me, "You cannot sit on the fence." You need to be in and committed to the business or retire and get out. We were talking about him retiring, so he could enjoy his life fully.'

No one goes through life without facing problems and emotional hurdles to overcome. The tragic loss of Alan Jarvis demonstrated this. As heartbreaking as the death of his business partner and friend was, some of Mahesh Patel's most difficult days were brought about by two separate fires affecting the CPL Group of Companies.

On 14 July 2015, a fire burnt to the ground the largest CPL Stop & Shop supermarket, Waigani Central, in Port Moresby.

'It was a new store,' says Mahesh. 'It was the largest one in Papua New Guinea—50,000 square feet. It is still our biggest store to date. At that stage, it accounted for 40 per cent of our company's turnover. It was a modern store, state of the art. Brand new. *Boom*. Gone. It opened in 2014 and was only eighteen months old.'

The fire broke out while the 2015 Pacific Games were being held in Port Moresby. Mahesh was at his apartment in Sydney at the time and flew back to Papua New Guinea the following day.

The report from investigators suggested the fire was started by rats chewing through electrical cables. No sabotage or human error was found.

'We had insurance with a private insurance company,' Mahesh says, 'to cover stock and loss of profit, which covers the staff payments. The problem was, the insurance company started paying out and then it went broke. That's really the problem which put us back. Till date, I'm still chasing about 8 million kina (174 million rupees). It was almost half of what we were owed, which we did not receive.'

The CPL Group kept their supermarket operational at the old site until the new supermarket premises were rebuilt. It did not occur quickly though, as the landlord was having their own insurance claim issues with an offshore insurer.

It took three years, but the new Stop & Shop supermarket eventually opened in 2018. But not before an even more catastrophic fire would bring Mahesh Patel and the CPL Group of Companies to the brink of total financial collapse.

The 2015 supermarket fire experience helped Mahesh Patel and the CPL Group of Companies prepare for any similar future disasters. But nobody could foresee the devastating impact a second major fire would have.

In 2008, the CPL Group moved their warehousing operation from the original head office and warehouse in Waigani Drive to an old warehouse site at Gerehu, which had been built in the early 1980s. Since that time, all of the company's offices, stock and vehicles were located in one massive warehouse.

On Sunday night, 18 June 2017, at 10.15 p.m., a fire started inside the Gerehu warehouse. Mahesh Patel was in Fiji at the time, which is two hours ahead of Papua New Guinea. He received the first phone call about the fire from his financial controller at approximately 12.30 a.m.

Realizing the types of stock and essential medicines held inside the warehouse, Mahesh immediately made phone calls trying to get additional fire engines to the warehouse site. He then tried to get on the first flight from Fiji to Papua New Guinea.

'I couldn't sleep,' he says. 'I was getting phone calls throughout the night from my staff at the fire. They were saying, "Everything is gone." Apart from worrying about the insurance claim, I was thinking, *What do we do?*'

Mahesh could not purchase a flight ticket online at short notice, so he arrived at Nadi international airport at 5 a.m. to try and get on the first flight to Honiara, which would then take him to Port Moresby.

'The airport staff were humming and hawing,' he says. 'I am saying, "This is an emergency, please help me." Luckily, one of the Fiji Airways crew recognized me and assisted.'

The Air New Guinea flight left Nadi at 8 a.m. It is a three-hour flight to Honiara, the capital of the Solomon Islands. The plane stopped for refuelling and then it was another two hours and twenty minutes to Papua New Guinea. Mahesh arrived in Port Moresby at 2 p.m.

'I got on the plane in Nadi,' he recalls, 'and had not slept all night. I have a good habit of just falling asleep on a plane. When I woke up in Honiara, I was saying to myself, *It's just a nightmare.* Somebody then walked up to me on the plane, tapped me on the shoulder and said, "Hey, sorry about the fire." I knew then the fire was real!'

After he arrived at the airport, Mahesh was interviewed by a local television news camera crew for NBC National News.

'It has just been the most horrendous night in the thirty-four years I have been here,' he said. 'It is just shocking. I don't have too much information. We are just going to the site now.'

At this point, it all became too much for Mahesh. He stepped backwards and to his left, away from the camera, extremely emotional, trying to compose himself.

'We are trying to regroup now,' he continued, shortly after, with red eyes, 'because we have got hundreds of people working there. We have to sort them out first, to see what is happening. Just rebuild. We have just got to keep the business going. We will see how we go. We will bounce back. We have to sort the issues out and make sure the stores are open and the stocks are back in and the staff are all OK.'

From the airport, Mahesh was driven directly to the Gerehu warehouse site.

Additional fire officers from the airport emergency crew, arranged via a series of phone calls by Mahesh, had arrived overnight to assist in getting the fire under control. Even from a distance, the blistering heat was like a blast in the face.

No one was allowed onto the warehouse site when Mahesh arrived. Flames were still smouldering and fire officers were still trying to extinguish them.

Fortunately, all CPL staff were accounted for and no one was inside the warehouse when the fire started. There were security staff on site, but they were stationed at the main entry gates.

'If anyone had been inside,' observes Mahesh, 'they would have been roasted, because the warehouse was generally locked up at that time of night on a Sunday.'

Surveying the damage from afar, with toxic burning smells filling the air and everything inside the warehouse destroyed, Mahesh was already thinking about what needed to be done next.

'My mind was running a hundred miles an hour,' he says. 'From thinking about my team members to the stock loss, the business continuity, the supply lines. There were already people saying the business would not survive. What would all my staff do? How would they put food on their tables for their families if the business folded? I had to make sure we had the support of the banks. From my perspective, failure was not an option!'

The next morning, all the CPL stores opened as usual and had stock on hand. The two key problems Mahesh now faced were keeping the stock supplies flowing and the morale of the staff upbeat and positive. Neither was easy.

Fortunately, the company had a policy of offsite data backups which had been implemented. They did lose some information because the backups were not live, but in the coming days the information technology (IT) team were able to set up new servers and reinstall the backed-up files. It was not perfect, and there were some corruptions in the files, but it worked well enough so the stores were able to continue with sales as normal. This was vital because every cent was going to be needed to get through this unprecedented crisis.

They started storing new stock arrivals at their old warehouse and office in Waigani Drive. Going from one distribution nerve centre to a series of satellite distributions centres caused much frustration and confusion. It took time and leadership to completely reorganize the team's systems and processes.

'I was so lucky I had Ravi Singh as CEO then,' observes Mahesh. 'He took charge of regrouping the team. We moved back to our original office site. We started ordering goods manually.'

Reorganizing all the staff was also complex. The warehouse staff had to be re-assigned to new locations, which were still being found. All the support staff had to be coordinated: the staff who ordered the goods; those who picked, packed and stored the goods. Having everything under one roof has huge advantages, but now, with the team spread out, everyone had to adapt quickly.

Keeping everyone in a positive mindset was vital. The fire started on Sunday night. Mahesh arrived in Port Moresby on Monday afternoon. On Tuesday, he held a staff town-hall style meeting.

The Stop & Shop supermarket which had burnt down in 2015, was still being rebuilt and had not yet reopened. Mahesh called all the affected CPL staff together to speak to them as a group. Approximately 200 people had been working at the warehouse site.

'All the staff were nervous,' says Mahesh. 'They were thinking, *We'll be out of a job*. I will never forget that meeting. Some of the older girls who had been with us for years and years. They were bawling their eyes out. Just so worried about it all.'

Long-time CPL staff member Tracey Gotele was at the meeting. She still gets emotional today thinking about it.

'Everybody was in tears,' she says. 'We just all sat down on the floor and humbled ourselves. Everybody was crying because of the fire. I thought, *This is not a good day for CPL*. We had confidence that we would not vanish and that CPL would return. Whatever our bosses say, we will stand with them. Whatever they have planned, we will work towards it.'

'When Papua New Guineans work for you for a long time,' observes Mahesh, 'they feel it's their home. The allegiance builds, and that's what we thrive on—the loyalty of our staff. Here I am supposed to give a positive message and I started bawling my eyes out. I cracked. I'm saying, "Listen guys, we will bounce back. We will come back. We just need to hold on."'

While the smaller logistical details were being attended to by his staff, Mahesh Patel was focusing on the bigger challenges facing the company.

'The accounts were chugging along because the shops were trading,' says Mahesh. 'But there was a whole list of problems: managing the banks, managing the suppliers, and trying to process the insurance claim. Director John Dunlop started getting calls from suppliers asking, "What is going to happen to CPL? Are you going to pay our bills? Are you going to go under?" The whole situation was just bizarre.'

To help instil confidence that the CPL Group would in fact survive, a newspaper advertisement was published by company directors John Dunlop and Stanley Joyce. It listed loyal CPL suppliers who were publicly standing with the company.

'I rang twenty of our suppliers,' recalls Joyce, 'and we formed the CPL supporters' group of suppliers. I said, "You are either in or you are out." If they were in, it was not for me to tell them what to do or how to do it, but they needed to give CPL a deal on trading terms.'

One nervous supplier to CPL was owed 6 million kina (130 million rupees). Mahesh Patel took it upon himself to call all their suppliers to reassure them that their invoices would be paid.

A supplier told him directly, 'I'll keep giving you credit. But if the company doesn't pay us, I'm going to come after you. I am only doing this because of you.'

This is where all the personal contacts Mahesh Patel had made and the networking he had done throughout the years came through for him. It would have been much harder for a business such as CPL to survive in these circumstances if they had not had a figurehead like Mahesh Patel.

Antoinette Amputch was the CPL insurance broker and managed the new insurance claim.

'The clauses within the policy were fine,' she says. 'The rats came and ate through the wiring, and 90 per cent of fires here are electrical fires. I was just thinking, *how am I going to get their money back as soon as possible so the company can re-build.*'

While the insurance claim was being investigated through a normal process of due diligence, Mahesh Patel had to immediately go around raising capital to keep the CPL business afloat while they awaited the decision of the insurer.

'I was literally out there with a begging bowl,' admits Mahesh. 'I approached anybody and everybody who I thought would support us. We didn't have cash lying around. We had to borrow. Nobody would lend at that point in time. We had to raise fresh cash from shareholders.'

A rights issue or rights offer is an offer to a company's existing shareholders to buy more shares, usually at a discounted price, within a particular period. It is a method of raising funds for a cash-strapped company when it cannot borrow. When the banks in Papua New Guinea or Australia refused to lend, CPL raised funds through a rights issue to continue running its businesses.

'Our banks said we had to get our current shareholders to put more money in,' recalls Mahesh. He personally approached everyone who owned shares in the company, asking whether they were willing to take up the rights issue. Before the fire, the company had been trading on the Port Moresby Stock Exchange at one kina (twenty-two rupees) per share. An independent valuer was engaged by CPL and reported the company should now be valued between 0.50 to 0.65 kina per share.

At this stage of his working life, Mahesh had already been considering retirement. To ensure enough capital was secured to guarantee the survival of CPL, he even offered some of the big company shareholders the opportunity to increase their shareholding and thus decrease his.

'I didn't mind being diluted,' he explains. 'I would just stay in as a minor shareholder. I was on the way towards retirement. I accepted I would own less of the company, but it would be a successful company.'

Some of the institutional stakeholders, however, looked at the capital-raising in a different way. Mahesh was leaked a copy of an email where some owners discussed not taking up the rights issue, allowing the company to collapse, and then picking up ownership of the entire shareholding at 0.05 kina per share.

'That's when I got my back up,' fumes Mahesh. 'That was just taking advantage of the situation. Usha, Nikhil, Ajay and I had a family meeting and asked ourselves, *What do we do*? Just virtually give the company away, or do we fight for it?'

There was unanimous agreement that they would not be pushed out of CPL or Papua New Guinea. Usha Patel was particularly strong in her stance.

'Usha holds everything together,' observes Jagdish Patel, Mahesh's friend and business confidante. 'The decision was, he would either go back to PNG to rebuild, or let the business go and have somebody else take over. Or we had to group some new investors together to make up for the shortfall. We talked about getting value out of it: "You are not just going to give it away. It has been built up by you, Mahesh." Usha said, "I think you will regret it if you walk away."'

Mahesh was comfortable with the decision, even though he knew they were in a desperate financial situation. 'We mortgaged our home and got friends and family to raise the capital,' he said. 'Special thanks to Christian Vinson, the Reddy family and my brothers Pravin and Anil.'

There was a clear, new goal. 'It was a conscious decision to stay in Papua New Guinea,' explains Mahesh. 'Firstly, for the staff who always saw me out front. Obviously, new owners with a majority control would bring in their own people. Secondly, could I have lived with it? I spent thirty years building the company. Could I have just walked away?'

Antoinette Amputch was in constant contact with Mahesh during the fire crisis and the attempted company recapitalization.

'Mahesh went through a tough time,' she recalls. 'I remember I would be sending him notes at night—affirmations and positive words. The moment he would say something negative I would say, *Stop*. This is how you are going to verbalize it. Forget the business side; he saw his entire life's work for thirty years gone in a flash—now what?'

Cousin Daksesh Patel saw first-hand how hard the fight weighed down on Mahesh physically, mentally and emotionally.

'Mahesh was very down in that point in time,' says Daksesh. 'He was not his usual self. I felt very sorry for him then. When I shared this with my dad, he said to me, "Mahesh is very smart. He will find his way. But if it really comes to the end where he is going to fall, *then* we will address it and give him a hand. But if we give him a hand now, he will not try hard." I thought it was cruel. But my dad is a self-made man, who came from nothing and left school at the age of fourteen and worked hard all his life. When I reflected on his statement, I think it is one of the best that I have taken into my mind and my heart. You've got to be pushed to the boundary to fight.'

Mahesh Patel not only fought; he won too.

'The institutional shareholders were really playing a bluff,' he says, 'thinking I would not be able to raise all the money needed. Then they could just take up all the shares and ownership of the company cheaply. They got a shock when they rang me, asking how much more money I needed, and I said, "I don't need any more."'

That was because on 28 July 2017, the news Mahesh Patel, his family, friends and all of CPL Group staff had been waiting for was finally made public. Pacific MMI Insurance had accepted the insurance claim. An initial payment of 10 million kina (217 million rupees) was being made by the insurer, with more to follow, pending further assessment of the final amount to be paid.

Mahesh Patel attended a media conference where he received a large novelty cheque from a Pacific MMI Insurance director.

'It gives me great heart that we have partnered with PMMI,' Mahesh was quoted. 'It's a great day for us to get this relief and also to show the public that we are here to stay.'

Investigators found there was no human error involved in the fire. The insurance company would later pay out on the full claim amount.

While there was much rejoicing upon the announcement, there was still much complex work ahead, rebuilding the company and its processes. Mahesh needed help from people he could trust completely. He asked his sons to move back to Papua New Guinea to work alongside him.

'I was talking to Dad on the phone quite a bit,' says Nikhil Patel, who was entrenched in work in the US at the time. 'I knew the gravity of the situation. Dad asked that either my brother or I come back to PNG to help out. I knew it was a challenging time. Luckily, Ajay was able to go.'

Ajay Patel had been working for a contract manufacturing company making furniture for designers out of Sydney and Melbourne. In March 2018, he relocated to Port Moresby to work at CPL.

'Honestly, I had no idea what I would be doing there,' he recalls. 'I knew it was going to be 100 per cent CPL work. We didn't even think of the Foundation at that point.'

'Ajay was going back and forth, helping out,' recalls Mahesh. 'Then I asked him to come over and work full-time. The banks had sent in their own forensic accountants to keep an eye on things. I told one of their senior consultants that my son was coming to assist. Where could I use him? Where I needed trusted people with passion for the job. We had set up a Project Management Office (PMO), and their job was to look after all the business improvements. The consultant said to put him in the PMO role, so he would have oversight of the whole business rather than just the one brand.'

'I originally started off in process improvement,' says Ajay, 'looking at how we could become more efficient in certain parts of the business. I had a couple of portfolios of the business that I was purchasing for, as well as the agriculture development work, which was swinging towards the Foundation side of things.'

For Mahesh and Usha, now back in Port Moresby full-time, having Ajay alongside them certainly lifted their spirits.

'Apart from the work itself,' says Mahesh, 'it was good moral support to have Usha and Ajay with me to bounce ideas off.'

As part of the rebuilding process, CPL came up with a forty-eight-point plan to re-energize the business and get it moving forward again. It would be some time before the warehouse site operations could be rebuilt, and there were many operational challenges to overcome. One of the major changes made was the appointment of a new CEO.

On 1 March 2018, Mahesh Patel stepped down as company chairman to once again become chief executive officer. Director John Dunlop became interim chairman.

'I talked to our bankers,' says Mahesh, 'and it was one of the primary recommendations that I work in an executive role. We had to go back to basics.'

In May 2018, the Stop & Shop supermarket in Waigani Central finally reopened, almost three years after it had burnt down. The unresolved insurance claim and subsequent warehouse fire had made it extremely difficult for CPL to come up with the funds needed.

The renovation, including refrigeration, fixtures, fittings, and additional inventory, cost 15 million kina (325 million rupees). Most pleasing for Mahesh was that the now larger supermarket would employ additional staff.

'Our staff numbers went up from 200 to 300, which was a big positive for us,' he says.

Looking back at the warehouse fire and what it took to not only survive but thrive again as a business, Mahesh Patel says he could not have done it without the love and support of those closest to him.

'The nights were sleepless,' he admits. 'Just waiting for morning to come, so we could get the rebuild going each day. Credit to Usha and the boys for their constant encouragement. Especially Usha, who was my rock. Thank God, she had encouraged me to do meditation and simple yoga some years earlier. This gave me a lot of comfort and peace of mind each morning when I practised it and continue to do so.'

Asked if he would have changed anything he did, Mahesh replies forthrightly.

'I don't think I could have done anything differently. I shouldn't say this, but I seem to excel at crisis management. Because it just gets me going, to say, *I'm going to do it*. That's what happened when I first started business—I said, *I'm the master of my destiny. I will make sure it works*. Because when you start a business, there is no surety that it is going to work. It is just about believing in yourself.'

Mahesh Patel and his family had endured much anguish in 2017 and 2018 as they worked to re-build the CPL business. Just when things seemed to be on the rise again, and with Christmas approaching, his beloved mother Savitaben Patel passed away in Fiji on 11 December 2018 at the age of ninety-three. Mahesh was in Papua New Guinea when he received the sad news from his sister Kusum, who was staying with their mother in Fiji. Later that morning, Mahesh and Usha took the first flight from Port Moresby to Brisbane and then another flight to Nadi.

'It was devastating, but we all knew it was coming,' concedes Mahesh.

All of Mahesh's brothers and sisters made it to the funeral. His sons Nikhil and Ajay were also there.

'I think it is important to pay your respects as a family,' says Usha. 'That's their last day on earth, as it were. It doesn't matter what you do, that is the most important thing.'

'It was a big funeral; the whole town was there,' says Mahesh. 'She was the local aunty. The saving grace was we were half-prepared. It did come as a shock, obviously, when it happened. But when you do sit back and think about it, it was her time. She knew. She had planned it. I think she was wanting to go. She didn't suffer. She didn't have to be hospitalized or get put on oxygen.'

It was a deeply moving moment for the family when Savitaben's casket came back from the morgue—where it was sent for preparation—for last prayers at her home. Her family had purchased an electric chair lift for her to get up and down the stairs. She hardly ever used it and preferred to walk up and down herself.

'We tearfully had to unscrew the chair to take it off,' recalls Mahesh, 'because the casket would not fit in the stairwell. That brought tears to all our eyes. That's it, she's gone forever now. We do cremations in our culture, so later, we scattered her ashes in the river there, which backs onto our property. Then I took some ashes to the Ganges in India. I did a little prayer and immersed her ashes there.'

There was another death in the family when Usha's father Manubhai Patel passed away peacefully in his sleep at home in Chatham, Kent, on 10 April 2020.

The timing of his passing was unfortunate. It was just one week before Mahesh and Usha had booked a trip there.

'Our plan had been to go to London and meet up with Mum and Dad,' Mahesh says. 'Then go on to New York to celebrate Nikhil's thirtieth birthday. Dad died on Easter weekend, which was 10 April. Usha could have gone by herself, but the new Coronavirus vaccine wasn't available then. If Usha picked up COVID-19 on the way, Mum could also have been vulnerable. Usha still wanted to go, so I rang the British High Commissioner in PNG and asked what were the chances of the UK allowing people in. Usha could go, he said, but the only way she could get in was through Doha, Qatar. But if Qatar closed its borders, she would not be able to get to London [and be stuck in Doha].'

The funeral proceeded without Usha and Mahesh. Usha's brothers Sunil and Rakesh were both living in England and attended, along with the priest. It was the Patels' first-ever internet-streamed funeral.

'When we were allowed to travel the following year,' said Mahesh, 'Usha had a real tough time visiting without her dad being there. Mum was still getting over it. But you never get over it at that age. Usha's mum, Kamlaben, is strong. She catches the bus. She wheels her little trolley with her shopping. Her neighbours there are also friendly and help her out. Usha's brothers live close by and they also help but respect her need for independence. But it is nothing like having a daughter close by there with you, where you can have a chat and cook in the kitchen.'

Chapter 14
Knight Bachelor

A knight is a person granted the honorary title by a head of state or their representative for service to the monarch, the church or the country. Originally, this was usually in a military capacity. Some may immediately think of the tales from the twelfth century of King Arthur and his Knights of the Round Table, and we still think of the United Kingdom when we think of knights. However, the issuing of knighthoods is not exclusive to the British monarchy. Knighthood origins can be found in ancient Greece and Roman times. In the early Middle Ages in Europe, knighthoods were conferred upon mounted warriors. By the late Middle Ages, the rank had become associated with the ideals of chivalry, a code of conduct for the perfect courtly Christian warrior.

The British government says the title of Knight or Dame is now 'awarded for having a major contribution in any activity, usually at national level. Other people working in the nominee's area will see their contribution as inspirational and significant, requiring commitment over a long period of time.'

The title of Knight Bachelor is the rank granted to a man who has been knighted by the monarch but not inducted as a member of one of the organized orders of chivalry.

Knights Bachelor are the most ancient sort of British knights and were established during the reign of King Henry III in the thirteenth century. A man who is knighted is formally addressed as Sir and his wife as Lady.

In 2012, Mahesh Patel received from Queen Elizabeth II the award of appointment as Officer of the Most Excellent Order of the British Empire, also known as an OBE.

The five classes of appointment to the Order are, from highest to lowest grade:

- Knight Grand Cross or Dame Grand Cross of the Most Excellent Order of the British Empire (GBE)
- Knight Commander or Dame Commander of the Most Excellent Order of the British Empire (KBE or DBE)
- Commander of the Most Excellent Order of the British Empire (CBE)
- Officer of the Most Excellent Order of the British Empire (OBE)
- Member of the Most Excellent Order of the British Empire (MBE)

Famous celebrities previously knighted as Officers in the Most Excellent Order of the British Empire (OBE) category include actor Sir Patrick Stewart and singers, Sir Cliff Richard and Sir Tom Jones.

On the 10 October 2020, an official announcement was issued from St James's Palace, London:

THE QUEEN has been graciously pleased, on the occasion of the Celebration of Her Majesty's Birthday, and on the advice of Her Majesty's Papua New Guinea Ministers, to signify her intention of conferring the honour of Knighthood upon the undermentioned:

KNIGHT BACHELOR—*Mahesh* PATEL, O.B.E., *For services to Commerce and to Healthcare.*

While personal recognition has never been a priority for Mahesh Patel, even he was stunned by this honour from Queen Elizabeth II. He would now be known as Sir Mahesh Patel, OBE, and his wife, Lady Usha Patel.

'I think I was shocked and blown away for being recognized,' says Sir Mahesh. 'Wow! An award from the Queen! I thought, *This is great.* I was also happy that my family would be very proud of it. And the family was. It was a big, big thing for me personally. You've been recognized, so just move on and keep doing the work. But the knighthood itself has never been the motivation to do the work. If it happens, it happens.'

'I think it is very well-deserved,' says Lady Usha. 'I wouldn't have said that if it was ten or twelve years ago. But now, it is absolutely the right time for him to get it. He deserves it, because I think what he has done for Papua New Guinea is priceless. He is well-respected and people love him.'

'Dad sent me something and I had to look twice,' says Nikhil Patel, who was working in New York. '*What, is this knighthood real?* I gave him a quick call: "What's going on? Congratulations." He said it was real. I was then like, *Whom can I tell*? I told my flatmates and one of them was English. He asked what do I call him now? I said, *I guess Sir Dad and Lady Mum.* I don't tell too many people, but those I do tell, they are pretty speechless about it. Because how many people do you know who have been knighted?'

It was later revealed that Sir Dadi Toka, who had originally recommended Mahesh Patel for his OBE, had also played a part in him being knighted.

Sir Rabbie Namaliu, who served as the fourth prime minister of Papua New Guinea from 1988 to 1992, also endorsed Mahesh.

'The biggest satisfaction I get,' Sir Mahesh says, 'is not for me so much, but that of actually contributing to Papua New Guinea and its people. Because that is where I feel the closest to home. While I was born in Fiji, PNG is probably the place I am most proud of. The knighthood was awarded by that government. It's a place I've always called my home. In any of my speeches I don't just say, "Papua New Guinea", I say, "our nation".'

Like for his OBE, Sir Mahesh had no hesitation in deciding that he wanted to go to London to be knighted. But in the midst of the worldwide COVID-19 pandemic, he would have to wait for this new honour to be bestowed in person.

At the time, Sir Mahesh was one of only three people from Fiji-Indian heritage who have been knighted. In 2021, he received an unexpected treat.

'The Fijian community in PNG,' he says, 'did what they call a kava ceremony for my knighthood. Kava is the national drink of Fiji. They even offered the Queen to drink it when she last visited Fiji. It is a ceremony which they only do for dignitaries.'

The kava ceremony is a communal ritual centred round the kava tanoa (a large bowl). Participants sit in a circle around the bowl, which is placed in front of the leader of the ceremony. The ritual begins by producing kava from the root of the yaqona plant. The root is pounded and the pulp placed in a cloth bag in the tanoa and mixed with water and strained. The result is a brownish liquid—the kava gold. This is then offered to the guest of honour and others.

'The Fijian High Commission arranged it specifically for me,' says Sir Mahesh, 'and that was very touching. I was extremely honoured.'

In March 2022, as lockdown restrictions were lifting, Sir Mahesh received confirmation from Buckingham Palace that he could now apply for a date for his knighting.

'They were not doing investitures in Buckingham Palace due to renovations,' he explains. 'They gave me options for locations and three dates to choose from.'

Confirmation was received. Sir Mahesh would be knighted on Wednesday, 8 June 2022 at Windsor Castle in the English county of Berkshire. The original Winsor Castle was built in the eleventh century, after the Norman invasion of England by William the Conqueror. Since the time of King Henry I (1100–1135), Windsor Castle has been used by the reigning monarch and is the longest-occupied palace in Europe.

The timing of Sir Mahesh's knighting was an added bonus. It would occur immediately following the four-day weekend celebration of Queen Elizabeth II's Platinum Jubilee, marking seventy years of service to the people of the United Kingdom, the Realms, and the Commonwealth. An exciting time to be in London.

With the date confirmed, Mahesh and Usha were able to book their travels leading up to the big day.

They would arrive in the USA on 16 April and stay in New York with their son Nikhil for one month. After a stopover in Los Angeles for the wedding of Mahesh's brother Jagdish's son, Arkesh, who was marrying his fiancée Reetika on 21 May, Mahesh and Usha would fly to London to visit Usha's mother. Mahesh would then travel to Paris, where he would attend the Champion's League football final between Real Madrid and Liverpool on 28 May.

Mahesh and Usha would then meet up in London again on 6 June. They booked a stay at the historic Cliveden House.

'It's a beautiful property,' gushes Mahesh. 'It's a magical place about ten kilometres from Windsor Castle.'

There was then discussion as to how Mahesh would celebrate his knighting.

'My cousins and nephews were asking what we were going to do,' he says. 'I told them, "Nobody is to organize anything. I will find a place."'

What started off as plans for a small celebration quickly turned into a major event.

'The numbers started at twenty and soon we find it's become forty or fifty,' Mahesh notes.

He booked the classy May Fair Bar in London for 11 June and made all the arrangements. A private area would be allocated for the gathering, with the serving of cocktails and finger food.

When the official invitations were issued, the design was so impressively royal-looking that there was some confusion amongst the recipients as to what they would be actually attending.

'I've got a friend in PNG, Lata Milner, a Kiwi of Indian descent,' says Mahesh. 'She is a real royalist, so she helped me design the card and the invitation with the wording. Most of the people we sent it to thought it was an official function being held by the Queen. I told them, "The Queen is not going to turn up at the May Fair Bar at 7 p.m.!"'

Mahesh and Usha Patel spent one month in New York through April and May, as planned, with their son Nikhil. It allowed the three of them to have some quality time together. But discussion of Mahesh's upcoming knighting was never far away.

'Yes, I was very excited about it,' Mahesh admits. 'I had been talking to the suit-hire places in London and made appointments to go and see them. I booked a car to take us to Windsor Castle. Booked the dinner and high tea on that day. It would be just the two of us.'

'I was the one who kept things calm,' smiles Usha. 'One of us had to. I was excited, too. Grounded? Yes, I think that is the word to use.'

While Usha was shopping in New York for her dress for the cocktail party celebration, a sales assistant at the famed Macy's department store was extremely impressed when told what the occasion was.

'She curtsied,' smiles Usha, 'which was unexpected in New York.'

On 13 May, Queen Elizabeth II made a rare public appearance at the Royal Windsor Horse Show, which was taking place in the private grounds of her castle. She was pictured smiling in the front passenger seat of a Range Rover vehicle as she watched some of her own horses compete. Later, she took her seat in the grandstands, with the aid of a walking stick.

The Queen had been rarely seen in public since October 2021, when she was hospitalized and had suffered what Buckingham Palace described as 'episodic mobility problems'.

The day of Sir Mahesh Patel's investiture had arrived. All the preparation and planning would be put into practice.

Mahesh and Usha rose early. They had breakfast and got dressed. Checked and re-checked their clothes. At 9 a.m., their driver collected them from the hotel and drove to the nearby Windsor Castle, arriving approximately twenty minutes later. Official check-in time was 9.45 a.m. Accompanying guests were taken to a seated waiting area in the main hall, while those receiving awards were given their official briefing. At this time, the attendees were informed that the Prince of Wales, the future King, would be deputizing for his mother.

'I think one of the most important aspects of the investiture,' said Prince Charles, speaking generally about the awards, 'is to be able to reward in a suitable way, the selfless service and dedication of so many of these remarkable people.'

The awardees were separated into groups depending on ranking. Mahesh was in the first group of twelve people, along with Sir David Attenborough.

'While I was getting the brief,' says Mahesh, 'I suddenly realized Sir David Attenborough was standing next to me!'

The beloved environmentalist would be receiving the Knight Grand Cross of the Order of St Michael and St George.

'It was quite nerve racking,' Mahesh admits. 'There was a lot of retired military personnel guiding us. My heart started beating hard as soon as they finished the briefing. I was asking myself, *Will I say the right thing? Will I take the correct knee?*'

The official ceremony commenced at 11 a.m. Sir David Attenborough was the first to be called. Sir Mahesh Patel was the fourth awardee summoned.

Dressed in his royal-blue morning suit, with a white shirt, light blue vest and matching tie, Mahesh Patel strode forward with purpose, albeit a little nervous, towards Prince Charles. The future monarch was dressed in his Royal Navy military uniform.

'I walked in,' recalls Mahesh, 'obviously making sure my steps were right and I did the correct nod. I put my right foot on the little pedestal. After he did the sword knighting, the first thing he asked was, "Have we met before?" I told him we had met ten years ago in Papua New Guinea. He asked if I was still living in Papua New Guinea. One funny thing: I was talking about the work we do with women's empowerment, issues with gender-based violence, and family-planning issues. He leaned in and corrected me quietly, saying, *birth control*, and started smiling.'

Dressed in a champagne-and-gold-coloured sari, Usha watched proudly from the guests' waiting area.

'In one of the photographs you can see me,' she says. 'They allowed the partners or friends to stand towards the side. I could watch quite nicely from where I was standing. When Mahesh finished, we walked out of the hall together. I started tearing up. It was such a huge moment for him. A very special moment for all of us.'

'I think we were both happy,' gushes Mahesh.

'You did well,' praises Usha.

'Once you enter the room,' Mahesh continues, 'you are waiting in queue, and as soon as you enter the room, it becomes quite surreal. You are in your own zone and not sure what is happening. You come out and you think, *What happened?*'

'They do it so well,' said Usha. 'To a T, with the exact timing. Everything is done perfectly.'

'My heart was still beating hard after I left,' says Mahesh. 'It was so unreal.'

Prince Charles placed the knighthood neck badge, on a red ribbon with gold trim, around Mahesh's neck. The badge has its own official red display box, all made by the Royal Mint.

In 1926, King George V issued a warrant authorizing the wearing of a badge on all appropriate occasions by Knights Bachelor. The breast badge, a little larger, is worn on the left side of the coat or outer garment. In 1974, Queen Elizabeth II issued a further warrant authorizing the wearing on appropriate occasions of a neck badge, slightly smaller and also in miniature.

The design is described as: 'Upon an oval medallion of vermilion, enclosed by a scroll a cross-hilted sword belted and sheathed, pommel upwards, between two spurs, rowels upwards, the whole set about with the sword belt, all gilt.'

After finishing the presentation, Mahesh and Usha posed for official photographs. They then proceeded out onto the castle grounds where they took some photographs of their own. The couple met the Honourable Paul de Jersey AC CVO, Governor of Queensland (2014–2021) and his wife Kaye de Jersey. A Companion of the Order of Australia (AC), he had now been invested as Commander of the Royal Victorian Order (CVO).

Mahesh and Usha were thrilled to have national treasure Sir David Attenborough present on the day. The ninety-six-year-old wildlife filmmaker was awarded his Knight Grand Cross of the Order of St Michael and St George (KCMG) for services to television broadcasting from fellow avid environmentalist Prince Charles. Sir David, was first knighted by the Queen in 1985.

'It was interesting, looking at Sir David Attenborough,' says Mahesh. 'I don't think I'll have the same energy when I'm ninety-six. It is quite daunting.'

'He doesn't use a stick to walk,' observes Usha. 'He walks well. I stood right next to him. It was a very special moment to watch him receive the Knight Grand Cross.'

Overall, it was a fabulous experience for both Mahesh and Usha.

'It went exactly as planned,' says Mahesh. 'I could not have asked for anything more.'

'Mahesh was very nervous,' smiles Usha. 'He had sweaty palms. Then, afterwards, he was happy and back to normal.'

The report on Windsor Castle itself?

'It was fabulous,' gushes Usha. 'It is so magical there. Everything we saw was just perfectly done. The rooms are just beautiful, with all the old history … all those paintings and artworks. It was nicer than Buckingham Palace. Definitely.'

The May Fair Bar in London is unmistakably sophisticated and modern, elegantly designed to match its clientele. Sir Mahesh and Lady Usha Patel gathered there with their family and friends on Saturday, 11 June 2022, to celebrate Mahesh's knighthood. It was an opportunity for those closest to him to express their appreciation for his achievements, but more importantly, it gave Mahesh the chance to let those in attendance know how much they meant to him.

Along with their sons, Nikhil and Ajay, some of the others on the guest list, which numbered nearly sixty, included Mahesh's brother Anil and his wife Manisha. From Usha's side of the family was her brother Rakesh, his wife Sonal and their children, Ashani, Nyal and Siyan, along with nephew Sachin.

Mahesh's friend Rohit Reddy from New Zealand, along with his sisters Kamini and Sandra attended as well. Sandra's husband Vimal helped Mahesh immensely with the planning of the gathering.

Cousin Sanjeev Patel, also known as Sanju, was the master of ceremonies for the evening and also assisted with planning. He was joined by his wife Merlin and his parents, Mahesh's aunt Jaya Masi and her husband Narendra Masa ['masi' and 'masa' are one's mum's sister and her husband].

With red London double-decker buses cruising past behind him on Stratton Street, emcee Sanju Patel welcomed all the guests.

'This occasion is to celebrate a culmination of a lifetime's work and achievement,' he said, 'which has resulted in Sir Mahesh Patel, OBE, being awarded a knighthood by Prince Charles.'

There were warm cheers from the audience and a loud, 'Hear, hear!'

'Now that he is part of British establishment,' continued Sanju, 'maybe, as his family, that makes us part of British establishment?'

Lady Usha was asked to speak first and stepped forward in a white floral full-length sleeveless dress. She had a small attack of nerves at the thought of speaking to such a large group, but once she started, she settled in.

'We, as a family,' she said, 'including our late parents Savitaba, Maganbhai, my dad Manubhai, and my mum Kamlaben, who could not make it here today, Jaya Masi, Narendra Masa, our CPL family in PNG and friends, are all immensely proud of you, Mahesh, for the recognition given to you for all your business and philanthropic contributions to PNG for over thirty years. We feel blessed by our parents and thankful to them for instilling good values in us and in gratitude for the Hand of Grace that has always guided us.

'CPL Group was born out of Mahesh's tenacity, hard work and never-give-up attitude, especially through some really tough times. I am grateful for the good Lord's guidance that has always been with us and thank everyone who stood by us, including our sons Nikhil and Ajay. Ajay, I know you were only meant to stay and help for a few months in PNG, but you decided to stay on when we needed you the most.

'CPL Foundation was created primarily to help women and children, particularly for our need to give back to the community. Whether it's helping one person or thousands, it's all important, as my late dad used to say: the one person you help may go on to light pathways for many others. We can never truly know the bigger picture of anything we do or don't do.

'I think for me this quote from Nelson Mandela sums up Mahesh's attitude to life: *There can be no greater gift than that of giving one's time and energy to help others without expecting anything in return.*'

Usha became very emotional, and her sons, Ajay to her right and Nikhil to her left, stepped forward and put their arms around their mother to support her.

'I am honoured and humbled,' Usha continued, 'to be part of your journey, Mahesh, as I would never have made it to PNG through my own volition and am grateful to PNG for all the opportunities it has given us in so many ways and for your well-deserved recognition.'

Then, raising a toast for her husband, Usha said:

'To Sir Mahesh ... and that's the only time I'm going to say that.'

The crowd laughed in approval and Mahesh walked over and kissed his wife.

'Thank you everyone and enjoy your evening,' she finished.

The older son Nikhil, in a cream Indian-style jacket, blue trousers and brown shoes, was the next to speak.

'I'm going to keep this speech short and sweet,' he said, 'just like Mum.

'I could list Dad's achievements. I could tell you about every moment I've seen him in action, which has led to me being who I am. Even to the point where in moments of doubt, I often thought to myself, *What would Dad do?*

'Although I've been through countless iterations of this speech, each time I start with a different concept. Nonetheless, there is one commonality between them: family. Now, how does one define family?

'There is the obvious: my brother Ajay, Mum and Dad. But it, in fact, goes beyond that, right? Beyond our blood, beyond our bas [matriarchs] and dadajis [patriarchs]—our ultimate guides—it is, essentially, everyone in this room. I believe this achievement comes down to my family and the support system they have provided.

'This is not about one lifetime; this is about the people he has influenced today, and the generations of people his efforts will impact tomorrow and beyond.

'All in all, a central concept to Dad's life, which is highly correlated to the knighthood, is to selflessly serve others. The reason we are here—he has impacted every one of our lives in one way or another over the years.

'Here's to Maverick, or Superman. Also known as the hero of the story ... Here's to you, Sir Dad.'

Younger son Ajay Patel, wearing a dark grey suit and white open-necked shirt, next took the microphone enthusiastically. He requested a round of applause for his mother Usha, who is not normally used to public speaking, and got a loud response.

'One of the essential terms that I am going to talk about,' he said, 'is the 2018 decision that Dad took to come out of retirement—and a pretty good retirement you know, all things considered—to return back to business full-time. The reason why we are all here today. Why his knighthood was signed off after thirty-eight years in Papua New Guinea.'

Mahesh and Usha looked on proudly at their younger son.

'The decision to come back out of retirement,' smiled Ajay, continuing, 'was not one taken lightly by him or our family. The decision upended a lot of our roots to move and come back to a place that is incredibly challenging. A place where, through blood, sweat and tears, he has been able to create more than just an empire; he has created communities. He has created a sense of connection between people across the twenty-two districts and 800 languages of Papua New Guinea. If you think disjointedness comes in communities of four or five languages, come and give us a visit over at Port Moresby.

'He came back and saved the company in a place commonly referred to as the "land of the unexpected", for so many, many reasons. The cohesion of Papua New Guinea's disparate variety—the languages, the people and the environment—is a reflection of Mahesh himself.

'What he has been able to do, is to bring these seemingly disjointed places together. I think that is one of the biggest testaments and what I am really proud of him for. He will talk to the prime minister one day and a farmer the next, and he will treat them with the exact same respect.'

Ajay paused for a second and then said, 'Dad, I don't know what else to say.' He walked over to his father and hugged him warmly.

Mahesh's youngest brother Anil Patel then stepped forward to speak, with Mahesh standing a few metres to his left.

'For me, it is very special to be able to look up to an older sibling,' he said, 'who, despite all his professional and personal achievements, still manages to be so caring, selfless and devoted to helping shape the lives of others around him.

'My dear brother, Sir Mahesh, you are an exception to the rule. The qualities and values you have inherited from our beloved parents Maganbhai and Savitaben are so beautifully reflected in your personality. We know that our dear and beloved parents, Bapuji and Ba, would be proud of what their son has achieved with the help of their guidance and eternal blessings. May this latest recognition motivate you to continue with good work. I wish you many more successes in the future.'

Anil raised a toast to Mahesh. They clinked their drinking glasses and embraced warmly.

Finally, Sir Mahesh Patel addressed his family and friends. Dressed in a dark-blue suit and white open-necked shirt. His Knight Bachelor medallion on red ribbon with gold trim around his neck and his medals pinned on the left side of his chest.

'It has been a great privilege and honour to be out there at Windsor Castle,' Mahesh said seriously. 'It was an amazing feeling. My heart beating fast. After meeting Prince Charles, as I came out, they asked, "How are you feeling?" I said, "My heart's still racing. I need a downer."

'First and foremost, I would like to acknowledge my parents who are no longer with us. I believe values and your own personality grows from them. I wish they were here today but they are not. I thank them for my upbringing. Their values and existence. Thank you, Jaya Masi—she is hiding away in the back; she is my mum's younger sister—and to my Uncle Narendra Masa, for being here.

'The most important person in my life, as most of you have acknowledged, is my dear wife Usha. We have been married thirty-four years. If she had not been bold enough thirty-four years ago, a girl from London going to Papua New Guinea to reach me, I don't think we would be standing here.

'I remember picking her up from the airport and thinking, *What the hell is she thinking?* I had just started the business, so all I had was the utility van. Without her support, we would not be hosting this function today.

Father and Mother:
Maganbhai Patel and
his wife Savitaben Patel,
parents of
Sir Mahesh Patel.

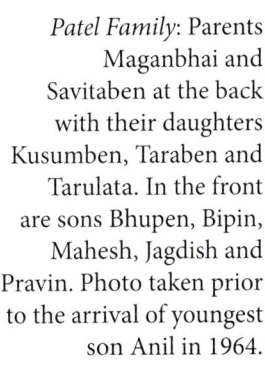

Patel Family: Parents
Maganbhai and
Savitaben at the back
with their daughters
Kusumben, Taraben and
Tarulata. In the front
are sons Bhupen, Bipin,
Mahesh, Jagdish and
Pravin. Photo taken prior
to the arrival of youngest
son Anil in 1964.

Mother and Son:
Sir Mahesh Patel with
his beloved mother
Savitaben Patel, in Fiji,
in 1962.

New Zealand Student: Parents Maganbhai and Savitaben visit Sir Mahesh Patel (third from left) in New Zealand in 1975. Brother Jagdish is on the left. Behind Mahesh's father, are friends Sailesh and Devan. Cousin Nalin is on the right.

Business Planning: Sir Mahesh Patel working on plans for his first pharmacy in Port Moresby, Papua New Guinea in 1986.

Wedding Day: The marriage of Sir Mahesh Patel and Lady Usha Patel in Port Moresby, Papua New Guinea, on 20 February 1988.

Bride and Groom: Newly married Sir Mahesh Patel and Lady Usha Patel, with Usha's mother Kamlaben Patel and brother Sunil Patel, on 20 February 1988.

Taj Mahal: Sir Mahesh Patel and Lady Usha Patel with sons Ajay (left) and Nikhil, at the Taj Mahal, on the banks of the river Yamuna in Agra, Uttar Pradesh, India, in 1999.

City Pharmacy: Lady Usha Patel poses in front of the City Pharmacy delivery van in Buka, Papua New Guinea, in 1994.

Public Company: Sir Mahesh Patel with CPL Group co-founder Alan Jarvis (left) and staff member Geoffrey Aimatu, at Port Moresby on 20 February 2002. The public listing of the company took place on the Patel's fourteenth wedding anniversary.

Opera House: Lady Usha Patel with sons Nikhil (left) and Ajay in front of the iconic Sydney Opera House in Australia.

Drummer Boy: Sir Mahesh Patel and Lady Usha Patel with sons Ajay and Nikhil at home as Nikhil plays his new drum kit.

Darling Harbour: Lady Usha Patel and sons Nikhil (left) and Ajay, receive a visit in Darling Harbour, Sydney, from Usha's father Manubhai, mother Kamlaben and younger sister Ragini.

Kokoda Track: Sir Mahesh Patel, Lady Usha Patel and sons Nikhil and Ajay, completed the arduous ninety-six kilometer Kokoda Track trek with family and friends over eight days in July 2008.

Fiftieth Birthday: Sir Mahesh Patel with Forest Essentials founder Mira Kulkarni (center), her son Samrath Bedi and his wife Karishma Bedi, at Mahesh's birthday party at Centrepoint Tower in Sydney, Australia, in November 2009.

Community Connection: Sir Mahesh Patel meeting with the Eastern Highlands Women's Group in Eastern Highlands, Papua New Guinea, on 4 March 2010.

Farming Tour: Sir Mahesh Patel is welcomed to a village in Highlands, Papua New Guinea, on 4 March 2010.

Brazil: Sir Mahesh Patel and Lady Usha Patel with sons Nikhil (left) and Ajay, in front of the iconic Christ the Redeemer statue in Rio de Janeiro, Brazil in 2012.

The Palace: Sir Mahesh Patel and Lady Usha Patel in the grounds of Buckingham Palace, London, during the visit to receive his OBE from Queen Elizabeth II on 21 November 2012.

The Queen: Sir Mahesh Patel shakes hands with Her Majesty Queen Elizabeth II at Buckingham Palace, London, on 21 November 2012. Their meeting occurred forty-two years after eleven-year-old Mahesh had waved a British flag as the Queen drove by him in Fiji in 1970.

Football Friends: Sir Mahesh Patel with his closest friends, Jagdish Patel (left), Jiten Patel and Vasant Bhuta, at the FIFA World Cup in Brazil on 5 July 2014.

Underground: During a trip to Vietnam in 2013, Sir Mahesh Patel inspected the tunnels in the Củ Chi District of Ho Chi Minh City. The tunnels were dug and used during the Vietnam War, 1955 to 1975.

Family Reunion: Sir Mahesh Patel was one of the driving forces behind a reunion of the Patel siblings and their offsprings in Fiji in December 2013.

Savitaben's Birthday: In July 2016, the Patel family gathered in Fiji, to celebrate matriarch Savitaben Patel's ninetieth birthday.

Usha's Parents: Manubhai Patel and his wife Kamlaben Patel, the parents of Lady Usha Patel. This photo taken in London, England, in July 2016.

American Summer: Lady Usha Patel and her siblings, Yamini, Sunil, Ragini and Rakesh, held their own family reunion at Jackson Hole Mountain Resort in Teton Village, Wyoming, USA, in July 2014.

Warehouse Fire: There was nothing but ashes and charred remains in the CPL Group's Gerehu warehouse in Port Moresby, Papua New Guinea, after a fire engulfed it on the night of 18 June 2017.

Sir Lewis: Sir Mahesh Patel poses in front of the Formula 1 motor racing car of Englishman Sir Lewis Hamilton, at the German Grand Prix in Hockenheim, Baden-Württemberg, Germany in 2019.

The King: Sir Mahesh Patel talks with the then Prince Charles and future England monarch, during his Knighthood ceremony at Windsor Castle in Berkshire, United Kingdom on 8 June 2022.

Teacher: Sir Mahesh Patel is an accomplished public speaker and willingly takes the microphone at his many speaking engagements to share his life lessons and business knowledge.

Pride of PNG: Sir Mahesh Patel with the 2022 *Pride of PNG* Award winners. From left, Hennah Joku for Bravery & Courage, Theresia Bafui for Education-Role Model, Susan Case for Community Spirit, Annie Varo for Young PNG and Ann Hewago for Care & Compassion.

The PM's: Papua New Guinea Prime Minister James Marape (right) introduces Sir Mahesh Patel to Australian Prime Minister Anthony Albanese in Port Moresby on 12 January 2013.

The Ganges: Rishikesh is a town on the banks of the Ganges in the Himalayan foothills in India's northern state of Uttarakhand.

Happy Birthday: Sir Mahesh Patel with his mother Savitaben, wife Lady Usha and sons Ajay (left) and Nikhil, at Mahesh's fiftieth birthday party in Sydney, Australia, in November 2009.

Patel Pride: Sir Mahesh Patel with wife Lady Usha Patel and sons Ajay (left) and Nikhil, at his celebration dinner in London, England, upon receiving his Knighthood from Prince Charles in June 2022.

Corner Pocket: Sir Mahesh Patel playing pool in Sir Richard Branson's Necker Island, in the British Virgin Islands, on 26 May 2023.

Seeing Red: Sir Mahesh Patel and sons Nikhil (left) and Ajay, with Virgin Group co-founder Sir Richard Branson, at Necker Island, in the British Virgin Islands, in May 2023.

'And my two boys, Nikhil and Ajay. Thank you for your love and support. I love you both. I keep calling them boys. They will always be my boys.

'I acknowledge that this award has come at a huge personal cost; while it is largely all glory to see ourselves celebrated, it came at a very big personal sacrifice, where I was away from the family a lot. I travelled a lot and in hindsight, it is a big lesson for all of you with young children as well. Spend the time with the family while you can, because I missed out on a lot.

'Usha and I started liking PNG and supporting the communities. We worked with a passion. On our Foundation website is a picture of her going through Bougainville, which was under civil war. We started our first pharmacy there, and she was the one who got a ride in a military truck to get there. The passion has always been there.

'We never imagined that this would turn out to be a full-fledged programme: healthcare in remote villages; empowering women and girls; fighting gender-based violence; mentoring young kids in business. As life goes on, Usha said to me last year, "You're busier now in retirement than you were when you were working."

'I could go on for hours and hours, but that's for another day. But thanks to you all for being here. Let's just enjoy the evening and have fun.'

On 8 September 2022 at 3.10 p.m., Queen Elizabeth II, the longest-reigning British monarch, passed away at Balmoral Castle in Aberdeenshire, Scotland, at the age of ninety-six. Her death was announced at 6.30 p.m. that night. She was succeeded by her eldest son, King Charles III.

Sir Mahesh Patel was in Port Moresby, Papua New Guinea, when he received the distressing news at 5 a.m. local time.

'I was deeply saddened,' he says, 'and rushed to wake Usha up, so we could say a quick prayer for her.'

It had been an amazing year, personally, for Mahesh, to be in London for the Queen's Jubilee celebration and receive his knighthood from the now King Charles III. His thoughts and memories were now with Queen Elizabeth II, who awarded him his OBE and knighthood.

'While we all knew that this day was coming due to her declining health,' he says, sombrely, 'I did not expect it to come so soon. This will really be felt in the coming days as we reflect on her life and the brief moments I was fortunate enough to have with her during my investiture ten years ago. Her Majesty will always be in our hearts. May her soul rest in peace.'

Chapter 15

Business Life

The business and personal success for Sir Mahesh Patel throughout his life has been overwhelmingly positive. Starting as a contract pharmacist in 1984, he made moves to open his own pharmacy in 1987, and then, with the help of others, built it into a public company, which reached revenue sales of 606 million kina (13 billion rupees) in 2022. In 2010, he was named Director of the Year by the PNG Institute of Directors.

But how exactly did he do it?

'I can't comprehend it, to be honest. I can't,' Mahesh frankly admits. 'Because I never, ever imagined what we have done. When you blink and ask, "How the hell did it happen?" It feels just like yesterday when I started.'

'I thought we would stop at eight or nine stores,' says Lady Usha Patel, 'because I thought, *This is it. This is right for me and you.*'

When Sir Mahesh Patel and his business partner, the late Alan Jarvis, opened their first City Pharmacy store in 1987, there was no long-term plan for expansion. Alan's son Caleb Jarvis, who would later become the company CEO, confirms that his father would have been initially testing the business plan to see whether it was sustainable, before investing more money into it.

Mahesh admits, 'I didn't even think about expansion in the early days.'

Not only did the first City Pharmacy store business prove itself sustainable, but fit for expansion, which continued with a second store in 1988. Then two more in 1990 and 1991. By 1992, the business was ready to expand outside the Port Moresby city area, and five new stores were opened in regional Papua New Guinea.

If you ask Mahesh what the one key component of his success was, he answers simply, 'Taking the risk.'

Of course, there are all levels of risk. Reckless risk should always be avoided at all costs. But calculated risk, where you have formulated your business plan and tested it in practice to a point, can produce extremely positive results.

'Taking the risk goes along with believing in yourself,' explains Mahesh. 'It goes back to asking, *Why did you start a business*? I had no market research to say my business would be successful. I said, *Okay, I'll start it up, and the ball is in my court*. I will have to make it work, and if it doesn't work immediately, at least I know I have a network of people who will come and shop with us.'

Self-belief and investing in yourself is one of Sir Mahesh Patel's key factors in the success of any business.

'The big thing is believing in yourself,' he says, 'that you are the one who can make it. If it doesn't work one way, twist it around and make it work another way.'

As with personal life, so in anyone's business life, there will be setbacks, problems to overcome and failure.

'You need to have a lot of self-confidence,' Mahesh reiterates, 'and not let setbacks get to you. Otherwise, you could say, *Oh, well, it's too hard*.'

Mahesh talks about tough times and how he responds to them by using the example of the aftermath of the fire in 2017, which burnt the CPL Group's warehouse and offices to the ground. 'I remember sitting in my apartment,' he recalls, 'when we decided in 2018 that I would move back to PNG in an executive role to rebuild the business. We could have taken the easy way out. We could have said, *We've done well, if the business doesn't get back up, it doesn't matter.* But then you say, *No. We will re-build.*'

Everyone brings unique skills to any business. Mahesh openly admits that problems with the business have often brought out the best in him.

'I think I'm better at crisis management,' he declares. 'If things go too smoothly, I get bored. That is when I start diversifying and doing other stuff. If there is a problem, I dive in. It seems the energy level comes back in. I say, *I'm going to fix it.* I think it is taking the challenge and believing in yourself. It is easier said than done. But that is what has got me going all the time.'

Lady Usha Patel points to how City Pharmacy was built over time, and the way they treated customers and other important strategies were utilized to develop their business.

'I would say it was step by step,' she suggests. 'I'm not sure it was in Mahesh's mind to have a big company. It was built brick by brick. We built a strong foundation, and from that, it grew because of his personality, because of the way he interacted with people, and the way we did business.'

The passion for your business and the self-fuelling energy you bring to each day are also important to your success.

'Mahesh is intelligent, focused and knows when he sees an opportunity,' says former CPL CEO Ravi Singh. 'But his best trait is his exuberance and the energy he brings to all who are around him.'

Without paying customers, you have no business. Similarly, if you cannot keep the customers you already have, you will also soon have no business. One of the areas where Mahesh Patel has excelled in business has been in identifying his customers' needs and consistently delivering what they want, while making them feel valued.

In 2003, City Pharmacy launched Papua New Guinea's first customer loyalty program: Real Rewards.

When Mahesh and Usha were involved with a pharmacy in Mascot, Sydney, in 1995, they inherited a manual in-store loyalty programme.

'It cost the customer nothing at all,' explains Mahesh. 'The customer gets a little card. You just stamp on it each time a customer spends 30 dollars (1,500 rupees), and by the time they get to ten purchases, they get something free for the eleventh visit. I thought this was simple, because there is no technology involved. I kept that in mind and we created a loyalty programme stamp with a passport-style card. That has now developed into an electronic system and we have now got 350,000 members.'

It was only years later in 2019, when one of Mahesh's mentees, Jaive Smare, drew Mahesh's attention to how much the rewards programme was valued by his customers.

'Jaive told me,' says Mahesh, 'that his mother still had the same rewards book from when we first started the programme in 2013 and she was very proud of it.'

'I used to go to second-hand book stores and buy *Time* magazine,' recalls Jaive. 'Once I picked up *Fortune* magazine. There was a story about Jeff Bezos at Amazon in the very early days—he used to have his value system with loyalty points. Then I saw my mother using the rewards card at CPL. This is what I just read about and they were already doing it at this store. CPL were a step ahead.'

Jaive suggested to Mahesh that the programme was something CPL should be promoting more, recognizing the attachment some people have to it.

'That reminded me of the importance of the programme,' says Mahesh, 'and that we were way ahead of anyone else in Papua New Guinea with our loyalty programme. That's what we have prided ourselves on: being the first to market. Just like waste management, recycling, environment controls, and saving the oceans. They are all fantastic initiatives and we at CPL want to be first.'

Working long, difficult hours is an accepted practice for any business person, particularly when starting up a small business or expanding an existing one. It is a necessary sacrifice which cuts into personal time and, in the case of Mahesh Patel, would lead to regrets later. But when it comes to getting ahead, there are few alternatives.

'When I start looking back through my old diaries,' says Mahesh, 'back then, I didn't realize how hard we were working. I spoke recently at a conference for small to medium enterprises, all new startup businesses. I told them, *there is no alternative to hard work*. Sunday was a normal work day for us.'

On the issue of time management, Mahesh Patel cautions people on spreading themselves too thin by taking on new businesses that are very hands-on.

'Sometimes, as they say, you run off the smell of an oily rag,' he says. 'I have made mistakes by going into small businesses in later life and they are only suitable to be owner-operated. I don't want to be doing that hands-on work or the nuts and bolts of it. I think that is where I have made a mistake by going into some businesses where I shouldn't have. I am learning now: don't get involved in small businesses because you have moved beyond that. Ten to fifteen years ago, I'd be there—not anymore.'

Similarly, going into businesses you don't really know or understand is another pitfall to be avoided.

'Mahesh was looking at a building investment in Brisbane with some friends,' says Jagdish Patel. 'I asked, "Have you seen the building?" He said, "No." I said, "Do we know anything about construction?" He said, "No." I took the paperwork and threw it in the rubbish bin. My wife Sangita asked, "Why did you throw the papers in the bin?" I said, "Because it is rubbish."

'People were trying to suck Mahesh in. There is a philosophy you should have. You do what you understand and you do what you know. It is Warren Buffet's quote: *Never invest in a business you cannot understand.*'

Another contributing factor in Mahesh Patel's success was having talented people working with and for him. As a qualified pharmacist, Usha Patel brought her own expertise from working in the United Kingdom. While his core business had been property development and construction, their partner Alan Jarvis brought enormous business experience and acumen to City Pharmacy.

Mahesh Patel was the company CEO when he started the City Pharmacy business with partner Alan Jarvis, who was the chairman. Mahesh became the company executive chairman in 2009 upon Alan's passing, with a CEO working under him. In 2015, he stepped back from day-to-day involvement and became a non-executive director. It was at this time that he started thinking about the future and who would chair the company into the future.

'I needed somebody who knows Papua New Guinea,' says Mahesh. 'Someone who is honest and trustworthy. Somebody who has got good ethics. Stanley Joyce is the guy who came to my mind.'

Mahesh has known Stanley Joyce for over thirty years. He started working in Papua New Guinea for a snack food company. Then he became marketing manager of the local brewery and, eventually, managing director of the brewery.

'In 2015, we were at the Rugby World Cup in London,' recalls Mahesh. 'We had been invited along by Heineken with a whole bunch of business people. At dinner one night, I asked Usha to sit next to Stan to see what kind of guy he is. Usha is a really good judge of character. Usha thought he was a very nice man. I asked whether he could become chairman of the company and without a flicker of doubt, she immediately said, "Yes."'

Stanley Joyce joined the CPL Group board of directors in 2016 and became the company chairman in 2018. He also chairs the boards of South Pacific Brewery and Westpac PNG

'Stan obviously has got impressive business credentials,' notes Mahesh. 'He is great in what he does because his heart is in Papua New Guinea, like mine. He is originally from New South Wales. We are both very alike. We came to Port Moresby in the early 1980s for work. He is not politically involved; he gets a lot of respect from the politicians and the business houses.'

Navin Raju was appointed as chief executive officer of CPL Group in October 2020 after working as the chief operating officer (COO) of the Group and previously as CEO of Hardware Haus Limited. Born in Fiji, Navin moved to New Zealand for schooling in 1988 at the age of fifteen. He earned his Bachelor of Commerce at the University of Auckland and his Master of Business Administration and Management from Southern Cross University.

Navin and Mahesh Patel have very similar backgrounds.

'I have known Mahesh for a long time,' says Navin. 'I was a friend before I became an employee. I met him about twelve years ago. We are both from Fiji. That relationship has always been there.'

In 2018, when he was recruited to join CPL, Navin made it clear to Mahesh that they had to keep their business and personal relationships separate.

'I told Mahesh,' Navin recalls, '"During our working relationship, I might upset you and you might upset me. We must remember that it is our working relationship." I told him if he could understand that, it would work.'

As an experienced businessman in his own right, Navin sees why Mahesh has been so successful.

'He is opportunistic,' he says. 'Mahesh is an entrepreneur. He has been in the right place at the right time and made the right decisions. He is also someone who takes advice from a lot of people. He understands this business. He has done it for so many years. For someone who is a pharmacist, he has a really good financial background and understanding; he says he doesn't, but he does. He is very strategic.'

Diversification of the business empire was another important component of Sir Mahesh Patel's business strategy. The purchase of the Stop & Shop supermarket chain by CPL in 2005 was a major step forward, but some questioned the logic of it.

'Because my family had a supermarket business in Fiji,' explains Mahesh, 'I always thought I could run Stop & Shop better. You always see the shortfalls. People sort of laughed at me and said, "What do you know about supermarkets?" I grew up inside a supermarket. There was a basic understanding. It all boiled down to customer service. Most people who shopped with us in the beginning came because they liked our service.'

Friend Greg Wisbey said Mahesh had to make some significant changes to get the Stop & Shop supermarkets humming along with increased efficiencies.

'He had to re-coach the management who were doing everything wrong,' Greg says.

'Mahesh has incredible skills in breaking down a profit-and-loss statement,' says Karishma Bedi, who has worked with him at Forest Essentials. 'Asking insightful questions that can start deeper conversations to improve efficiencies. He was always able to look at things from both sides and then share his opinion with pros and cons. He was always a call away for advice and assistance, no matter the ask.'

'Owning a business is in his blood,' says Usha Patel. 'It sort of drew him to it at a subconscious level because he was involved as a child doing odd jobs in the family business.'

But not all new business innovations work.

'We failed in a lot of diversifications,' admits Mahesh. 'Whether it is supermarket or hardware, it is still retailing—the basics are the same; the products are different. Whereas when we put up our hand for the cinema chain, it didn't work. We tried pizza. It didn't quite work. We went into manufacturing of kit homes. It didn't work. That's when we said, *Let's have our four-pillar strategy of retailing in different formats.* Now we stick to healthcare, food, shelter, and lifestyle. So, when people say now, let's do something different to that, I say *no*.'

Along with their City Pharmacies and Stop & Shop supermarkets, CPL has further expanded their business empire to include:

- Prouds, a chain of duty-free stores from Fiji, which sells fragrances, jewellery, liquor, and so on in its stores at the airport. They have downtown stores as well, now. In PNG it is a joint venture with the Fijian Motibhai Group;
- Jacks, an apparel store. It mostly stocks a lot of Pacific clothing and fashion. Again, it is a joint venture with the Jacks of Fiji;
- Fresh Express, their food bars, which sell salads, fish and chips, stews and so on;
- Hardware Haus, which sells hardware products;
- PWL or Pharmacy Wholesalers Limited is their Sydney office.

'Over time we've added a few businesses and retail,' says Mahesh, 'but we've got our four-pillar strategy for the business. That is our strategic plan, unless we decide as a group or a board to do a chicken farm or a brewery. That would be a decision by the board to say, *Do we move away from our four basic pillars?*'

The company changed its trading name from City Pharmacy Limited to CPL Group in 2005 to avoid confusion.

'We were a pharmacy when we started,' says Mahesh. 'Then when we bought the supermarkets, we'd send inquires to meat suppliers and produce suppliers and they wonder, *What does this pharmacy group want lamb for?*'

The Patel family supermarket business in Fiji has a long history. C.P. Patel & Company Ltd, named after Chhotabhai Patel and then continued by younger brother Maganbhai Patel, had established the first family grocery and general shop in Ba's main street in the late 1940s. The business was carried forward by Pravin Patel and other family members, eventually becoming New World Supermarkets. Their first big supermarket was opened in Lautoka in 1985.

'It was my brother Pravin,' recalls Mahesh, 'who in the 1970s opened a self-service super market, which blew my dad away. He was thinking, *How can you have self-service? People are going to steal.* Previously, it was only counter service. People would give you their orders, you fulfilled the order, and they paid you the money and went away. It was a new concept in the very early 1970s.'

Newworld Limited, now a private company, is one of the largest retail chains in Fiji. The retail activities are carried out via twenty-eight stores under the name of New World Supermarkets, Pots & Things, and Chilies. They are located across Fiji in Ba, Rakiraki, Tavua, Lautoka, Nadi, Suva, Nausori, and Labasa. Since 2014, the New World Supermarkets have partnered and branded with IGA, the Independent Grocers Alliance of USA.

'Mahesh was the guy who guided us all the way,' says company Chairman Pravin Patel. 'He gave us good advice on how to structure the business.'

Mahesh is on the Newworld board and has been the perfect adviser, calling on the successes of his own Stop & Shop supermarkets.

'There are congruencies between the two businesses,' says Newworld CEO and Mahesh's youngest brother Anil Patel. 'Part of his business is similar—the retail. So, we thought, let's exchange information and see if there are synergies in buying or ideas or new ways of doing things. The CPL team visit us every now and then when the need arises.'

In August 2022, work commenced on the construction of a new 45 million Fijian dollar (1.6 billion rupees) centralized distribution centre in Wairabetia, Lautoka. It will take approximately two years for the new warehouse to be fully operational, but will add another 100 employees to the companies' current roster of 1,200, more than half of whom are women.

It wasn't until 2012 that Mahesh started to receive significant dividends from his ownership in CPL. Prior to that, he was living off his salary as an employee.

'It was after the liquefied natural gas (LNG) boom,' he says, 'that CPL started paying out reasonable dividends. That's when we had spare cash, so Usha and I invested in a few other companies. Our rationale was, why leave it in the bank or in managed funds when we have got a family member starting a business and we have good faith in them. That is when a lot of these things happened.'

Amit Patel is Mahesh and Usha's nephew. He is the son of Usha's sister Yamini.

'Amit is the firstborn on my side of the family,' says Usha. 'He is and always has been special. When my sister was pregnant with my niece, she was not keeping well, so we took care of Amit in London. I have always had a strong connection with him.'

Amit was starting up a new business in the USA where he lived. He asked Usha and Mahesh if they could invest.

'We did and, obviously, he was grateful,' said Usha. 'But he was worried, because he didn't want to let us down. So, I wrote him an email to say, whatever happens, I'm giving you this money because if you succeed, all well and good; if you don't succeed, still all well and good. I didn't want him to feel stressed.'

'Mahesh and I talk on a business standpoint,' said Amit, 'and the relationship has grown over time. He is readily available at any time. No appointment required. He continues to be very casual and informal and that is both ways. Even if he is looking at something and wants my advice.'

The initial business was a success and now their partnership has continued into second and third businesses.

'We are at that change stage of our life now,' said Mahesh. 'We are downsizing and simplifying, and getting the kids involved in investment. We have some joint investments with Nikhil and Ajay. A lot of proposals come to me which I send over to them to look at and say, *Are you interested*? If yes, we do it jointly.'

When looking at the business success of Sir Mahesh Patel, it is important to recognize the personal characteristics of the man, which have complemented his passion for work and readiness to work long hours. These include his business knowledge acquired through successes and failures, an openness to seize new opportunities, his willingness to listen to others more knowledgeable in any subject, and his leadership. But, most importantly, he treats all the people he deals with, in whatever capacity, as real people.

Dr Shetal Desai, affectionately known to her uncle as Tiku, runs a chain of medical diagnostic centres in Gujarat.

'Mahesh is a staunch personality' she says, 'no tolerance for nonsense, sensible. He likes to talk straight. He is punctual and very active. I am in awe of his business acumen and have a lot to learn from him.'

'Even when he was asked to chair Telikom PNG,' notes friend Udhay, 'it was not a commercial enterprise for him. It was more of a public service. In that period, he would consult me, not on the nature of the business, but on macro and global communications matters. He was a quick study. This was not his industry, but he tried hard and talked to me a bit about where technology is going and where are business models going; he really applied himself, as if he owned the business.'

'I have been with Mahesh on business trips to Hong Kong, the Philippines and other places,' says friend Gareth Joseph. 'I have seen how he does business, who he does business with and how he does it. How he recruits people. He has asked me to sit in with him when he has recruited people in the Philippines. He would say, "I'm not sure about that person, what do you think?" I would reply, "I think that person is right for the company." He listens to a variety of opinions. He makes people feel valued.'

'What I admire about Mahesh,' says cousin Daksesh Patel, 'is that he is never shy about admitting to his problems. He is the one who raises his hand and apologizes. He will admit a cockup or a stuff up and say openly, *Listen, I stuffed up.*'

Why does he do this?

'It drives him to become a better person,' suggests Daksesh. 'I think his experience in India may have mentally changed him, his perspective on life.'

'CPL was a small organization,' says Mahesh's mentee Vani Nades, 'which was growing and then diversifying into different businesses and spreading its wings across the region. That shows leadership. At the same time, when it is branching out, it is providing services to other parts of the country where you were previously unable to find these things. It is an amazing, successful story to tell. Very inspirational.'

'Mahesh pigeonholes his activities extremely well,' observes friend Greg Wisbey. 'When he's with you, he'll focus on what he is talking to you about. Then he will close that drawer and next he is on to CPL Group or Forest Essentials. Okay, then he'll close that and he's talking about schools. Close that and then he is talking to someone about something else.'

Long-time business associate Ramesh Mahtani puts Mahesh Patel's business success down simply to four words: 'Hard work and honesty,' he says.

Former City Pharmacy CEO Caleb Jarvis suggests that Mahesh's business traits may be rooted in his cultural beginnings.

'He is, obviously, extremely entrepreneurial,' he observes, 'being a good Gujarati from a good Gujarati background. They are renowned as being top businesspeople, top traders in a great historical sense. Anyone who has done business with Gujaratis knows how proficient they are at it and trading.'

No one should ever underestimate how difficult it was for Sir Mahesh Patel to arrive in Papua New Guinea as a foreigner, start his own business and build the CPL Group into the behemoth it is today.

'Mahesh has always been driven, ambitious, smart and innovative,' says friend Vasant Bhuta. 'He ventured into Papua New Guinea, a place that is most definitely not for the faint-hearted, and made it his own turf.'

'Mahesh has always been very fortunate in business,' says friend Jiten Patel. 'Anything he touched turned into gold. With Usha being a pharmacist, he was off to a good start. His business partner Alan Jarvis gave him a great opportunity, and with his hard work, he never looked back. He just went from strength to strength.'

The ability to conduct business in a country which has had its problems with political instability, is also remarkable and praiseworthy.

'What I am most proud of,' says Usha Patel, 'we have created the business honestly, without getting involved with anybody in a nefarious way. That has always been our intention. We both worked very hard. But Mahesh's main aim was more to give than to get. I think that when you have that attitude, your energy is different. Whether you believe in this or not, the universe reads that on some level and I think you get that back. I think if you do it with a good heart, it works differently.'

'Mahesh was successful in Papua New Guinea without wielding his political influence or an iota of corruption, which speaks volumes for a person's courage and conviction, resolve and sheer determination,' agrees Daksesh Patel. 'I think my only regret is this: if the same resolve and determination had been applied by Mahesh in Australia, he would have been much bigger.'

Mahesh occasionally looks back at the businesses he has created and the success he has had.

'It gives me immense satisfaction and pride,' he admits. 'Especially now. You get more pleasure in giving than making. I try and do something to serve somebody else. I'm busier now than when I was working, because I have all this responsibility. Actual added responsibility. I think, looking back at it, we always say, *We should have done that, we could have done this.* But it's all behind us. You have to look forward. It gives me great pleasure spending time in Papua New Guinea. It's frustrating sometimes, because the country is a developing nation. You see a lot of corruption. You see a lot of wrong things where people get short-changed. Infrastructure is not done. You could turn your back and walk away, or you could make a little difference. I choose the latter.'

Chapter 16

Mentor

If you were to draw a pie chart showing how Sir Mahesh Patel distributes his available time, the largest slice will be the hours he puts into the CPL Foundation's charity work in Papua New Guinea. But a close second will be mentoring young people trying to start their own businesses. Passing on the vast business knowledge he has accumulated gives him immense joy.

'Every time I meet people,' he says, 'they ask: *Why did you come to Papua New Guinea? What happened here? Where did you start from?* I mentor people and they inspire me. They are the ones who made me want to have my life story documented, so it can be used by others as a guide. My target audience is the youth of today.'

Whether they are in Port Moresby, Delhi, Sydney, Nadi, London, New York, or anywhere else in the world, people are always asking Mahesh questions about his unique life and how he got started.

'I was in Fiji recently at a barbecue,' he recalls. 'I met a youngster, introduced by his dad. He started asking me all these questions about my life. His father said, "Oh, stop nagging him." I told him, "It's fine. I don't mind." Because everyone wants to know about all the decisions I made.'

Mahesh is currently closely mentoring four business operators in Papua New Guinea. There are also hundreds of others he has advised over the years. He also regularly speaks at small business startup conferences.

Mahesh usually starts any discussion by asking the same question. *Why do you want to do it?*

'I am looking for their passion behind it,' he explains.

Mahesh gives a specific example of how that question affected a woman who sought his advice.

'She had a great little café,' he said, 'but she was struggling to make money and pay the rent. We started to break down the costs of the business. It was me trying to impart logical business etiquette. Because I have been doing business for the last forty years, I assume things, like everybody knows what their gross profit is, what their costs are. But not everyone does.

'Finally, and this was a defining moment. I told her, "I'm going to ask you a question. Don't answer it now. Go home and talk to your husband and your children and come back and tell me the answer tomorrow."

'I asked her, "Do you want to be a really good cook, or do you want to be a businesswoman?" That sort of threw her a bit and she went away to think about it.

'She rang me the same night and said, "I have spoken to my family and I want to be a good cook." So today, she is creating recipes and charging a royalty. She will make more money than running her own business.'

Mahesh's strategy when mentoring anyone is to try to drum into them making commonsense decisions for their business.

'I don't tell them what to do,' he says. 'I question them. First, do you have passion for the business? Second, what is your goal for the business? And third, what is your business speciality?'

'Having passion. That is the key,' he says. 'Some kids don't come back after I ask them these questions. Because they realize what it takes to be successful.'

Mahesh also cautions about jumping straight into a new business unprepared.

'Do not leave the job you are doing now to start a business,' he warns. 'You have to burn candles at both ends. Do something on the side. Retain your current job, it puts food on the table. Because a lot of new businesses fail.'

The Young Chamber of Commerce in Port Moresby arranges for leading CEOs to speak to young business owners. One of their monthly events was hosted by CPL, and Mahesh was the keynote speaker.

'I was talking to some of the people there and they were all quite sheepish,' he recalls. 'They were scared to talk to me. I tried to break the ice with them.'

Two men told Mahesh they ran a car rental business in a regional area outside Port Moresby and wanted to expand their business into Port Moresby to attract more clients. Mahesh asked them, 'Why? Have you thought about who is going to run it? You will have to invest in more cars.'

Mahesh asked the men whether there was a taxi service where they currently operated.

There wasn't one.

'I suggested to them,' he said, '"Why don't you start there? Saturate your market and become the king of that. There are online startups now where you can book taxis online. Partner with them. You don't have to create your own app." They said, "Wow, that is a good idea." They can stay in their province.'

Mahesh's friend Udhay can see how his mindset for business is also applied when he is mentoring others.

'It is something similar to what he did in India,' Udhay says, 'where he had this idea of going to India, and setting up a chain of pharmacy stores, and then off the back of that experience, he discovered or identified other opportunities. That's Mahesh. He will start with something and figure out something else around it and then create another company.'

Mahesh advised another lady who is on his mentee list about not undercutting herself when it came to recouping her costs.

'She is running guided tours,' he says. 'She had some well-known Hollywood stars she was escorting across the Kokoda Track. I asked her how much she was charging and she told me. I said, "No, you should charge more." Because they are Papua New Guinean, they are too shy.'

She was booking all their domestic tickets and travel, but was not adding a margin. Mahesh encouraged her to add an administration fee.

'You are running around and doing work for them,' he noted, 'so, you are entitled to add a fee.'

Mahesh invited her to his office so he could look at her business's financial figures.

'I asked her to do a spreadsheet,' he said. 'I wanted to see all the costs. She had one line originally. I sat down with her and had to extract all the information we needed. She wasn't making any profit. What she needed to do first was work out what everything costs and then apply her fees accordingly.'

There was another person who produced virgin coconut oil. They had problems with packaging.

'I used a supplier to source bottles from China,' said Mahesh. 'I got our internal graphics team to design the label with the barcodes, etcetera. I said, "You focus on what you are good at, making the product. I will do the marketing for you." That's what really excites me. Using all I have learnt.'

Helping the women of Papua New Guinea has always been a priority for Mahesh. A young woman entrepreneur is making great progress with the same people in mind.

'She is working with reusable sanitary pads,' says Mahesh. 'Her research done in the villages showed that when girls start menstruating, their school attendance drops. Two out of three girls stop coming to school during menstruation. Because the subject is sensitive in the village, they don't know about sanitary pads or know how to use them. It is sad. So, we supported a new programme with this young woman. Our CPL stores would have donation bins, and we'd encourage other working women to buy and put pads in the donation bin, and we would match that. We would give her support from the CPL Foundation staff to run the education programmes in villages, schools and classrooms.'

Another man had started a taxi service in Port Moresby, and at a business startup conference, he approached Mahesh for advice.

'Nine out of ten people in the room didn't know about the taxi business,' said Mahesh. 'He came to me and asked if he could talk to me about it. I did a bit of mentoring with him and said the best way I could help him was to give his business a pilot through CPL. That's what we do with many local businesses. I asked, "How many taxis can you muscle up?" because security is a big issue in Papua New Guinea.'

Security for female CPL staff has been an ongoing issue. When their Stop & Shop supermarkets close at 9 p.m., there is no public transport for staff to get home.

'The trust factor was missing at that time,' explains Mahesh. 'Even the buses would stop at 6 p.m. We used to hire security buses which would park outside our supermarkets at 6 p.m., 9 p.m. and 10 p.m., whenever the staff finished. The staff would then be dropped off home. But a twenty-minute run could take an hour and a half for the staff to get home. It has always been a concern and we had been trying to crack that problem.'

The taxi company committed to Mahesh to supply a set number of taxis and the drivers would be fully trained.

'I said to them,' Mahesh recalls, 'we will hire thirty taxis, every night, seven days a week, 365 days a year. Line up here and drop our girls home. There were a few false starts, but the business is up and running.'

But then the owner wanted to expand his business in a different direction.

'He wrote to me, wanting to start a pest control business,' said Mahesh, 'and then he suggested a security business. I said, "Stop. Your speciality is taxis. Why don't you talk about food delivery or business delivery?" I then reminded myself: *I was exactly the same*. Why don't we do this? Why don't we do that? There is always a desire in people to just bounce into new things.'

The advice Sir Mahesh Patel gives anyone trying to start up their own businesses is varied, but can be summarized in ten key points:

- Have passion for the business—this is the key. It is not only about profits, but about creating solutions for our communities and the environment.
- Be disciplined and have belief in yourself and your abilities.
- Do not be afraid to ask for help or guidance, no matter how small the issue—you learn by talking and opening up.

- You need sheer determination to succeed and work hard—never give up.
- Align with intelligent people you can learn from.
- Practise humility, empathy, transparency with your team—have honesty and integrity.
- Reinvest in yourself.
- Know what the customer wants.
- If diversifying, stick to what you know and your skill set.
- Follow-up, follow-up, follow-up. And hold people accountable—including yourself.

Anyone attempting to create any sort of business should always remember that varying levels of failure are a natural part of working life.

'People only see the success that we have had,' says Mahesh. 'But we have had some really tough times, where we had our backs to the wall. There is no choice but hard work. It is not easy. You see our success now but not the troubles we have been through and the sacrifices we have made with our family. In hindsight, sometimes you think, *Would you do it again?* The answer is probably, *No.*'

Jaive Smare is a Papua New Guinean business entrepreneur who is being mentored by Sir Mahesh Patel. He is a perfect example of someone who had a great idea, but didn't have the business expertise to make it work.

In Papua New Guinea, many people survive from day to day on pre-paid electricity.

Pre-paid electricity meters installed in homes by PNG Power required tokens to operate. But many people found it difficult to purchase the physical tokens, which were dispensed by vending machines and other methods.

A random violent attack on a woman trying to buy electricity tokens prompted Smare to make the system more accessible for all communities.

Prior to Jaive's innovation, there were over 500,000 houses in the country with pre-paid electricity meters, but only eight outlets where the tokens for them could be purchased.

'It wasn't enough,' he laments. 'You had these long lines of people queuing for power, which took forever. It was ridiculous.'

Jaive was living in Koki in Port Moresby, considered to be one of the rougher neighbourhoods in the capital city. A woman he knew had walked five kilometres to purchase an electricity token, but at the outlet where they were sold, their point-of-sale system was not working. On her way home, she was attacked, stabbed, and robbed.

'I wanted to help her,' said Jaive. 'She was only trying to buy power. I thought if I could put more electricity token outlets in our neighbourhood and other places, it was less likely she would get victimized. People shouldn't have to travel outside their suburb to buy electricity. The problem weighed on me so much that I had to fix it.'

Jaive grew up in a small village in the Highlands. He graduated from the Divine Word University in Madang with a degree in journalism. But after working in the media for a few years and enjoying it, he decided he wanted to do something else.

While he didn't consider himself an expert in computers or the internet at school, 'I liked writing about technical stories. I like seeing end results,' he says.

He complemented his one year of internet courses at the Divine Word University by travelling to the Papua New Guinea University of Technology in Lae to learn to write computer script and coding.

'I used to hang out with the computer science kids to try and learn what they were learning as well,' he said. 'I had an interest.'

Jaive then went to New Zealand to do a programming course where he learned high-level computer programming skills. But after two years there, he became homesick.

'I just wanted to go home,' he said. 'I would work at whatever people gave me. When I came back to PNG, I wanted to work on a project that was good for the country.'

Back in Papua New Guinea, he was helping missionaries repair aeroplane air strips, figuring out emergency evacuation of women from rural areas to hospitals for childbirth.

It was at this time in 2017, that he started working on solving the residential electricity supply problem.

'I never aimed to make a business out of this,' Jaive explains. 'But I started working on it really hardcore. I put everything I had into it, all the money I had saved.'

In conjunction with PNG Power, Jaive built a new web platform which would allow people to purchase electricity via their mobile phones or at retail outlets.

Easipay is a user-pay system where customers who buy power receive a computer-generated sixteen-to twenty-digit number. By entering the number into their electricity meters at home, they are credited with the kilowatt hours purchased. Jaive took the existing system and created a new, more reliable phone app and computer interface.

'It came to a point where I had built everything,' said Jaive. 'I had to figure out how to do it at the lowest cost possible. Once I figured out how to get past those firewalls, I was able to build a better integration. When I got past that process, people started using it everywhere, but the power company said my volume was too low. They said, "We are going to cut you off."'

PNG Power told Jaive he needed to achieve 1 million kina (22 million rupees) in sales per month to make the new system financially sustainable, or they would discontinue it. With mobile phone and credit card use in Papua New Guinea still limited, compared to other countries in the world, he needed a way to get into enough retail outlets where people could easily access it.

'That is when I started going after Mahesh Patel,' said Jaive. 'I was problem-solving and looked at the biggest retail chain in the country, which is the CPL Group.'

On 17 September 2018, Jaive emailed Mahesh seeking his assistance in making his Easipay platform available in CPL outlets.

'I can integrate the purchase process into your current point-of-sales system,' wrote Jaive, 'and you can print out the vouchers on a thermal receipt printer as you currently do.'

Mahesh emailed Jaive back and suggested they talk the next day.

'I immediately thought, *This is a good idea*,' recalls Mahesh. 'We installed it as a pilot in one store and, *bang*, it took off.'

Jaive learnt a big lesson from Mahesh the very first time he met him at the CPL head office.

'I was ten minutes late,' admits Jaive. 'Mahesh said, "Are you going to use the traffic excuse? I know all the excuses." Since that day, I have never used an excuse with him, ever. If I am late, I am late. If I don't want to do what he told me to do, I just tell him, "I'm not going to do it." Our first meeting taught me how to deal with him, but it also changed me.

'Now, I don't make excuses anywhere. I am straightforward. It was a good thing because it taught me how not to waste energy making excuses. I didn't actually know what I was doing, but Mahesh did not care, he just said, *get it done*. "I'll give you access to all the CPL stores, but I don't need your excuses."'

The store pilot programme commenced in November 2018. There were some problems with integrating the new Easipay platform into the CPL stores point-of-sale software.

'When we installed the sales machines,' recalls Jaive, 'Mahesh got angry and said he wanted the integration happening quicker. He would call me and say, "I don't know what you are going to do, Jaive, but you better fix it." He would call me at one in the morning, yelling, "What the hell are you doing?"'

Over time, Jaive learned that Mahesh Patel does not waste his time.

'A friend of his son Ajay,' he reveals, 'told me that Mahesh only swears at people he likes. He doesn't waste his time on people or things he doesn't believe in.'

On 3 April 2019, Jaive emailed Mahesh seeking his formal mentorship in business.

'I have always been the dreamer,' he wrote, 'because sometimes, when you are hungry, all you can do is dream. I really want to build a company that millions of Papua New Guineans can draw lessons from. But there are too many people talking to me, and though business speak is great, the danger is I may lose the vision.'

Mahesh replied the next day.

'I am very happy to assist,' he wrote. 'You have the passion and drive, and as I warned you in one of our meetings, you do not want to lose sight of your vision in the journey!'

Mahesh knew that he needed to try to get Jaive better educated in basic business practices.

'Jaive is a really smart guy,' observes Mahesh. 'But he is one of those typical IT geeks who is all over the shop. My task was to streamline him and instil a business sense into him.'

The power company had wanted Jaive to achieve sales of 1 million kina (22 million rupees) per month. They are now beating the numbers.

'There are all these reasons why my relationship with CPL shouldn't work,' remarks Jaive. 'But Mahesh didn't care. I pushed the entire CPL team to get this done. I worked my ass off. I guess everyone identifies him with the CPL chain. But it's not just that. People like him are very rare. I got my break through him. My technical innovation was big, but what made it sustainable was my break with Mahesh. Not just selling in the stores—it was him talking to me to fix things up.'

Jaive willingly admits that without Mahesh's guidance, his business venture would most likely have failed.

'Everything I have learnt in business is from Mahesh,' he declares. 'Without him, I would have stuffed up this project a long time ago. There are times where I have lost so much money trusting people. I have zero brilliance in business, how to understand the difference between low-margin products and high-margin products. He sat me down and talked me through it. This was all bigger than I had planned. I was building it to sell to someone else. But I'm glad I didn't. I am not a businessman, but I want to be.'

Interestingly, Jaive admired Mahesh and his success, and in the back of his mind, he had always wanted to work with him in some capacity in the future.

'At university, I used to have a picture of him on my wall,' he said. 'CPL was the first retailer to do the value rewards card. We weren't well-off then. I dropped out of school to help my siblings to ease the pressure off. Working for Mahesh was something that I thought of as a kid, and it came full circle. He is the only person I know who has built something from nothing in PNG. It is a hard country to do that, but he did it, starting from one pharmacy. I had ambitions to build software to change the country, but I didn't have the business acumen to do that.'

When asked the best thing Mahesh has taught him about business, Jaive thinks for a while before replying.

'Just about things having balance,' he says thoughtfully. 'The other thing Mahesh has taught me is you can't do things on your own. For a long period of my life, I did a lot of things on my own, just because of the way we grew up. We were homeless at one point … It is in the culture here—it is very hard here to make it on your own.'

Jaive is also complimentary about Lady Usha Patel and the role she plays in the life of her husband.

'She gave me this book about drinking water,' he says. 'Just a simple book about staying hydrated, some things you forget to do. Usha is not like Mahesh; she is calm. She has a calming influence on those around her. If you were an ambitious person and you needed someone to keep you centred, even when you totally stuff up, she is the one you want there. That's the feeling I get from her.'

Giving back to the community has always been something which Sir Mahesh Patel has strongly believed in. Jaive Smare has a similar focus.

'Mahesh has helped people get lifesaving drugs they couldn't afford,' he says. 'The guy is recognized everywhere in Papua New Guinea. I wouldn't say he is a celebrity; instead, he is intensely respected. Celebrity is a phase, and they fade away. As he gets older, Mahesh becomes more respected. After I talk to him, I get emotional. I can't thank him enough for taking a chance on me.'

Vani Nades grew up in Papua New Guinea's Central Province, with no running water or electricity. After dropping out of high school in class 10, she began working at the Institute of Business Studies, now IBS University. Later, she went on to study in Australia at Southern Cross University's Coffs Harbour campus. In addition to graduating with a bachelor's degree in accounting, she was the 2018 winner of the Southern Cross University Entrepreneurial Award. Vani first met Sir Mahesh Patel in 1995 when she was working as an innovation and development officer at the Institute of Business Studies. He has been mentoring her ever since.

'Being around Mahesh and others like him motivates me to grow,' she says. 'I was a dropout. The system rejected me. But I never quit because of people like this who help you and boost you to keep growing and achieve your dreams. From dropout to degree holder, I am so grateful to the people who have been part of my journey. They empower us and education is key. Apart from my father, Sir Mahesh has been a part of my growth.

'Education is knowledge. Education is power. Education is what enables people to make a difference and bring our kids to the next level. It is re-engineering our education system. It is breaking the cycle to have all the children in school.'

'Vani is a great advocate for the next gen of PNG,' said Mahesh, 'in education, in the startup space, and for empowering women.'

In 2015, Vani started her own consultancy business, Emstret, to help small, and medium-sized enterprises get the startup help they need to survive and grow. In 2019, she launched Emstret Space as a working space to further help small and medium enterprises.

'We run startup programmes and we need mentors,' says Vani. 'Mahesh is also on one of the judging programmes. He gets himself involved. There was a woman's startup and we saw the potential in her, so we brought her to be mentored by Mahesh, and the lady and her business just took off. It was exhilarating to see.'

Vani recognizes the dedication that Mahesh has towards helping the women of Papua New Guinea as a priority.

'You can see the amount of passion he has,' she says, 'to help women grow to the next level in business, education, or other aspects they are focusing on. He takes it to heart because he believes in the potential and the capabilities of women, knowing that women are great managers and can progress. If you help women, the women also help the community. The community benefits from that.'

In addition to her work helping startups as the CEO of her company Emstret Holdings Limited, Vani has a number of businesses she operates, including providing internet connections to Papua New Guineans, particularly in rural areas.

Vani has tried to run her businesses with a social responsibility in mind, like Mahesh has done with CPL.

'I grew with a passion to learn,' she says, 'and a passion for the community, for impact, and looking at your business differently. I resonate a lot with Sir Mahesh. He has been such a wonderful mentor to me and others as well. Being around this sort of leadership encourages us to be confident in ourselves and do business and give back at the same time.'

Asked to describe Mahesh's mentoring style, Vani is direct, just like him.

'He is very critical,' she smiles. 'If he doesn't like something, he tells you straight. You have to be very open to criticism and Sir Mahesh is someone who will give you positive criticism. You have to take it because you want to grow in business. No sugar coating—he is very straightforward. If you are serious about mentorship, you have to commit yourself. If you don't commit yourself, then just forget it.'

But why does Sir Mahesh Patel, a man who could be doing some many other things, give his time and expertise so willingly?

'His story is about having a heart for people,' suggests Vani. 'Because he is passionate about what he does. He loves it and he wants to make an impact and give hope to someone else. He has done a lot of giving back to the community, empowering and inspiring, recruiting a lot of Papua New Guineas and giving them second chances. That's how we connect. People come into your life and support the journey that you pursue.'

Not putting himself above others has always been important to Mahesh's success and how he is perceived and relates to others.

'Humility and humbleness are absolutely the keys,' he declares.

Mentoring anyone is a commitment, and if you do take on the responsibility, says Sir Mahesh Patel, it is important to truly commit to it.

'Mentoring takes a lot of time,' he says, 'and you need to be dedicated. Otherwise, you are letting these kids down. As it is, they are too scared to come and talk to you, because they think you are a big man and too busy. I say to people, "Don't take a mentorship if you don't have the time." If you take it on, you must devote the time.'

Keeping a healthy work–life balance is one of the topics that Sir Mahesh addresses when he mentors the many young people who seek his business-building wisdom.

'I keep telling them,' he says, 'that they have to focus on getting that home balance right because there will be a time when you look back at your life, regardless of the financial success and question whether it was all worth it.'

Jaive Smare now has a young son with his fiancée.

'Mahesh told me,' he says, 'I need to spend more time with my child. By the time they get to ten, you have lost them. I could feel what he was saying. He was talking to me not like a mentor, but like a brother. I asked Mahesh, "How did you make the life balance?" He replied, "I didn't have a life balance." When he was talking about his kids, he said he did some crazy stuff and "my kids probably hate me for that". He was saying that and I took it very deeply. Mahesh was telling me to make the right decisions. He was mentoring me. Now that my baby is born, it stays in my head.'

The regret within Sir Mahesh Patel burns deep.

Chapter 17

Missteps

Everyone lives their life with regrets. Some are minor and easily forgotten as you move on. But others tug at your heart and soul for years and years. Some regret will always be there, eating away at your emotional and mental well-being. For all his successes in life, there is one major regret which Sir Mahesh Patel lives with each day.

From: Sir Mahesh Patel
Sent: Tuesday, 18 October 2022 4:57 a.m.
To: Paul Upham
Subject: SMP book

Dear Paul,

I was just thinking that while I and most of the people you talk to will give stories about me in positives only, there are some points I would like to stress on.

There has been nothing more important to me in my journey than my family—Usha, Nikhil and Ajay, for they are the ones that keep me going!

It is their love I thrive on… despite all the lost time being away from home, and the mistakes I have made along the way. Usha, being the rock behind me—always supportive, come rain, hail or shine; keeping me on the "straight and narrow", helping out, looking out for me with her unconditional love!

And my love for my boys, despite not giving them the time I should have, growing up—that's what has made me who I am and where I am today.

In hindsight, I did have a choice, but sometimes I took the wrong one, at the expense of my family. I will always regret this!

Now, trying to make up for all the lost time is difficult. But we are united as a family.

And the thought of working with the CPL Foundation, in a way giving back to the community, is what will keep me going for a very long time.

Mahesh

When Mahesh and Usha Patel moved to Sydney to live with their sons Nikhil and Ajay at the end of 1994, it started an endless spiral of nights away from home for the husband and father, travelling between Australia, Papua New Guinea, India, Fiji and many other countries in Asia. Mahesh doesn't try to sugarcoat what he did and speaks openly about how his absences have affected his relationships with the three people who mean the most to him.

'I look back at my diaries,' he says, 'and I feel really sad at the way I travelled like an idiot when I was young. I'm angry for not making the time to spend at home.'

'I acknowledge,' says Usha, 'that my situation was not unique in that a lot of women both work and look after children without partners to support them, and they have it quite tough on their own. With

Mahesh, it was always pluses and minuses. He has not been the most perfect husband ever, but he has done amazing things others haven't accomplished, though that shouldn't be my judging point. His good side pulled me through, otherwise I would have left a long time ago.'

A normal routine for Mahesh would be to arrive back in Sydney on a Friday afternoon and then fly back out again to Port Moresby or elsewhere on a Sunday. But there were times when he was away for much longer.

'When I would go to India,' he admits, 'I would spend four or five weeks at a time—not a week here and then a week there. I would be away a whole month.'

Mastering the battle of work versus life balance is one of the most difficult conundrums for anyone, where the lure of financial security for one's family is offset by the time away needed to obtain it.

Does Mahesh think he was a terrible father because of all the time he was away?

'I do,' he agrees. 'Because that's the lasting impression the boys have as well. *You were never here*. When you think, you actually were here, but because of that inconsistency of being in and out, there is a lot that got missed.'

Mahesh's friend Udhay recalls him being an active and engaged father to Nikhil and Ajay when he was around.

'Whenever I caught up with Mahesh,' he recalled, 'we would have two types of catch-ups. Sometimes he and I would just have a meal. But it was also with his boys. We would do a lot of stuff together with the boys. I thought when he was there, he was very involved.'

There is one incident, however, with younger son Ajay, which remains burned in Mahesh's mind.

'I used to take the boys for a haircut,' he recalls. 'You know hairdressers, they like chit-chatting. Ajay was having a haircut, he must have been seven or eight, and it was the end of the school year, so the hairdresser asked, "How's it going?" He replied, "We had the last soccer match last week, but Dad never comes to our soccer matches." I was thinking, "That's pretty bad." I had missed just one match.

'I would come back, making sure I was at home on Friday. I'd be tired on Saturday. One son would go east and one would go west; I'd be driving—on Saturdays I was the glorified taxi driver. But for me, that's a great thing I did. But obviously it didn't make an impact on the boys. Because their feeling was, "You were never here." That makes me sad because it was because of the lack of consistency.'

Told the haircut comment story, Ajay Patel chuckles that he would have said it.

'Yeah, definitely,' he smiles. 'It was the same thing with soccer or cricket or softball. Dad could be there the entire season, but if he missed one game, that is, of course, what I am going to remember.'

Ajay thinks about it further and laughs.

'I am sorry,' he says honestly, 'because I know that must have upset Dad a lot. But I kind of laugh that my little shit self would have said that. I know when I got older, Dad made an effort to be there almost every single Saturday. But that would have been a rough comment to come from your son, and so it stuck with him.'

Older son Nikhil recalls that his father's absences were an accepted part of their normal routine.

'That was life,' he says. 'It was sad to see him go, but it wasn't like a dreadful shock or a serious upset. It was always saddening when he had to leave. But I understood: that is just the way it is.'

Now in his thirties, Nikhil has a greater appreciation for what his father has achieved businesswise, and how hard it must have been to juggle all his commitments.

'I have a better understanding,' he says, 'of how much he had to do and how much he had to put into everything that he has built. It puts all of his work into perspective, especially in recent times, as we are adults with similar challenges. It was obvious that to have the opportunities that we did, it took a lot from him, and we are grateful for those opportunities. It's more—how he managed to balance everything at my age, like having kids, running a business, and all the charitable efforts, and the ninety-nine million other things he was doing. Just how was all that possible?'

Ajay wrestles with trying to balance the positives and negatives of growing up with his father's constant work travels.

'I remember once what I said to mum when I was young,' he recalls. '"Forgo the trips; it would be nice just to have Dad home." But now,

I know the sacrifices and what they were for. Maybe now I would say, "Trade in that trip for this and we can do a bit of horse trading on the time frame."'

For Mahesh, it is something that he cannot let go. His thoughts consistently return to what he views as lost time, which can never be replaced.

'Usha keeps telling me, "Move on",' he says. '"You can't keep crucifying yourself." But it still lingers. Especially when I'm travelling and I see families with kids. Even though I did it, I suppose I would have been miserable if I was at home all the time. But the travelling gave me the break. Like they say, you appreciate a thing more when you don't have it. When I came back home, I really appreciated it. But I suppose, growing up as kids, they would have liked their father to be there. Even though they won't interact with you on a daily basis.'

Would life have been better for Sir Mahesh if he had remained a single small-business owner-operator pharmacist?

'Life would have been different,' he admits. 'It is hard to balance. Which is why I keep reminding myself, *You have to move on*. But I'm an emotional guy and it gets to me. Kids grow up, and hopefully the boys will reflect on it and say, *It was okay*. We get on now, but there were times when there was quite a lot of tension that I was not at home.'

Friend Greg Wisbey witnessed over many years the difficulties Mahesh's absences were causing for the family.

'Mahesh was distracted,' he said. 'He had so much on his plate. He just left Usha to look after the boys. He would fly in and out. When he was in Sydney, it was a maelstrom. It was just chaos. Usha used to tell me, he would come in, there would be a massive storm of things to do, and then he was gone.'

While conceding his time away from his sons would have been a negative for them, Mahesh feels that the constant travelling they underwent growing up, both in residences and holidays, gave them advantages in learning.

'There was a difference between my life growing up in one place,' he observes, 'and ours, where we kept moving constantly, is that the boys would have been disorientated, but I saw it as a positive experience for them.'

Mahesh remembers attending a seminar at Hamilton Island many years ago run by an organization called Family Business Australia. One of the other attendees was a fourth-generation farmer. The wife explained what happened when they took their children out of school to attend the conference. The headmaster said to her, 'Don't let school get in the way of education.'

'The meaning,' summarizes Mahesh, 'was that kids would learn more at the seminar and in family travel than in the school when missing out on two days. Such a powerful statement. What you learn when you travel and meet people, you will never learn in school. It's a very important lesson. That's the way I saw it. Travelling is an education for the kids. We were fortunate to be able to do that.'

Asked if he thinks all the amazing extended holidays, unique experiences, and life opportunities afforded to his sons offset his time spent away from home, Mahesh replies bluntly, 'I don't know. That is a question for them.'

Looking back at their lives and the time missed with their father while they were growing up, Nikhil and Ajay are both honest and philosophical about the positives and negatives.

'The amount of time together has been spread out at different points,' observes Nikhil. 'Although Dad may have had to travel through our school years, we also did have the opportunity to take extended vacations with Mum and Dad. Altogether, if you just look at life in a holistic sense and the total time spent together, I think we spent quite a bit of time together compared to the general family on average. It's just how the hours added up.'

'I definitely had points where I would accept it,' says Ajay, 'and then there were points when I was asking, *Why is dad not here for this special event of this day? What's more important than me?* It came down to an ego thing in a certain sense. In hindsight, there were times when I looked back and saw some negatives in him not being there every day, but I think it was more to do with my perceptions on the day I was thinking about it. I think there were definite points of anger. There were points where I was upset with him.'

Ajay describes a specific memory of the effect on the family routine, to highlight this anger.

'This is what I felt at the time,' he says, emotionally. 'When Dad wasn't there during the week—that was the norm: the way we would do our homework, the way we would sit, the way we would have dinner. But when he was home, *No, now it is his way*. Now we have dinner when he says, the way he wants, the way he expects—that was more disjointed, more disruptive, than when it was just the three of us. Which is another comment he is not going to like to hear, but I think I have mentioned it to him before.'

To be fair, Ajay also recognizes the effort his father made to attend some of his important school events and how he often turned them into something extremely memorable.

'Dad really made an effort for the big events from his perspective,' he says. 'I remember one of the best ones was when we went to Brisbane for some state robotics championship. We were quite young, maybe eleven or twelve. He was there and we had a lot of good memories of him chaperoning my team. There were three of us on the team, and on the way back home, our flight got cancelled. But because Dad flew a lot, he got our team, plus another one of the teams that was travelling with us, into the VIP lounge in the airport. We were like, *Wow, we can sit here and get free food*. Of course, him being there was really important. Seeing our wins, seeing our losses. Just being supportive.'

Ajay's overriding memories seem to be, 'Dad was always there for the big events, which I think were important in his mind, but I think for a lot of the smaller things that make up the surrounding environment, he was not there.'

Both Nikhil and Ajay have discussed their experiences with their father.

'We have discussed it to the extent,' said Nikhil, 'that we aren't holding anything against him. We can understand that you just have to go out there and do what you have got to do.'

'We have discussed it multiple times, sober and drunk,' reveals Ajay. 'When I was a lot younger, I was holding on to a hell of a lot more anger and white-knuckling my emotions that I had not unpacked. But as I have grown up over the years, I let go of it, a fair bit of time ago. But especially coming back to live with Mum and Dad in PNG, seeing the two human beings existing together, you just remember that, right, everyone goes through their struggles and challenges.'

Now that he is much older, has it given Ajay a better understanding of what his father has achieved and what all the time he spent away from home was for?

'Absolutely,' he says. 'Do I think he did the right thing? Not all of the time—as he says, as well. I think he could have made different decisions.'

Does Ajay think his life would have been better had his father had a job close to home and been around all the time?

'I think I would have rather just had him at home,' he replies. 'It was cool that we were able to go and do that stuff and have epic memories in a certain sense, and have great photos, because I don't think I remember a lot of them. You could ask me on a different day and a different week and I would be like, *That was a really cool trip.* But I think I would have just preferred to have him at home.'

But having said that, Ajay still recognizes the advantages in life his father's work has provided him.

'The opportunities afforded through his network,' he acknowledges, 'through the success he has had, they have made our lives unbelievably more enriching. The past seems hard because I am sitting here, in the shoes of one who has all those advantages. I imagine if I had to go through the usual hustle and grind in all I had to do, I might feel different. I'm not sure.'

Repairing his relationship with wife Usha was even more difficult for Mahesh over many years.

'It was a very tumultuous time,' reveals Greg Wisbey. 'When he wasn't in Sydney, he didn't have any clue, really, of what was happening. Mahesh delegates, and he would give Usha a great long list of things to do. They were off his mind then and he would go off and do his thing. She had her own regrets with Nikhil and his foot medical issues and how that happened with him.'

Sandra Diaz-Twine is an American reality television personality who became known for her appearances on the show *Survivor*. She won the first two seasons she appeared on *Survivor: Pearl Islands* and *Survivor: Heroes vs. Villains*, making her the show's first-ever two-time winner. Competing for thirty-nine days, along with the preparation and return home, she spent long periods of time away from her children.

'I didn't focus a lot on my children,' said Diaz-Twine, 'because I had left them with my husband and my mother. So, I felt like I had left them with the two most capable people to care for them. My focus wasn't on my kids. From time to time you wonder, *What are they up to? What are they eating?* Silly things like that. But I never sat out there and cried about missing them so much because I knew—and I had just got out of the army where I had spent five years—I guess I was already acclimated to leaving my family from time to time.'

Perhaps Mahesh simply felt comfortable knowing their sons were with Usha, and it removed any concerns he had about being away from home for long stretches?

'Absolutely,' he agrees. 'Usha did everything. My attitude was, *Okay, it's all taken care of.* I don't remember any time where she nagged me or told me I wasn't playing my part or not contributing or not sharing the load. She just took the load on.'

'To be fair to Mahesh,' says Usha now, 'he was setting up a business and I was contributing to that in some way. But that was his main focus.'

But Mahesh's time away from home was causing great conflict, to the point where his sons, over time, become aware of the rift between their mother and father.

'Tension? Absolutely. But they hid it well,' says Ajay. 'There were times where I was asking myself, *Why is mum losing her shit on the phone? Who is she talking to?* Then I would figure it out, who else would she be talking to. I think once she threw the phone across the room or I heard a crash and was like, *What happened?* And she replies, *Oh, nothing, I'm just on the phone.* And I'd be like, *Hold on a second, that doesn't really connect.*'

To give some context as to how much Mahesh was travelling, in 2005 his personal diary records him being at home in Sydney for only 132 days. Interestingly, his 2022 diary records him being home for a very comparative 139 days.

'But Usha would have been with me for half the days I was away overseas in 2022,' notes Mahesh.

In 2001 and 2002, prior to meeting Samrath Bedi and Mira Kulkarni and his investment in Forest Essentials, Mahesh was spending so much time in India away from his wife and sons that he nearly lost them.

'I think through all his trials and tribulations and the journey he took,' says Samrath, 'Mahesh came to a point where he realized that Usha was probably the best thing that ever happened to him.'

The positive effect of Usha on Mahesh, should never be underestimated. It is a resounding belief among those who know them both well.

'Usha's strength comes into it,' says Daksesh Patel. 'She has done an amazing job. Mahesh recognizes now the sacrifice Usha made to be with him side by side and do it with him without an iota of complaint. You reflect that back in a relationship. It is worth something.'

'Mahesh and Usha, they are almost opposites,' says Greg Wisbey. 'They are very different. Usha is very humble. She is not interested in gold chains and perfume. She is very spiritual. The thing about Usha I so admire, she is a lady that has a very strong faith, and nothing shakes her faith. This is what has driven her and allowed her to come through the storm. She was left on her own for a long time. Usha is incredibly loyal. She hitched her star with Mahesh and she was prepared to go through hell and high water, and now they are through to the other side.'

'Usha talks about philosophical things a lot,' says Daksesh Patel. 'She is very spiritual. But she confronts Mahesh when he becomes aggressive. He can be pretty blunt and sarcastic. He has got a problem of being too opinionated. Then he'll become aware of it and begin making jokes to lighten up. I think Usha brings him back to ground and tells him, *Look, this is not right. You can't take that view. You can't make an assumption about a person. What if that guy was struggling in life and you weren't aware of it?* She brings that sense of balance in his mind.'

'Usha believes in forgiveness,' says sister Ragini Shah, 'because she feels it's the only way to overcome unpleasant things that happen in life and have gratitude for all the good that comes our way. She always said that you can forgive but never forget.'

Usha explains: 'By practising true forgiveness, the negative impact of the situation loses its potency to affect our minds, mentally and emotionally, in a negative way. After a while with diligent practice, this turns into compassion for self and others.'

'It doesn't take a lot to poke Mahesh,' observes Daksesh Patel. 'This is his weakness. You can pinch Mahesh with philosophical debate. He can be very argumentative. When that happens, he becomes a little disrespectful at times. Which he probably does not realize. But again, no one tells him that. Usha will counsel him, but only when it happens in front of her. But it doesn't get reinforced, and nobody wants to reinforce it with him because he will just argue again. Whereas with Usha, he doesn't argue. He just says, *Okay*. Because Usha can say, *If you don't listen to me, piss off*. The spouse has a different relationship.'

Anyone who spends time with Mahesh and Usha now can see that they are in a very happy relationship. There is love and respect. Mahesh constantly defers to Usha's judgement in most matters.

'Mahesh has told me,' says Samrath Bedi, 'that he really regrets not spending enough time with his wife and sons. About his time over here in India, it is a situation he regrets greatly, but having said that, I know how hard he has worked to make it right. It has been a very difficult path for him. A very difficult journey. Usha and him are in a better place now. A good place, I would say.'

Asked if he is happy in his marriage, Mahesh replies enthusiastically, 'Absolutely! It has blossomed into an amazing relationship and my eternal thanks to Usha for sticking by me.'

Does Mahesh think Usha is happy?

'I think so,' he says. 'I think we are in a good place. One positive thing that came out of the COVID-19 pandemic was that we spent nonstop time together. The longest time ever in our lives. That is the most time we have spent together without a break in our married lives. Your priorities change as you mature. We have a great time together. We are both different people. But when we are together, it has really blossomed. Actually, it has blossomed more now than when we were younger.'

Mahesh Patel also regrets not spending more time with his mother Savitaben. A simple interaction with her, when he travelled to Fiji for a milestone birthday, opened his mind to the importance of simply spending time with family without doing anything in particular.

'I went and surprised her on her ninetieth birthday,' he says. 'I told my brothers not to tell her. She came out of the prayer room at

7.30 a.m. I'd always be one of the first to call her on her birthday. The moment she said, "I haven't had a call from Mahesh," I walk in the door. She got the shock of her life. The brothers had breakfast with me and Mum had tea. I had changed into shorts and a t-shirt. I was walking around the house on the phone or was on the internet. All of a sudden, it was 1 p.m. I had not spent much time talking to Mum, because she was busy in the kitchen and I was on the phone and internet doing work. And she said, "See, you don't have to travel overseas, you can just come and stay with me and work from here." It dawned on me how selfish we have been at times. I tried to make that effort, but we always get distracted. That's what I tell the kids I meet now. You don't have to go and sit down and talk with your parents. Just go and be there, while you are doing your own stuff. She knows you are there. Your presence is so important.'

Another realization for Mahesh later in life is that parents do want to be included in family activities, even if they don't initially agree to it.

'I found out from my mum's own book,' he says, 'when she was young, living in India, anytime they got a chance to go and swim in the river or in a pond, they'd go in. I didn't know that. But growing up in Fiji, we used to go out for picnics to rivers and beaches. We would always think, *No, Mum won't be interested in swimming*. And initially when you asked them—and Usha's mum would be the same—they'd say, "No, you go on, I'll be fine." They would not expect to go.

'But if you ask them three times, they will say, "Okay, I'll come," very enthusiastically.

'That was a big regret—not knowing your parents properly. That she would have loved to have gone. I think if we had taken her out to picnics in the early days, she would have gotten used to it. Half the time Dad did not come either, so she would stay home. We never thought of it that way.'

Mahesh Patel has regrets in his business life, too. One of the toughest roles he ever took on was the chairmanship of Telikom PNG, which he held from January 2014 to December 2017.

'There were just a lot of challenges,' laments Mahesh. 'It was a constant battle over four years.'

Telikom PNG is the country's leading telecommunications company, owned by the Papua New Guinea government. In operation for over six decades, it offers voice and data services.

'The prime minister asked some private sector leaders to take on the chairmanship of various struggling government entities,' Mahesh says, as he explains how he ended up in the role.

His initial response was to reject the offer.

The prime minister insisted, saying, 'It's about time you guys give something back to the country.'

Mahesh then reluctantly agreed to accept the position but said, 'I don't know anything about telecom.'

'Good, you'll learn,' the prime minister replied.

In his usual thorough way of doing business, the new chairman took a hands-on deep dive into the companies' activities to fully understand where the problems lay.

Telikom PNG in the 1980s was state of the art. They employed the best Papua New Guinean engineers to work at Telikom, and also hired engineers from other countries to work in Papua New Guinea. Their communication service was better than Telstra in Australia. Then, somewhere along the way, service standards declined.

'There was something wrong,' he says. 'I would be out at the Telikom office every day looking at things.' Neglecting his own CPL business, he spent hundreds of hours going through the company's accounts.

'I got accused by the unions that I was micromanaging,' says Mahesh. 'The company had a monopoly at one stage and we were still not making money.'

To ensure their survival, the board of directors agreed to a series of staff reductions to streamline the business. Initial cuts were from 1,400 employees down to 900 and then eventually to 600.

'The unions were outraged,' recalls Mahesh. 'I got abused on social media. They were saying, *You're ripping our people off, you are putting them out on the streets*. I was quite active as the chairman on behalf of the board, so I was the public face.'

Mahesh clearly remembers his first town hall meeting with the hostile staff.

'Everyone was standing around waiting for me to speak,' he says. 'It was like those Roman stone-throwing events. I'm standing there thinking, *I'm the new chairman, what do I say?*'

Mahesh had prepared a long speech about commitment and ownership in an attempt to engage the staff and explain to them the future vision for the company. But before he spoke, a prayer was held, as is the usual custom for the predominantly Christian country. The new chairman immediately discarded his prepared notes and tried a different tack.

'The preaching you just heard,' he told the angry audience, 'if everybody could just follow that, we will be a better organization.'

He then calmly walked off.

The employees, who had waited to hear him speak, were stunned.

There were further problems with basic assets and documentation.

'Telikom had towers and a massive amount of land ownership,' says Mahesh. 'I was having trouble locating half of the documents proving it. We know we own it, our towers are there, but the papers are missing. I had two or three staff full-time just sorting that out.'

Mahesh stopped a contract deal that was not in the best interests of the company, which upset some people.

'I was not a Papua New Guinean citizen at that time,' Mahesh says, 'and I was threatened with being kicked out of the country!'

The stress and pressure he was under eventually began to affect Mahesh's health.

'My blood pressure went up,' he says, 'whenever I got a call about Telikom. With my own business, I was calm.'

While he regrets his time at Telikom PNG and the negative effects it had on his own business, Mahesh does not regret the decisions he made or the way he acted.

'I just got undermined,' he says. 'The ministers got involved. The politicians got involved. *You have to employ this person, so this and the other, etcetera.* But my conscience is clear.'

After the devastating CPL warehouse fire in Gerehu in 2017, Mahesh stepped down as chairman of Telikom PNG.

'I told the prime minister,' recalls Mahesh, '"I've got to go and re-build my business."'

Chapter 18

Where Are You From?

For most people, it is a simple question, often asked in social settings, which is easy to answer: *Where are you from?* But for Sir Mahesh and Lady Usha Patel, it is a much more difficult task, raising questions for them and their sons, Nikhil and Ajay, about their place in this world.

'I ask people, have they got five minutes, when they ask me,' smiles Mahesh, 'because I tell them the whole story. I think that question is massive from our kids' perspective because they are totally confused as to who they are. They are of Indian heritage. I'm from Fiji. Usha was born in Africa, and lived in India and England. The kids were born in London, and spent the first few years of their lives in Papua New Guinea. Then they became Australians. They also lived in India. I think sometimes in school they had issues like that. Because they were kids, they struggled to answer, like we did. *Are you Indian? Are you Australian? Are you Fijian? Who are you?*'

In a column for the *Sydney Morning Herald* newspaper on 31 May 2022, Abbir Dib wrote, 'I am a walking game of "guess the ethnicity". Strangers strike up a conversation by asking a variation of *what are you?* at least four times a week. The curiosity is understandable—humans are inherently fascinated by each other's walks of life. But as someone at the receiving end of these questions, there is often a lack of good manners when people converse about race.'

Similarly, Mahesh Patel can also get frustrated when people are told about his origins, only for them to then question what they have just been told.

'I am very sensitive about it,' he agrees. 'I say I'm from Fiji. I had, well not an argument but a bit of a tiff, with somebody some years ago. He said, "So you are Fijian Indian." I replied, "No, I'm Fijian." And he looked at me strangely. I said to him, "What are your origins?" He said, "Italy." So, I asked, "Are you Australian-Italian?" He looked at me, confused. I continued, "That's what it means to me when you say I'm Fijian-Indian." Nobody asks that. That's what Fiji is now saying, that everyone is a Fijian. You are not an Indian. You are not Fijian Indian. That's how culture has to mix. In Papua New Guinea now, in all my speeches, all my comments, I say *my country* or *our country*. I have assimilated to say it is *my country*. Even though I have only just recently become a citizen. Nearly forty years on, Papua New Guinea is the closest place I feel I belong. Irrespective of which passport I have, or which nationality I've got. It is where you feel you belong. That's the place I feel at home. It has been the longest stretch that I have ever spent in any country.'

Pranab Mukherjee is an Indian politician and statesman who served as the thirteenth President of India from 2012 until 2017. When he visited Papua New Guinea, it again reminded Mahesh of others' perception of him, including that of some senior politicians.

'A minister who knew me well,' says Mahesh, 'nudged me at the official welcoming ceremony and said, "Go and say hello to your President." I told him, "I'm not an Indian citizen so we will let others go first."'

'Our heritage is obviously Indian,' explains Lady Usha. 'But having lived away from India for so many years from such a young age, I feel I am now a sum total of all my experiences of all the countries and places that I have been fortunate enough to live in. I will always be in gratitude to my wise ancestors who took the first brave, courageous steps to better their lives and ultimately ours. Through it all my connection to India in memory of my ancestors will always be strong.'

India will always play an important part in Sir Mahesh's life, even though he was not born there.

'We are Indian culturally,' he says, 'spiritually and religiously as well. Fiji was home, but we had a lot of Indian practices.'

'Fiji was a little India for you anyway,' Lady Usha tells her husband. 'I think Fiji is a great place to bring up kids with a good, strong foundation.'

A demonstration of their connection to Indian culture is the fact that the couple renewed their wedding vows in India in 2013.

'We enjoy going to India,' says Sir Mahesh. 'Our favourite place is Rishikesh. It's up in the mountains. Our business partner has a property there right on the Ganges River. We renewed our vows on our twenty-fifth wedding anniversary there. We did not have a proper ceremony when we got married. Not a proper traditional Indian wedding. So, we had a proper traditional Indian wedding, where they get you to do your seven vows around the sacred fire.'

Mahesh Patel has an Australian passport and is an Australian citizen. He is also a dual Papua New Guinean citizen. He has a Fijian birth certificate.

Usha Patel has an Australian passport and is an Australian citizen. She has dual British citizenship.

Both have also been given Overseas Citizen of India cards by the Indian government.

'You have all the rights without having to vote,' explains Mahesh. 'It's like a permanent residency. We don't have to apply for visas each year.'

When Mahesh obtained his Australian citizenship, he had to give back his Fijian passport.

'I can get it back if I want to," he adds. 'I had to give it away in the early days, because Fiji did not allow dual citizenship.'

Obtaining his Australian citizenship wasn't as easy for Mahesh as might have been expected, for geographical reasons. He was living in India at the time.

'It's interesting how I ended up with the Australian passport,' he recalls. 'When we were living in India in 1999 and 2000, I still carried my Fiji passport. At that time, there was a big military conflict between India and Pakistan. Pakistan actually threatened a nuclear strike. Usha used to get a call every week, first from the British High Commission, advising her of evacuation plans in case of security threats, where the British citizens in India would go for evacuation. Then from the Australian High Commission. After a couple of weeks of this, I said, *Nobody's calling me.* Because Fiji didn't have any representation in India. Usha rang the Australian High Commission. Australia was the closest connection for us. Australian officials said, "No, unless Mahesh is a citizen, we won't evacuate him."

Meanwhile the British said, "If he's your spouse—and you have to prove it—we will evacuate him." That's when I thought, *What am I carrying this Fiji passport for*? I had to apply for my Australian passport.'

After making an application, Mahesh was granted Australian citizenship, but he had to go through a citizenship ceremony in Australia to finalize it.

'After living in Sydney for two years,' he says, 'in 1996, I was eligible for citizenship. By the time I applied for it in 1999, we were living in India. I applied after Usha and the kids had already obtained theirs in 1998. The Australian foreign affairs department wrote to me to say the citizenship ceremony was on a certain date. I had to come and recite the oath. The first time they asked, I said, "I'm overseas, I cannot make it." So, they gave me an alternative date. I said, "I can't make that either." They said, "If you do not make the third one, you'll strike out and you'll have to start applying again."'

Mahesh then called on close friend Andrew Petrie, who was the Mayor of Woollahra, to give him some guidance on arranging a citizenship ceremony he could actually attend.

'I rang Andrew for any guidance or assistance,' recalls Mahesh, 'because I was genuinely unable to come back to Australia. Could they give me a bit of a leeway? He rang me back a week later and said, "Don't worry about it". The next time I was back in Australia, he would work something out.'

When Mahesh and Usha were next in Sydney, visiting at the end of 1999, they were invited to a dinner by Andrew and Edwina Petrie.

'Edwina had called Usha and made the arrangements,' recalls Mahesh. 'Before dinner, we were to go for drinks at the Petries' house. But when we arrived, we found his house was full with about fifty people. Andrew had the Australian flag set-up, and a picture of Queen Elizabeth II and a Bible. They also had some friends over. I was just so surprised. Andrew made me take my oath in front of everyone and the clerk. That's how I got my Australian citizenship.'

'Mahesh didn't know it was going to be a party,' added Andrew Petrie. 'Because the Council was closed, we decided we would do it at my home. What he also didn't know was that I had invited all these people. I managed to get the flags from the Council and we all sang "Advance Australia Fair" at the end. Just like we used to hold for any other citizenship ceremony when I was mayor at Council. It was run exactly the same way. It had to be slightly formal because that is what is required. It was just all done with drinks in hand.'

Was there any emotion or regret for Mahesh when giving up his Fijian passport?

'No, it had to be done,' he says. 'I have sort of moved away from Fiji, emotionally. More so since my Mum's passing. I don't feel any link. With what's happened in the country, the way it's progressed, I really lost that loyalty. It is a small place. I find that I have grown into Papua New Guinea more and more. I have sort of ventured away. Really, I feel very little connection with Fiji now. I have been offered some board positions. I said, "No, I have my schedule full in PNG." I have really cut off quite cleanly. Remember, I left Fiji when I was fifteen for school in New Zealand. All my friends have moved on as well. When I go to Fiji now, there are hardly any links available. Before, I would go and spend a day with Mum.'

As complicated as his heritage may be for Mahesh Patel, their own backgrounds may be even more complicated for his sons.

Nikhil and Ajay are both Australian citizens with Australian passports, but they also have dual British citizenship. They were born in London and have British birth certificates. They both also have American Green cards and Nikhil has been living and working in the USA since 2016. Ajay has spent the last five years living and working in Papua New Guinea.

'For them,' says Usha, 'it is like they were kids of personnel in the military or a high commission. They moved around quite a lot. When you talk to them, it is exactly the same issue for them about where they belong.'

'It causes a lot of confusion,' adds Mahesh. 'That sense of identity plays a major role in your life in understanding who you are. Because you have a different cultural background, a different upbringing—and then you are living in this different environment, with different value systems as well. I feel for them. We went through that, but we were living for large blocks of time in each different place, but Nikhil and Ajay have moved quite a lot over the years.'

'We've had some guidance,' says Nikhil, 'because we have discussed this as a family. I have my little elevator-pitch story. Being from such unique places—people are always interested in these mystical types of places that are highly valued in terms of travel.'

'I usually say I'm from Australia,' says Ajay. 'The issue of identity is an intense sort of topic to think about, being a third-culture child. Having Mum from one end of the planet with Indian heritage and Dad from the other end of the planet, also with Indian heritage. There is a nice connectivity. But it is all that distance in between which carries significance in its own way. It is unique. When people ask, I sigh a little and think, *where do I begin? What do I say, what do I hold out on?* I do say my family is from India.'

Asked if Fiji fits anywhere in his explanation, Ajay explains further.

'I mention India,' he says, 'because that is the short version. But then I say, "Actually, Dad is from Fiji, Mum was born in Uganda"—and that throws everyone out. It kind of gets complicated. I still think I am from Australia. I like Australia. If someone asks me how to get around Sydney, how to get public transport somewhere, or drive your car someplace, I can tell them. I know the streets, the restaurants and the nightlife and things to do. Granted, Sydney has changed a lot, but it is Sydney.'

Mahesh Patel has a little chuckle to himself when he thinks about the time his wife Usha had to give back her British passport when she obtained her Australian citizenship.

'When Usha got her Australian passport,' he smiles, 'she had to send her British passport back to the Australian Department of Foreign

Affairs. They sent it to the British High Commission who then sent it back to her. They said, once you're a citizen, they will never take your passport away. I found that quite funny.'

With all their experiences moving around so often, the Patels really are world citizens.

'The problem is we got so used to it,' agrees Mahesh, 'to moving around. For me, particularly, it is hard to stay put. Unlike me, Usha is very happy to settle into once place. I'm still coming to terms with it. It's difficult.'

Asked if his primary residence will ever be outside Australia again, Mahesh laughs aloud.

'I can't,' Usha interjects firmly.

'Only recently,' reveals Mahesh, 'we were talking about living in New Zealand. It's a nice country.'

'Maybe not live there permanently,' suggests Usha. 'Just to go and stay there for a while.'

'Try it out, maybe,' continues Mahesh. 'Do a month of Airbnb and see how it goes. It's a pretty country. But again, we are not sure.'

'I would always come back here to Australia,' says Usha.

Mahesh Patel's family and friends have their own perspective on where they think he belongs, both culturally and geographically. Some relate it to their own views on their place on planet Earth.

Pravin Patel: 'I was born and bred in Fiji, so I say I'm Fijian. I have a Fijian passport. The route is from India. Our parents are from India.'

Anil Patel: 'I say I am from Fiji. Born in Fiji. Australian? Not yet. I should be.'

Manisha Patel: 'I say I am Indian and brought up in England. But I live in Australia.'

Daksesh Patel: 'The good old Ba town in Fiji, which is God's country, is Mahesh's spiritual home, as much as he may deny that. His naturalized home is Papua New Guinea. While I admire him, and he may disagree with that, you have to have an origin, and I think that is his. He is a boy from Ba.'

Samrath Bedi: 'Earlier, I would say Mahesh was from Australia, because a lot of people would not know where Papua New Guinea was. It made conversation easier because you would not have to open up a larger conversation around it. But now, I say Papua New Guinea. Because that is where his entire business is based. His OBE and knighting is because of Papua New Guinea. To me, that is what defines Mahesh.'

Stanley Joyce: 'I think Mahesh is just as proud of being a Papua New Guinean as he is of his knighthood.'

Daksesh Patel: 'I am an Australian citizen. But I say I am a Fijian too. Because you don't say you are a Scottish Australian. Mahesh is entitled to have Fiji citizenship as well. He doesn't have to renounce his citizenship. Fiji will recognize his citizenship as well, because they do not restrict what countries you can be a citizen of. He is definitely attached to Papua New Guinea and that's fine. But I think Ba has given him that origin and you can never forget your origin. That's where I connect myself very closely with Mahesh. It was in Ba.'

Udhay: 'I usually say, and I've had to do it a few times, that Mahesh is from Fiji originally. But he is a very global person. He has lived in multiple countries. I start with Fiji and I think that is probably defining.'

Amit Patel: 'I say Mahesh is from Fiji. I think where your family primarily has resided and the environment from which you emerged is where you are from.'

Jagdish Patel: 'I say Mahesh is from PNG. If I am referencing where he is from region-wise, I say Papua New Guinea. I say I am from Fiji. It is not just by birth. It is also a question of your formative years and your career.'

Vani Nades: 'Mahesh is part of Papua New Guinea. He is an asset to the country. I don't see him as different or as being an outsider. People recognize him and see the work that he has done. He has really planted himself here and done amazing things.'

Daksesh Patel: 'Mahesh is madly in love with Papua New Guinea. In fact, he considers Papua New Guinea as his home of origin.'

Sir Mahesh Patel's connection with India will always remain emotionally strong, regardless of where he lives or what others may believe.

After his mother passed in December 2018, he took some of her ashes back to her spiritual home. His father's ashes were scattered at the same location years earlier.

'The waters of the Ganges,' he explains, 'are called Ganga jal, meaning water of the Ganges. It is supposed to be holy and pure. She always kept a bottle of Ganga jal in her little temple at home. Apparently, that's the holy grail. We do cremations in our culture, so we scattered her ashes in the river there in Fiji, which backs onto our property. Then I took some of her ashes to the Ganges in India. I did a little prayer and scattered the ashes. Dad is there too. They will always be happy in India together.'

Chapter 19

Passion and Perspective

If you were to describe Sir Mahesh Patel in two words, *passion* and *perspective* immediately come to mind. After everything he has accomplished in life, all the travelling and the many different places he has lived in, and the people he has met, Mahesh has a unique view of the world.

'I get bored very quickly doing the same mundane stuff,' he concedes. 'I think it is reflected in my life. Usha gets quite annoyed, because we keep changing. She reminds me, in thirty-odd years of marriage, we have moved seventeen times. I suppose it is in my nature. No sooner than I land I say, *Where am I going to go next? What am I going to do?* It's both good and bad, because you constantly want to be moving, you can't sit still. I think it is more of a thrill-seeking thing, not really to go out and make lots of money and be successful. It was like a challenge to say, *Can I go and do this?*'

Mahesh has a passion for life which is infectious. But along with that passion comes a lot of emotion, which can sometimes complicate his life.

'That's a good side of me,' he says, 'because sometimes I get overly concerned about people. I forget that I don't have to really worry about everyone. I guess there is a balancing act. From a corporate view, I was hopeless, because I wasn't able to sack somebody. There are positives and negatives in having that passion.'

If you are ever in a movie theatre and the sad storyline results in an audience member crying, it could be Sir Mahesh Patel.

'Oh, I get very emotional,' he admits. 'I'm getting teary-eyed now just thinking of this. The animated movie *Lion King*. When Simba's father died, I was crying in the cinema because I could relate that to my dad. I like F1 motor racing. I was watching Ayrton Senna's documentary. When he passed away, I was bawling my eyes out. Then, all of a sudden, I realized the guy next to me was looking at me strangely. I'm overly emotional sometimes.'

It has been said that travelling and seeing the world gives one a great perspective on life. Mahesh Patel has a lifetime full of it.

'When I look at Auckland now,' he says, 'it seems so small to me compared to when I went to school there. I remember the days when the bus fare was ten cents and we couldn't afford that bus fare to go to school. When you come through all that, it builds certain values. It carried through in Papua New Guinea. Why do I get angry when people are washing down the pavements with continuous running water? I just cringe. Because we had days in Papua New Guinea where there was no water supply. It's life experiences that bring that to you naturally. That's why when we had the opportunity to move to India, I took the boys. I said, *You've got to see both sides of people's lives*, meaning poverty and wealth. I think that's a problem with the world over, that people complain, *Oh, Sydney rail is stuffed*, if it runs late. I go there, get on a train and say, *This is perfect*. Because there are places in the world where there is no public transport service. In Papua New Guinea, there are some people who walk for a whole day just to come into town.'

'I think there are definitely two sides to the coin,' Nikhil Patel says, of his travelling and living experiences. 'In terms of getting exposed to different cultures, meeting people from all over the world and still being friends with some of them—that certainly was a benefit. On the flip side, not having that consistency and structure and predictability of the future. *Oh, we are going to have to move again*. Some of those things are neutral and some were an advantage.'

'To be brutally honest,' says Ajay, 'the best learning we had was not from the trips to all the cool places. It was from going back and visiting Mum and Grandma's village in India. Our lives would have been insanely different if my grandparents had not moved to Fiji. We would have been farming.'

'Nobody really has a choice,' continues Nikhil, 'in what they want to do as a child, where they want to be. Although we did have to move around, it was also a nice environment. I loved being in India. I have great memories there. It's tough to speak of the other side: what if we had stayed in one place? I can only hear it from friends. People who have lived in the same place all their lives, they have complaints about that as well. There is good and bad with both. But I think the positive is that we had those journeys. It's not the first time we've been abroad, meeting new people and getting out there. It has made it easier in my adult life, considering the path that I have taken. By attacking any challenging issue as a child, you don't have a fear of that. There was always some uncertainty, which is natural. But the lack of fear probably stems from my experience and memory as a child.'

Family has always meant so much to Sir Mahesh Patel. He has never forgotten the sacrifices his father Maganbhai and mother Savitaben made for him and his brothers and sisters. He was particularly close to his mother and respected her immensely.

'She was looking after the kids, running the home and working in the shop,' he recalls of his time growing up in Fiji. 'We used to take a freshly cooked lunch every day to school—she made roti rolls. Then she would start cooking lunch for the elders. That finished. Then she would start preparing for dinner. In the evenings we would all have our milk before we went to bed. We had a pretty healthy lifestyle in those early days. Mum would be up at 4 a.m. to prepare our breakfast and school lunches.'

While he was close to his parents, they never directly expressed to him how proud they were of his success in Papua New Guinea, though he did find out in other ways.

'Mum's friends would know all the things that I did,' Mahesh says, 'so, it would obviously have come from Mum. I think culturally they would not say, *Well done, son*. They just wanted us to succeed and be happy and united as a family.'

'Our parents said Mahesh was a good son,' recalls brother Anil, 'and they were very proud of him. My father was not disappointed that he did not start his own pharmacy in Fiji. They would guide us, but they would never hold us to account in whatever we were doing.'

'Mum's saying was,' continues Mahesh, '*Whatever happens, we need to have family unity*. It was very important for her. Unfortunately, as we all started living all over the world, it's become harder and harder.'

But as difficult as it is to physically connect people from around the world, Mahesh was the driving force behind the Patel family reunions in Fiji. In July 2016, they gathered in Fiji as one, to celebrate Savitaben's ninetieth birthday. There were four generations in attendance, comprising over fifty people.

'It was spread over four or five days,' says Mahesh. 'It was quite a blast. Mum loved it. Having so many people around her. The kids put sunglasses on her and put a baseball cap back to front on her head for photos. I think she treasured that.'

'Mahesh was the guy,' says older brother Pravin, 'who was trying to keep the family together.'

Another special talent of Mahesh, which became apparent to family members at their gatherings, is his love for dance.

'Mahesh likes to party,' says brother Anil. 'He likes to party into the wee hours of the morning. Not drinking. Partying. He dances. On the table. On the sofa.'

'Mahesh enjoys himself wherever he is,' says sister-in-law Manisha. 'He makes the most of the time. If there are any parties, he'll be the first on the dance floor. He is very comfortable within himself. He doesn't really care if anybody else is dancing. If he likes the music, he'll dance.'

'Anyone who knows Mahesh knows he is a party animal with a knighthood,' observes brother Bipin Patel. 'In 2020, we were in India and he got everyone dancing. He jumped up on the table, and then my son jumped up, and they got everyone dancing. That is typical Mahesh. If you want to have a party, you just turn him loose. He will be the real Mahesh. You will see. He is a fun-loving person and he loves to party in a good way.'

But is Mahesh's dancing ability impressive?

'In his own mind, it is,' smiles Anil. 'He thinks he is a good dancer. We all get up and dance with him.'

'Mahesh loves to dance,' says sister Kusum. 'I like his moves, I'm telling you. I feel so happy when I see Mahesh because he reminds me of our dad. I miss my dad and when I look at him, I see our father. It is a happy feeling when I see him.'

Sister Taru Patel reveals that the phenomenon of her brother dancing is nothing new. He has been doing it for years.

'One day I saw a cake on the table,' she recalls. 'I asked my mum, "How come there is a cake here?" My mum said, "Mahesh got a prize for being a good dancer." He was a teenager then. Now, he dances on tables at parties. He did that in 2018 at one of our family weddings. He got on the table to dance.'

More and more these days, Mahesh Patel spends time thinking about his wife and sons. Not just what they are doing at the time, but what he has subjected them to in the past, both the good and the bad.

For many, travelling, particularly by oneself, can open up a whole lot of emotions.

This is true for Mahesh too.

'Sometimes,' he says, 'I've written some really sobby notes to Usha and the kids. You get emotional about things.'

Thinking about his life, Mahesh understands how difficult he made things for Usha, Nikhil and Ajay. His appreciation for how they coped with his absences from home over many years continues to grow.

'People see the front end,' he says of his success. 'But the struggles that Usha went through, just managing the kids, with me travelling continuously, went unseen. It just feels sad now that I was in and out so much. People forget that I was only able to do it because Usha was managing it all. A lot of credit to her because she gets shuffled to the side and I get the limelight.

'If I had my time again, I wouldn't do it. I just didn't understand; I couldn't comprehend what Usha went through. I was just so absorbed with what I was going through. When I speak to kids now at universities, I tell them, "You need to balance your work life." Alan Jarvis used to tell me that. And a lot of kids will say, "Well, you've made it now, so you can say that." Alan went through the same thing, because he was travelling around a lot. He said to me, "Listen, that's what I regret."'

Friend and business partner Samrath Bedi observed of Mahesh, 'Usha was probably the best thing that ever happened to him.'

'Yes, that is so true,' agrees Mahesh. 'I don't involve Usha enough in my acknowledgements. I can't stress it enough. Over time I have just not given enough credit to Usha for where I am today. We went through some really rough patches—financially, socially and in our relationship as well. It has been a tough road. But we have come out positive at the other end.'

Trying to move forward, Mahesh pushes himself to look to the future, rather than focus on the past and the things he cannot change.

'People sometimes forget,' he observes, 'that the rear vison mirror in your car is small, the front windscreen is much bigger. Why do you keep looking back? Your focus should be the bigger screen. That is so relevant to life. Because you can keep looking back, keep looking back.'

'Mahesh has tried a lot harder in the later years of his life to make up for it,' says Usha. 'Now we do spend more time whenever we can with Nikhil and Ajay as a family. It is more quality time than quantity.'

'Mahesh travelled a lot, but I think he was also very involved with his boys,' says friend Udhay. 'As they have grown into young adults, I have noticed he was always trying to weave them into things he was doing. Trying to get them involved and thinking about investments or how businesses operate. Try to connect them with friends in the business community. He was always trying to give his boys the best possible opportunities, ideas and support.'

Whenever Mahesh Patel talks about his sons Nikhil and Ajay, there is great pride. He also sees their own unique personalities and characteristics, and is often amazed at how different they can be, despite being only two years apart in age and having shared so many of the same experiences in life.

'Very different,' Mahesh observes, 'but their inner values are pretty much the same. Usha has instilled truly good values in them as human beings. Ajay, like Usha, is an avid reader. Nikhil doesn't enjoy it as much, like me. Ajay can live very frugally, like Usha. Nikhil likes his mod cons.

'I have spent a lot of time with Ajay over the last five years, so I may have moulded him towards my line of thinking in a business sense. But he is still very independent. They will both challenge your thought process.'

'For me,' says Usha, 'it is important that they have grown into good, kind and thoughtful human beings. That is all that matters.'

After so many years of flying and so many flights, Mahesh has a set routine when he travels.

'When I get on the plane,' he says, 'I shut my mind off. I'm looking at the destination. I don't suffer from jet lag as much as most people, because mentally I'm already in the time zone of the next place, especially on the long hauls. If I'm landing in London or Los Angeles at six o'clock in the morning, I'll be sleeping till just before we land there, so when I get in, I'm fresh. Or, if I'm landing in the afternoon, I make sure I don't sleep. I tire myself out, so then I can sleep in the evening.'

Mahesh finds it helpful to use the time on the plane and be productive.

'I don't do much of my reading when I am at home,' he says. 'In the past, I would take bunches of my magazines with me, and they would be in the seat pocket, and I would be ripping out any interesting articles and leaving the rest behind. Now, I'm reading things on the internet. I watch my movies. I am in my own zone.'

Considering the thousands of flights taken, Mahesh has been fortunate not to be involved in any serious incidents in the air.

'I've been in major turbulence,' he says. 'It's funny, when I'm sleeping on a flatbed on a plane, I actually enjoy the turbulence. Because it's like "Rock-a-bye baby". A lot of people get scared. I'm just sound asleep. Sometimes the stewardess gets quite envious, saying, "I can't believe you sleep so soundly."'

On a flight to Hong Kong one time, the plane Mahesh was aboard almost landed in Kowloon Bay.

'The plane was descending,' he recalled, 'then, all of a sudden, it went straight up and we are holding onto our seats. I'm thinking, *What the hell's happened*? The pilot apologized. When we landed at the old Kai Tak Airport, we found out he had overshot the landing and if he had landed, we would be on the water.

'We had another incident in Papua New Guinea where we were taking off and then the pilot slammed on the brakes hard; we would have fallen out of our seats without our seat belts on. At some of the regional airports in Papua New Guinea, the mountains surrounding them are so high, if you take off at the wrong angle, you can crash into them.'

The greatest scare Mahesh ever had involving a plane was a flight he did not take, in the Star Mountains Rural area of the North Fly District in the Western Province of Papua New Guinea.

'It was an Easter weekend in the 1990s,' he recalls. 'The Ok Tedi Mines at that time were the largest in the country—gold and copper. I went for a visit. CPL still supplies them pharmaceuticals. You have to go in overnight because of the flight schedules. The next day, my flight home got cancelled. I rang the office and pulled all the strings I had. I said, "I don't care, route me wherever." As it was Easter weekend, all the flights were full and these are small aircraft. I was prepared to get onto the jump seat (temporary crew seating) of any flight. I almost got onto one, but got bumped off by the airline at the last minute. The next day I was told that flight I missed had crashed and everybody on board was killed. I was going to be on that plane. Then, I wasn't. It was so sad, yet I felt so fortunate. I might have had a much shorter life.'

In-depth studies are regularly conducted on the characteristics of the most successful people to determine the personal traits that contributed to their achievements. Passion and perspective often feature prominently, but it is possible that perseverance in the face of obstacles in pursuit of goals could be the most important.

'I'm convinced that about half of what separates the successful entrepreneurs from the non-successful ones is pure perseverance,' said Apple co-founder Steve Jobs. 'Being an entrepreneur is challenging, and it's easy to give up and move on to something else. But the biggest part of being successful is having the stamina to stick through the hard times without quitting.'

Throughout his life, Sir Mahesh Patel has demonstrated the quality of perseverance in multiple circumstances.

In 1978 in New Zealand, he missed out on securing a position in the university pharmacy course. He instead did one year of commerce, and re-applied for pharmacy the following year and was accepted.

'Because I said to my father I would study pharmacy,' explains Mahesh.

In 1986, when he lost his position as a contract pharmacist at Chapman's Pharmacy, Mahesh could have easily boarded a flight back to Fiji with the ticket presented to him and started afresh. Instead, he stayed in Port Moresby and pursued his goal of opening his own pharmacy. With no income and unable to work, he had to rely on the help of others.

'I leveraged everything I could,' he says. 'You have got to have that friendship network.'

Looking back at the time when he lost his position as pharmacist, Mahesh is at peace with what occurred.

'I don't have any bad feelings about it,' he says. 'I was more shocked than angry.'

When he was suddenly unemployed, Mahesh says his mindset was, '*It's happened. Let's have a go at my own business.* There was no forward planning. I was at that age where you keep falling down and you keeping getting up and running.'

After being let go by Mr Foung, Mahesh never spoke to him again. He eventually moved back to Australia to live. But as evidence to Mahesh not holding a grudge in any form, he uses the services of Mr Foung's niece Joanne for a lot of his travel.

'She has three children and runs a travel agency in PNG,' he said.

In 2017, Mahesh was on the verge of retiring. But when the Gerehu warehouse fire threatened the future of the CPL Group, he jumped into action to rescue the business.

Seeing the success of the CPL Group now, does it give Mahesh great satisfaction?

'Absolutely,' he replies.

Again, it was the perseverance to work towards the bigger goal, and not taking the lesser and easier way out, which took Mahesh to even greater levels of success.

'We made mistakes for sure,' he admits. 'A couple of business decisions I made, I pushed through with passion and it bit us back. But again, we had to work hard to turn that around. There was always that time when we had our backs to the wall with the warehouse fire. The economy was down. The energy projects had wound down. The government owed us huge amounts of money. The insurance company from the first fire in 2015 went bankrupt. We had opened two brand-new stores and had invested a lot of money. We had given a loan to the landlord to fix the supermarket building. Because we were so cashed up, I sort of lost sight, to say, *What about the bad days?* It just got tighter and tighter and tighter and eventually it really hit us. I was caught between the ethics and the board that said, "No! Stop the medicine supplies to the government." I said, "Well, there will be blood on our hands if we do not supply the medicines to the hospital and you'll hear stories of people dying." At one stage the government owed us about 18 million kina (390 million rupees). The insurance company owed us 10 million kina. We had given the landlord another 16 million kina (347 million rupees) for their fit-out. All of a sudden, from being very cash-rich, and with the economy plummeting, we were stretched out. It was a lot of stress, and then the warehouse fire happened in 2017. That's when we thought, *That's it, game over.*'

How did Mahesh handle all that stress and pressure?

'It's been a big balancing act with Usha and the boys,' he says. 'They have been very supportive. I suppose I had to keep calm and just believe in myself. That's when I started doing a bit of yoga and meditation. Just to calm my nerves down. I'm not sure if it worked or not but it must have made some impact. There were some really stressful, sleepless nights. Because you think, *What's going to happen?*'

Usha's impact here, again, cannot be underestimated. She helped him stay calm and grounded through the crisis. Mahesh says Usha is a very spiritual person.

'Yes,' she replies, 'but not in a sense that I follow any religion. If it can help me live my life in a way that is good for me and for everybody else, then that is a good thing to follow. I don't necessarily have to label it in any way.'

Usha believes meetings are not by chance, whether it is spiritual or by some sort of other force, 'there is an exchange happening for a reason,' she suggests. 'It humbles me. You don't have to be spiritual. It doesn't matter. A good human being is a good human being. I don't see myself as being spiritual the way he sees me. I'm interested in the world beyond the five senses because I think there is a lot out there at play that we do not understand. It also helps me to think before I speak or act. I probably go against the grain in some ways a lot of times. Just because the majority think or act that way doesn't mean I will ... I won't. I think intuition is to be followed wherever it gives you that opportunity to do so.'

Over the years, Usha has seen Mahesh slowly open himself to different ways of living his life.

'I think Mahesh is a lot more aware,' she says, 'maybe not as open, but maybe he doesn't want to be open to it right now. I know spiritually he has a strong connection to things that we don't understand, but I'm not sure he is totally aware of that himself. I'm always trying to get him to stop looking *out there*. The answers aren't out there. They are within. But to look within is not always easy because I think we are afraid of finding things there that we don't want to confront. He's much better than he was, say, ten or fifteen years ago.

'I must have done something, because I said to him, "You owe me a week of your life to do whatever I want to do with it." He agreed to it. To get that kind of time from him was a goldmine. I thought, *What can I do?* I didn't hurry things on, but maybe a year down the line, I said, "Okay, we are going to a retreat in Bali. I found this holistic health place, which was more suited to his personality, because he would still want his phone there. But it was a vegan place, which was okay, because we are vegetarian at home anyway. But there were a lot of healing modalities there.'

[Healing modalities are therapeutic techniques that seek to balance the body, mind, emotions and spirit.]

'Mahesh started doing yoga there,' continues Usha. 'I didn't push anything, because he is the sort of person who, if you push, he is not going to listen. Instead, I said, *Let's just go and try it and see how this goes.* We went for a few sessions of yoga and I told the teacher to just teach him the Surya Namaskar (Sun Salutation) and the basic asanas so he is not too overwhelmed by it. Then I got him to have some other healing practices as well. Because we were eating a good diet, it cleansed our systems on all levels. He saw the difference from day one to day seven. He has kept up his yoga practice to this day. I think it really helped him to centre himself a lot more. Obviously, it's helping, otherwise he wouldn't continue with it.'

Mahesh Patel insists he never had a grand plan for his life. Much of it was about sensing opportunities as they presented, persevering and exploring new ways to be successful.

'It was only when I went to Papua New Guinea,' he recalls, 'that something clicked inside me, where I said, *What about me having a go at this?* Until then, I had no idea I would end up owning businesses. It was just that desire, or more so a challenge. It was the same when I went to India in 1999. People said, *What the hell are you doing?* There wasn't this big vision to go out and do business globally, I just saw it as a challenge. *Can I do it?*'

Mahesh also found it was often the little things that made the most impact on people's lives.

'When I was first working in Port Moresby in 1984,' he recalls, 'I could see people coming into the shop and they'll have a prescription for an eye infection. Normally I would see my staff give it out, and they would pay and go out. A couple of times I asked, "Do you know how to actually use the eye drops?" They replied, "Uh, just put it in." I said, "No, you have to tilt your head." It was such simple stuff nobody was taught. That's when I started engaging more and more in the front line. A couple of times the patient would come back and say, "The medicine you gave me has cured me. Thank you very much." I was thinking, "*Wow, you never hear comments back like that.*"'

Mahesh was always an excellent pharmacist, but there was much more to him than just that. Something deeper inside him, which wanted to reach for the stars and create a better life for his family and the people with whom he came into contact.

'I know I said to people,' he remembers, 'after I graduated, after seven weeks, "I think I have gone into the wrong profession." Because it was boring, just dispensing medicines. So, there was obviously something more in it than just counting pills. When you were doing your internship in those days, we got dispensing bottles and then reused bottles, and basically filled prescriptions. But what I did enjoy, was the customer interaction side of things. Talking to people and just getting out there from behind the counter, rather than just counting pills and typing labels.

'I had ambition to do more. I think I had the business side in me. But I am lucky I had a business partner in Alan Jarvis, from whom I learnt a lot. But I guess, growing up in Fiji, my dad had the corner store, so we were always part of that enterprising and business side of it all.

'I think the burning desire to do more was always there, but I don't think I realized that. It must have come naturally or it must have just flickered up from something when it naturally happened. I think 99 per cent of the kids just get a degree and then say, *What am I going to do with myself careerwise*? I was part of that boat. But I was never one to sit in one place and be a good old chemist for the next umpteen years. I think there was always this thing inside me wanting to do more and more and more.'

Chapter 20
Port Moresby, November 2022

Friday, 18 November 2022: 2.20 p.m.

Sir Mahesh Patel arrives at the National Parliament House in Port Moresby. It was officially opened by Prince Charles, the Prince of Wales, on 8 August 1984.

CPL holds the Pride of PNG awards at Parliament House. Guests are slated to arrive at 6 p.m. The Governor General is the patron and will arrive at 6.30 p.m. There are 148 people on the guest list.

'I just want to eyeball the table seating arrangements,' says Mahesh. He bounds up the stairs with enthusiasm and enters the Parliament State Function Room. It is abuzz with activity as parliament house staff, catering personnel, audiovisual technicians and CPL Foundation staff busily set up arrangements.

The Pride of PNG Awards is the CPL Foundation's flagship programme. The awards were created in 2007 and there have been twelve presentations over the last fifteen years, with missed years due to the COVID-19 pandemic. The local newspaper, *Post-Courier*, will be in attendance to document the winners. An edited video package for local television will be prepared by the CPL media team.

Independent judges are in place to assess the merits of each submission. From 150 applications, six winners will be awarded tonight. They receive medals and a lifetime of commitment funding for their project from the CPL Foundation.

'Whatever project they do,' explains Mahesh, 'we fund it, carrying on. It is a lifetime commitment. It is not just an award. One of the things we look at is: what is sustainable?'

Mahesh consults with his staff, paying close attention to the table seating plan.

'I seat the people according to the table map they give me,' he explains.

But there is a problem. The physical layout of the tables within the room does not match the seating plan the CPL founder received. There are still fifteen tables with ten people per table, but the tables are aligned differently in the room.

'Now the seating has gone haywire,' he says, with concern. 'I try to mix my people up.'

English and Albanian singer Dua Lipa's song, 'Levitating' plays in the background. It is appropriate, as Sir Mahesh Patel seemingly floats around the room, consulting with everyone who will play a role in ensuring the event runs smoothly.

'Did you check the PA systems?'

'Did you get the video that the tech prepared? Please, *check, check, check*.'

'Make sure the national anthem is set and ready to go.'

On the way out, Mahesh stops at the guest's arrival table and checks on the lighting and speaks again to staff members Regil Wanwanji and Joycelyne Tapo, who work full-time on CPL Foundation projects.

'I don't want people queuing up saying, "Which table am I on?"' he says. 'It's not nice to queue up when you are dressed up and it's hot.'

After praising his staff's efforts, Mahesh returns to his CPL vehicle.

'Certain things ...,' he breathes deeply. 'I learnt the hard way in the early days. I asked, *Why didn't you do this*? I should have come in and checked it. It is not the staff's fault, because they don't prepare these events all the time.'

Sir Mahesh instructs driver Joe Pato to go to the 9-Mile Cemetery. In his early days in Port Moresby, Mahesh used to drive everywhere himself. But a couple of near-miss crashes at a dual lane roundabout in Gerehu, going to and from the company warehouse, prompted him to get a driver.

'One day I told myself, *Right, wake up, you have got the resources, why are you still driving?*' he says. 'I get a lot of work done in the car. I'm supposed to be retired, but some days I leave home at 7.45 a.m. and I don't get back till 6 p.m.'

Friday, 18 November 2022: 2.55 p.m.

Driver Joe Pato guides the CPL vehicle off the main road into the 9-Mile Cemetery. There is a large garden nursery with plants for sale outside the entry gates. Sir Mahesh Patel is making a visit to reminisce on his first-ever day in Port Moresby, way back in 1984.

'Mr Foung was in shorts and a t-shirt,' recalls Mahesh. 'It was a Sunday. He went to visit his father's grave. He parked on the roadside. There were none of these pavements and fences. It was just a dirt road. He just parked here and I'm sitting in the car. He went out to lay a wreath for his father. My first day in this country. I didn't know anybody and I am here in the cemetery. In the middle of the heat, hungover from the night before. In my glitter shirt. I was in the car waiting for him for ten minutes, and then we were gone. I've driven past so many times, but this is the first time I've come in again. I was twenty-four years of age then and now I'm sixty-two. It has just gone by in a flash.'

Friday, 18 November 2022: 3.12 p.m.

Boroko is a suburb of Port Moresby. There is a residential area and a sporting precinct. This is where the business ownership career of Sir Mahesh Patel first started in 1987. The first CPL pharmacy was opened in a small mall at Garden City.

'I started the business calling it "The Pharmacy",' Mahesh explains, 'but found out when we spoke to people and mentioned that we had The Pharmacy, they would ask, "Which one?"' Then we changed the name to City Pharmacy in 1989.'

'The back was a supermarket and the front were specialty stores,' he recalls, driving along Angau Drive, looking out the car window and pointing. 'The pharmacy was inside the supermarket. The first local television station EMTV was in there as well. That was totally brand-new premises in 1987. There are so many memories in between. The very first hotel I stayed in, the very first night in Port Moresby, was just near here as well. It was really run down.'

When the Steamships Group moved out of the mall, there wasn't the same foot traffic anymore, so Mahesh moved the business in the early 1990s to another location further down the road. There is a new CPL pharmacy in operation now in a standalone building. Further down Angau Drive at the intersection of Nita Street is the Boroko Stop & Shop. Just adjacent is the blue-and-white building that was Chapman's Pharmacy, where Mahesh first worked as a contract pharmacist in 1984.

'This was the precinct for shopping in the early days,' recalls Mahesh, 'and they really messed it up with these one-way streets. It was open planning. The town planning now is really bad here. There is also a lack of public transport.'

CPL have standalone pharmacies like this one, as well as pharmacies inside some of the Stop & Shop supermarkets. Driver Joe parks the CPL vehicle outside the CPL pharmacy.

Mahesh gets out of the car and strides into the store. The security officer stationed at the entrance smiles and welcomes the company founder.

There are lots of people in the store on this Friday afternoon. On alternate Fridays, the government departments and the private sector do their pay runs, so people are usually out spending on a Friday.

Christmas decorations and festive stock throughout the store leave no doubt what season it is. Besides the usual pharmacy items, there are snack foods for sale. Overall, the store carries a diverse range of products.

'This is a large-format store,' notes Mahesh. 'It is one of our bigger turnover stores, which is surprising because it is tucked away. Yet, we get this high traffic coming through.'

Adding the supermarket chain and its supply line has allowed CPL pharmacies to greatly increase the range of products they sell. 'There is a lack of quality retailers, so if we see a gap, we say, "Let's do that,"' notes Mahesh. 'The beauty of Papua New Guinea is that you can import from all over the world.'

Recent sales show that 15 per cent of the overall CPL pharmacy business is prescription medicine, 25 per cent is over-the-counter medicines like Panadol and medical items. The remaining 60 per cent of CPL pharmacy business is beauty and other products.

Most pharmacy products are imported, but they do have some CPL house brand products. The bulk of the items come from Australia. CPL has a supply arm, Pharmacy Wholesalers Limited (PWL). They have an office at Strathfield in Sydney. They are a supplier, exporter and manufacturer's agent for wholesale pharmacy products. Established in early 2012, PWL supplies high-quality wholesale pharmacy products to the South Pacific region.

'A lot of suppliers don't want to ship by themselves,' Mahesh explains, 'so they send their products to Sydney and we consolidate. We send two full container loads every week. We use air freight every week for pharmaceuticals.'

Mahesh goes up to the prescription counter and greets all the staff individually. Pharmacies have long staff retention, while supermarkets, industry-wide, always face problems retaining quality staff. Mahesh knows many of the pharmacy staff in this store by name.

'It is a joy, saying hello to the customers and staff,' he says. 'I don't look at it from a sales perspective. If I told the staff I was coming today, it would be different. They would be all standing at attention. I like surprise visits.'

The manager Raynneil has been in charge of the store for eight months and previously worked at the Port Moresby General Hospital, where CPL also has a pharmacy. He has worked for the company for four years.

'Sir Mahesh always makes us feel very important,' Raynneil says. 'He is very friendly ... always.'

After a short ten-minute visit, Mahesh Patel exits the store. A nursing station is located outside to the side of the store, set up during the pandemic to provide auxiliary medical aid to the citizens. 'During COVID-19, we didn't want people entering the store,' he notes.

Mahesh Patel waves at Joe, turns right, and walks down Angau Drive to the nearby Stop & Shop supermarket. As he walks, he recalls another recent charity support opportunity that he will pursue.

'I met a guy on the plane, one of the regional managers from Swire Shipping,' he says. 'He has contacts with the Anglican and Catholic Church schools in Australia. Every few years, all their school desks get sent to landfill. "Really?" I asked, "You are a shipping company, why don't you send them to us?" He replied, "I didn't even think about working with CPL Foundation for distribution." They will ship the school desks free of charge as part of their contribution if we can help them distribute it. I said, "Absolutely." In a lot of the schools in Papua New Guinea, the students do not even have a school desk. The CPL Foundation will then donate and distribute the desks to PNG schools.'

Mahesh Patel crosses the intersection at Nita Street to enter the Boroko Stop & Shop supermarket. Two unknown men in a sedan wave at him out of a car window, 'Hey, Sir Mahesh,' they yell. Mahesh smiles and waves back.

Glancing over to his left at the blue-and-white building, where he once worked at Chapman's Pharmacy, he recalls, 'There was a German deli next door and I am still in touch with the family which started it.'

Outside the supermarket, there are lots of people milling around. Some are listening to Bible-reading sermons. It is a more run-down area than some other parts of Port Moresby City. The pavement is splotched with red stains spat by betel-nut-chewing passers-by. CPL rent these premises. Mahesh acknowledges, 'This is an older supermarket.' He walks in through the doors with a smile.

The supermarket is a hive of activity. The stores usually get busier at 4 p.m., when the government offices close each day. There is a large TV screen on the wall, playing a CPL Foundation video on loop. Mahesh's son Ajay is the narrator. 'It comes down to consistency and hard work,' Ajay says, speaking about CPL Foundation community projects they are undertaking. 'That is the only thing holding you back from building up resources.'

Suddenly, Sir Mahesh Patel's face pops up on the television screen, speaking. The timing is amazing. Customers looking up at the screen do a double-take as the same man walks right past them.

'If you ask people why they like us, they will say it is because we do community service,' says Mahesh, proudly, observing himself on the television.

One of the female staff walks over and greets Mahesh.

'Ruth is one of our longest-serving staff,' he says. Ruth has more than twenty years' service with CPL.

'Sir Mahesh loves his staff and we love him too. He is our man,' she says, warmly.

Walking along the store aisles, Mahesh inspects the fresh produce, some of which is from Australia. The share of local produce has risen dramatically in recent years due to the encouragement and support given to local farmers by CPL and the CPL Foundation.

'All of these greens, we did not have this ten years ago,' says Mahesh, pointing at watermelons, root crops, tomatoes, greens, capsicums and beans. 'We developed this supply with the local farmers. This comes in container loads from the Highlands. Before we started this new local programme, we were importing 80 per cent of our produce. Now, we are importing 20 per cent. We have swung the pendulum completely. When you tell that story to any Papua New Guinean, they are amazed and so happy. That is when they start getting emotional.'

Chicken is farmed locally. Ice creams are made locally. Pies are made at the new CPL warehouse bakery. Vegetables are local. Smallgoods are local.

Mahesh speaks with the store manager, Felix. He has been in this position for four months, and before that he was working in CPL merchandise planning and store fit-outs. He has been employed by CPL for nine years.

'I love CPL,' he says. 'That's why I'm staying. I love the company.'

This supermarket is open seven days per week, from 7.30 a.m. to 7 p.m. each day. Some of the CPL Stop & Shop stores are open 365 days a year. The Central Waigani store is open till 9 p.m. There are seventy people employed at this store.

'I try to get the store opened at 7 a.m.,' explains Felix, 'to target those early shoppers who are not currently shopping with us.'

Friday, 18 November 2022: 5.35 p.m.

Sir Mahesh Patel, Lady Usha Patel, and their son Ajay Patel arrive at the National Parliament House for the twelfth edition of the Pride of PNG Awards. A security officer gives directions on where to park. The day has been muggy and hot. A tropical storm is likely to arrive shortly.

After checking in with staff at the entrance, the three walk up one flight of stairs. Entering the Parliament State Function Room, Mahesh immediately checks in with the CPL Foundation staff, to ensure the table seating is as he planned. There is a large banner at the front of the room facing the guests which proclaims: 'Pride of PNG Awards—Real courage is doing the right thing when nobody is looking'.

Mahesh is now pacing nervously, awaiting the arrival of Governor-General Sir Bob Dadae. Government House will call ahead when he is on his way. Upon his arrival, guests will be asked to move to their tables and stand for the playing of the national anthem.

Nazar Shaffee is originally from Sri Lanka. He is the CPL Company secretary and general manager, finance, and has worked for the company for three-and-a-half years.

'Mahesh is a celebrity because he has done so much for the community,' says Nazar. 'He has always connected with the grassroots people and they love him. It is a two-way relationship with employees. He is invested in those relationships. To have someone like that to work for is very important.'

Tessie Soi is a social worker who was awarded an OBE by Queen Elizabeth II in 2005, for her outstanding community work with HIV-AIDS patients and prevention. She is also a past Pride of PNG award recipient.

Tessie is the coordinator of social work at Port Moresby General Hospital. She originally met Mahesh Patel at his first City Pharmacy store in 1987.

'It is good for someone to come in and do something for us Papua New Guineans,' she says. 'He is helping us when we are down. I have been working at Port Moresby General Hospital for thirty-eight years. I can pick up the phone and ask him for something as the head of the social work department. It is not begging. He has recognized my role.'

Jacquie Simons is the Lamana Hotel's Assistant General Manager and has been employed there for over twenty years.

'Mahesh is respected,' she says. 'We call him Big Man. It is a mark of respect we show to a father figure. He gives back to the community. You won't be given that same respect unless you have been here a long time and people have seen that you are different. Port Moresby is actually smaller than you think. Everyone at one stage might have worked with him or somebody related to them would have worked with him. They know his story.'

Governor-General Sir Bob Dadae arrives, and the master of ceremonies asks guests to stand at their tables. There is a formal entry ceremony as the Pride of PNG Awards patron enters the room with his wife, Lady Emeline Tufi Dadae.

The room then continues to stand, awaiting the playing of the national anthem. Sir Mahesh Patel looks over nervously towards the audio control technician, as there are a few awkward seconds of silence before it begins. He had reminded his staff earlier that afternoon to have the anthem cued up, ready to go.

'He usually knows what they are going to mess up,' son Ajay would later observe. Guests are finally seated. Mahesh is introduced to give his address to the audience.

In navy suit and official Papua New Guinea tie, and wearing his OBE and knighthood award pins, he walks up to the dais, adjusts the microphone, and then welcomes guests by rank and order.

'I am proud to share that the Pride of PNG Awards has come a long way since its inception,' says Sir Mahesh, 'with sixty-six winners, from amongst thousands of nominations over the years, continuing their work with our ongoing support. This is not a one-off recognition but a lifetime support for the projects our winners get their awards for.

'I'm standing before you today as a passionate champion for women's empowerment and protection, and as a champion, it distresses me greatly that our women and girls have some of the worst socio-economic indicators in the world. In 2020, PNG was ranked 161 out of 162 countries in the United Nations gender inequality index.'

Patel gives some harrowing statistics in his passionate but composed speech, about the reasons the women of Papua New Guinea need further support, pushing everyone in the room to up their own efforts.

'I would like to conclude,' he says, 'with a quote from Nobel Prize recipient Malala Yousafzai, who said, "I raise up my voice, not so that I can shout, but so those without a voice can be heard. We cannot all succeed, when half of us are held back."

'PNG, in that context, will never reach its full potential as a resource-rich and culturally rich country, unless all Papua New Guineans, men and women, girls and boys, can overcome barriers and have equal opportunities to reach their potential. I look forward to working with you on this important mission.'

There is warm applause as Sir Mahesh Patel steps down and returns to his seat at the head table.

Sir Bob Bofeng Dadae is the tenth Governor-General of Papua New Guinea. He assumed office on 28 February 2017, succeeding Sir Michael Ogio. Dressed in a stylish blue suit, the patron of the Pride of PNG Awards walks up to the dais and welcomes the audience.

'We are here tonight to honour Papua New Guinean women,' says Sir Bob, 'who are anything but ordinary. Their courage, their strength, their tenacity, and their dedication to their families and their communities and to Papua New Guinea define them as extraordinary, as heroes.

'These heroes have not, despite personal scenarios being against the odds, sat quietly waiting for someone else to come along and improve their lives and of those around them. They have stood up. In their selflessness, they have shown the true spirit of Papua New Guinea. They do this because they saw a need in their community and they knew they could do it.

'Tonight, everyone and I in this room, salute you, for without the presence of women such as yourselves, leading the charge, caring for and working tirelessly for the communities, Papua New Guinea will not move forward towards a stronger and better nation. Let's continue to honour them in our daily lives, by emulating their sprit, their bravery, and their commitment to service.'

The six award winners are then introduced and presented with their framed award certificates and winners' medals by the Governor-General and Sir Mahesh.

This year's Pride of PNG Award winners are Ann Hewago for 'Care and Compassion', Hennah Joku for 'Bravery and Courage', Annie Varo for 'Young PNG', Theresia Bafui for 'Education-Role Model', Susan Case for 'Community Spirit', and Naomi Longa for 'Environment'.

There have now been seventy-two award recipients over the award's twelve years.

Hennah Joku accepts her award for 'Bravery and Courage'. Her family worked in print media, but she started in television and then fell in love with radio.

With fabulous long blond dreadlocks, Hennah stands out in any crowd. But tonight, it is her powerful words and passionate delivery to the audience that demand people take notice.

'Nothing happens by chance,' says Hennah. 'Not the people you meet nor the events that happen. The only thing that changes is how you feel as you go through the different life experiences, and your response to it determines how you get through it.'

Standing bravely at the dais, Hennah recounts the night she was brutally beaten and raped.

'As my body kicked into fight mode from the trauma,' she says, 'with my mind racing to ensure that I walked away and survived, a lightbulb flicked. A voice told me that I would survive and tell my story to help others. That my purpose was to use my platform in media to be a voice for others.

'I tell the story I have for two very specific reasons. Number one, to protect myself and keep a spotlight on this case. Remember, this is Papua New Guinea, women are killed for a multitude of reasons, and challenging the status quo and daring to speak up can be the most basic one.

'Number two, to ensure that I do my part—my social obligation—to empower as many Papua New Guineans as possible with information that they may not otherwise have, and to show the government and the agencies responsible where the gaps in the system are so broken that they need to be fixed.

'Because my story is that of thousands of other women across the country. This recognition isn't mine alone. This award is for all the victims of violence, those still entrapped in violent situations. Know that you are stronger than you think and braver than you feel.

'When you look at me, I hope you don't just see a survivor, but a thriver.'

The audience connects with Hennah and responds with a round of standing applause.

Mahesh Patel says proudly to those close to him, 'She is so inspiring. Hennah interviewed me in 1998 when she was a cadet at EMTV.'

At the end of the presentations, guests mingle around the Parliament State Function Room. Sir Mahesh Patel is thanking the serving staff for their work.

One of the CPL managers catches Mahesh's attention and introduces him to a young woman from one of the CPL departments.

Leila thanks Mahesh for the opportunity to attend tonight and says, 'This is the first time I have been in Parliament House. Ten years later, I am going to come back as a member of parliament.'

Mahesh replies to her, 'You are an inspiration. Let's take a photo now in Parliament.'

He walks Leila up onto the stage podium, and they have their photo taken by the event's official photographer.

A few minutes later, on his way out of the room, Mahesh says profoundly, 'This is the house of the people. They should be able to come here.'

Saturday, 19 November 2022: 8.30 a.m.

Sir Mahesh Patel is picked up from his apartment on Ela Beach and is heading downtown to Crown Hotel, where the CPL Group of Companies is holding its annual management convention.

After the previous night's Pride of PNG Awards at the National Parliament House, Sir Mahesh and his wife Lady Usha Patel had attended an after-party at the Lamana Hotel. They then dropped Seema, the wife of CPL CEO Navin Raju, home and got back to their apartment at 12.30 a.m.

The company founder is looking refreshed, despite the late night. He will make a speech to the assembled group of over 300 CPL employees, representing the entire cross-section of the company's multiple divisions.

Three conference rooms have been booked to cater for staff in the three CPL brands—City Pharmacy, Stop & Shop, and Hardware Haus. A presentation for the entire group will begin the day's proceedings. Staff will then break up into the three divisions for specific briefings and coaching. The entire team will then reassemble later tonight for a sit-down dinner and staff awards presentation. Long-service awards will also be presented.

Arriving at the Crown's loop driveway entry, driver Joe is having trouble getting through. CPL company cars are parked everywhere outside the Crown Hotel. There is even a large white CPL bus.

'Dropping off and going,' Joe tells the security officers on the gate. They wave him through.

Dressed in his own conference shirt in CPL Group's signature bright-blue shirt, black business trousers and black shoes, Mahesh exits the car and walks purposefully through the hotel doors.

The conference is being held on the second level. Mahesh walks lightly up the stairs and has a momentary reminiscence.

'This is where Usha and I had our wedding reception,' he smiles. 'It was the Travelodge then and we had 100 guests.'

Stephen is in charge of CPL security and spots the company founder. He escorts Mahesh into the main conference room where CPL CEO Navin Raju is standing. CPL staff are milling around outside the conference room.

'Okay, come in guys, everyone in,' says the CEO, herding his staff into the conference room.

There is a sea of royal blue inside the room, with staff wearing their commemorative CPL conference shirts.

CEO Navin Raju commences formal proceedings, outlining the events of the long day and evening. He then introduces Sir Mahesh.

Mahesh steps up to the podium and caresses the microphone, looking relaxed. With a silent video of CPL stores playing on the big video screen behind him, he welcomes the staff.

'This year we celebrate thirty-five years of our existence,' he says proudly.

He captures the attention of the room, telling his 9-Mile Cemetery arrival story. Some of the staff look on confused, not understanding where he is going with the tale, but then break into laughter at its conclusion.

'It is quite challenging now to think back to all those years ago and what we did,' he continues. 'We wouldn't exist without the help of all you guys. Our team, our family, is what has got us here and what is going to take us to the next level in the years to come.

'I thank you all. You are the ones who make CPL. I'm out in the front and get in the newspapers and on television, but behind me is what you guys deliver, so credit to all of you.'

The audience applaud warmly. The company founder then progresses into the main part of his speech, talking unscripted, but using topic prompts from his mobile phone notes.

'Today,' he says. 'I want to talk about where we came from, what we stand for and where we are heading. Because that is very important. As thirty-five years have gone past, you do look back. I thought, *I won't be here for 150 years*. Now, I want to talk about something unusual. The world's most authentic brands are perceived as having a strong vision and values. They are happy to be transparent. I read in a global survey covering 395,000 people worldwide, more than 2,000 brands in 30 countries, and 21 industries—quite a large spectrum of research. It showed that 77 per cent of the brands are not meaningful in their lives.

'When they asked people, what does this brand stand for, they said, "We don't know or care". Only 47 per cent of the brands were trustworthy. It would be interesting to do a survey here, and I would put my money on it that CPL would be ranked highly in trust and being meaningful for people's lives. But that is to be tested.'

Sir Mahesh then retells his favourite netball player story and concludes 'She was six years old when CPL sponsored her Rebels netball team. That [chance meeting with her] gave me goosebumps. That's the impact we can have on people's lives. Our key value is that we care. We really do care and we have got to show that. For our community. For our customers. For our people—and that's you.'

The CPL CEO speaks next, and as soon as he finishes to applause, Sir Mahesh Patel stands up and leaves the room, smiling warmly at the staff and shaking hands as he exits.

'They have a huge team for planning this event,' Mahesh notes, as he walks out of the hotel. 'The problem is, though, as the company becomes bigger, everything becomes a little bit more impersonal.'

Saturday, 19 November 2022: 9.35 a.m.

A white CPL vehicle driven by Joe Pato enters the car park of the Stop & Shop supermarket in Konedobu. A suburb of Port Moresby, it is located in the valley between Touaguba Hill and Burns Peak. The headquarters of the Royal Papua New Guinea Constabulary is located nearby. The vehicle stops and Sir Mahesh Patel gets out. The supermarket car park is busy, with many people coming and going.

From a white van parked in a loading zone, two workers in green shirts carry buckets of fresh flowers for sale into the supermarket. There is a staffed *bilum* (tote bags) counter at the entry, where people can leave their bags while they shop.

Mahesh walks to the main entry of the Stop & Shop. A smiling security guard stands at the sliding entry doors, who immediately recognizes him, and says, 'Good morning, Sir Mahesh.'

There is no other big chain competitor to Stop & Shop in Papua New Guinea, only lots of individual operators. The supermarket looks brand-new and is extremely well-presented. Everything is neat and tidy, with wide shopping aisles. It looks like one of the larger Coles or Woolworths supermarkets seen in Australia. There is no surprise in learning an Australian consultant was used for the store design and layout. There are lots of festive Christmas decorations and flashing lights all around the store.

'Not our biggest supermarket, but one of the biggest,' remarks Mahesh.

At the end of one of the first aisles—a high-profile location—Mahesh stops and looks at the new galip nut range on sale. It is a local product he has been personally supporting in development and delivery, in partnership with the National Agriculture Research Institution.

'This is quite unique to here,' he explains. 'We are supporting this and we will be launching it next week as a new brand.'

Walking along the aisles at the front of the store, Mahesh suddenly stops. He walks back to one of the aisles and detours up it. Some customers have been spotted acting unusually.

There are three men and one woman, all white Caucasian, holding up products off the shelves and taking photos of them. They then replace the products back on the shelves and pick up some more. One of the men is wearing the yellow staff shirt of a food manufacturer and supply company.

'You have to buy that to take photographs,' says Mahesh, firmly, as he approaches. The four think he is joking.

'So, no photos?' asks one of the men, laughing.

'No. I'm serious,' replies Mahesh, walking right up to them.

One of the men then recognizes who is making the request. His expression and body language suddenly change. He gestures to his colleague to put the product in his hand back on the shelf.

'Ah, sorry about that,' he says, apologizing.

'I'm sure your company would not like someone from your competitor doing that,' Mahesh continues. 'We have a policy and we can't have two sets of rules.'

'Okay. Sorry,' says the first man. 'We know you own the place.'

Mahesh smiles, turns on his heel, and walks off along the aisles at the rear of the store.

The third man whispers, 'Is that him?' The first man simply nods in reply.

Mahesh continues his inspection of the supermarket.

'These expatriates come along and think they can do anything,' he says, shaking his head.

After the encounter, the four will have walked away impressed that the CPL Group's company founder and current director, knighted by King Charles, does his own foot patrols of the Stop & Shop supermarkets.

Mahesh does a full loop of the store and then walks back to the cash registers at the entry doors. He stops and talks to Emmanuel Mora, the assistant store manager. There is one store manager and two assistant managers for the supermarket.

'How are you doing?' asks Mahesh, immediately recognizing him.

'I'm fine,' Emmanuel replies, with a big smile. 'I really like it here.'

Emmanuel Mora is a perfect example of CPL's career path optimization. He first started work with CPL as a cinema usher, when the company owned the local cinema chain. He then progressed to management level at one of the Total service stations, another chain previously owned by the CPL Group. When it was sold in 2020, he moved into Stop & Shop store management.

Emmanuel Mora is the acting store manager today, while the South African-born store manager attends the CPL management conference. Mahesh gives Emmanuel a nod and heads towards one of the checkout cashiers. Emmanuel smiles again—he will make an even greater impression on Sir Mahesh later that night at the CPL staff dinner.

Mahesh exits the supermarket and gets back into the CPL car Joe Pato has parked nearby. He gives further thought to the four people he observed in the aisle checking products and taking photos.

'They were checking out the packaging,' he muses, rubbing his chin. 'All the Asian, Indonesian and Malaysian chocolates, even though they are international brands, the formula is different. The lady was holding up some sugar products. My guess is they are looking at bringing in sugar themselves, so they are checking out the competition.'

To the average person, the four people standing in the supermarket aisle looked like regular shoppers. But the experienced Sir Mahesh Patel spotted them immediately after a split-second glance.

'It was really tongue-in-cheek when I said, "You need to buy that,"' he smiles. 'But we don't normally allow people to take photos. That is the policy.'

Mahesh Patel is dropped off at home to prepare for a lunch meeting with one of his former CPL CFOs. Joe Pato drives back through Port Moresby city. There are council murals by local artists decorating the streetscape. Beautiful paintings and coloured clothes are for sale at a pop-up stand on a street corner. A couple sit under a tree with two little babies.

Joe has worked as a driver for the CPL Group for twelve years. He is Mahesh Patel's preferred driver and he also drives for CEO Navin Raju. He previously worked as a driver for another company and applied for this job when it was advertised. The allure of working for the CPL Group appealed to him

'Sir Mahesh is a great man,' says Joe. 'He looks after his staff.'

Saturday, 19 November 2022: 7.00 p.m.

The CPL Group is holding its annual staff dinner at the Crown Hotel in Port Moresby. Earlier in the day, the same conference room was filled with staff wearing their blue conference shirts. Now, everyone is back, dressed in their finest Pacific wear attire with a splash of CPL blue, as suggested on the invitation. Sir Mahesh Patel and wife Lady Usha Patel have arrived and are seated adjacent to the podium at the front of the room.

Emcee Paruru Lawrence attempts to settle the rowdy audience.

'It is an honour to be here in front of all you handsome gentlemen and beautiful ladies,' she says.

CPL CEO Navin Raju gets on stage to speak to his staff. He makes special mention of Sir Mahesh and Lady Usha.

'I've been doing a lot of talking today,' he says, 'so, I am going to keep my talking now to a minimum.'

A few of the staff seated at tables chortle to themselves in reply, doubting their boss's ability to stick to his promise. Navin mentions this morning's message that the company is celebrating thirty-five years of business.

'We have got the plan now,' he says, 'which is going to carry us forward over the next three years.'

CPL Chairman Stanley Joyce is then welcomed to the podium to speak.

'We were at Parliament House last night,' he says, 'for the Pride of PNG Awards. At the dinner were some of the big companies in town, like Exxon Mobil and Steamships, and I thought to myself, *This is a sign of what good looks like.* When other corporate companies show that sort of respect to us, for what the views of the CPL company are, and the work that is being done, and the leadership that is being provided through the Foundation of Sir Mahesh Patel, I think the first thing to do is thank him for everything.'

The audience responds with loud, prolonged applause.

The Chairman then acknowledges all the other CPL Board members present in the room. He announces that Eddie Ruha will be replacing the retiring John Dunlop, a former chairman of the company.

'There are times when boards change and people move on,' says Joyce. 'One of the first things to do tonight is pay our respects to somebody and to thank him for his service to this company, with more than seventeen years as director—and that is Mr John Dunlop.'

John Dunlop has worked in Papua New Guinea, Fiji, New Zealand and the Solomon Islands for forty-two years. A chartered accountant, John was always considered to be 'a financial man'. He was CPL's Group Chairman for two years. His corporate experience in Papua New Guinea first started with Steamships Trading Company.

'John always dealt in the facts,' observes Joyce.

John Dunlop walks up onto the podium and is joined by Sir Mahesh. Mahesh presents John with a commemorative award, shakes his hand and puts an arm around him warmly.

'I was very fortunate to be asked to go on some boards,' says Dunlop, 'and the first one I accepted an invitation to was CPL. The reason was because I have always seen it as a very positive company and one that did things slightly differently to everybody else. I thought by coming on the board, I would learn a lot from it, and in fact that has been the case. I have really enjoyed my time with CPL.'

Mahesh Patel then steps forward. He smiles as he looks at John.

'On behalf of Usha and me,' he says, 'we sincerely thank John for all his support. He looks like a nice guy, but if you do the wrong thing, he will really get on your case. I think Navin has been learning that quietly.'

Mahesh then shakes hands with John as the audience applauds.

'We have just been so lucky over the last forty years,' said Dunlop, sitting back down at his table, 'to watch the country grow. We got here eight years after Mahesh, and it was still very colonial.'

After a short break, Chairman Stanley Joyce introduces a video.

'The next part of the evening,' he says, 'is a tribute to what the heart and soul of what this wonderful company is all about. The culture of the business is a reflection of its values, and tonight we want to make a special recognition to the two wonderful people that this business is all about. I give you Sir Mahesh and Lady Usha Patel.'

The couple walk up onto the stage to enthusiastic applause from the CPL staff.

'They have put it out there for Papua New Guinea every time,' Joyce continues. 'The way they have lived their lives is the way they have built the company, their values. I am very proud to say that the government of Papua New Guinea and Her Majesty, in their wisdom, nominated and bestowed onto Mahesh a knighthood.'

A video recording of Sir Mahesh being knighted by Prince Charles is played on the large dual video screens. The audience watches, enthralled.

Stanley Joyce sits back down at his table adjacent to the stage and surveys the room. There is a positive vibe amongst the CPL staff.

'We have a rainbow team of people,' he says. 'It is amazing. You don't pull that off unless you put a true form of company culture together. Mahesh always puts the staff above him. That is pretty unique in PNG.'

Joyce first arrived in Papua New Guinea for work in 1980. His expertise is in food, beverage, and manufacturing industries. He was the South Pacific Brewery Limited's (SP) Managing Director for fourteen years. He now has over thirty years of management and board experience.

'The belief he had in what could happen,' recalls Joyce. 'Mahesh was proven and vindicated. This business using his fundamentals has all come together. I am very proud.'

After a further break for dinner, Sir Mahesh and Lady Usha return to the stage for the presentation of awards to long-serving staff.

'The whole value of CPL as a company,' says Mahesh, 'what Usha and I did, was about family. It is very heartening when you go around the room and see the people who have been with us for many, many years. They tell us it is a good environment to work in. They love the company and we love them.'

Awarded staff will receive a commemorative pin, certificate, cash bonus and a travel allowance.

Two long serving staff are not at the dinner tonight, but receive a special mention. Tuana Kamo started at CPL on 12 February 1993. She currently works in the office at the CPL warehouse. Tracey Gotele has been working for CPL for thirty-two years and is also not at the dinner. Her first job was at City Pharmacy in Boroko.

'Usha and I have worked with both Tuana and Tracey,' notes Mahesh, privately. 'They both started when our kids were born. Tuana and Tracey have both been amazing employees. They started off at a very, very junior level. They have really escalated in the organization. They may not have the big titles, but the sense of responsibility and the commitment—that they have got. Tracey was seventeen when she started. She is a grandmother now. They both have real history here. It is a pity they are not here tonight, but I am sure I am going to run into them at the offices on Monday.'

After the awards for long-serving staff, awards for employees from each of the CPL Group branches are presented. Following this, there is the unveiling of a new set of CEO Awards for 2022.

'Because I thought of a lot of people who were not getting recognized at the ground level,' explains Navin Raju. 'These are to recognize the people at the operational level.'

Floyd Tembon works in facility management. He has been with the CPL Group for six years. He had previously worked for a bank in their properties division.

Sitting at one of the tables to the side of the stage, he is relaxed and enjoying himself. When his name is read out for one of the CEO awards, it is totally unexpected.

'I am surprised,' he says, sitting back down at his table looking at his award certificate. 'Mostly with the awards, the shops are considered. In support services, we don't normally get anything. Because the shops are bringing in the money from which we get paid.'

'Over the years,' Raju later explained, 'Floyd has been one guy who has worked very hard for the company, yet he was never recognized.'

Asked about why he enjoys working for CPL, Tembon replies proudly.

'CPL is more like a family company,' he says. 'The culture of the company, the way they treat their employees. There are ups and downs; whenever there are issues, they get resolved and we move on. It comes from the top. It is a shared vision and mission. The staff drive it and make sure it happens. I have worked with a lot of other companies before and this feels different.'

Asked about the company founder, Tembon smiles widely.

'Sir Mahesh is the guy!' he declares. 'Whenever there is a crisis, he steps in, he solves it all. He is there. The staff love Mahesh. The way he talks to the people and addresses them—he treats everyone on the same level. There is a difference in the way Mahesh treats people. Whenever there is a crisis, the staff ask, *Where is Mahesh*? He is the only one who can fix it.'

Eunice Parua is a member of the CPL Group board of directors. She made history for Papua New Guinea as the youngest lawyer to make partner at a law firm. In 2019, she joined the CPL Group as a trainee director.

'You feel like this is one big family,' she remarks. 'Because of Sir Mahesh's spirit, his leadership, the way he has driven his organization. The culture is just so good. It is quite rewarding for me. When I was approached to start training to be a director, I talked to Mahesh. I said, "Yes, I would love to be a part of CPL because of what it represents and what it is." Everyone this evening, coming together, supporting each other and cheering each other on. You can tell it is just one big family. It gives me so much. There is happiness, joy, seeing everyone come together like this.'

Once the official presentations are completed, the music flows and the dance floor is energized.

CEO Navin Raju and his wife Seema are moving to the beat of Pitbull's 'Give Me Everything', featuring Ne-Yo, Afrojack and Nayer.

Company Secretary Nazar Shaffee is on stage, lighting up the room with his own moves. Theatrical smoke washes across the dance floor in a sea of blue.

Emmanuel Mora, the assistant manager at the Stop & Shop supermarket in Konedobu, to whom Mahesh had spoken to earlier in the day, is on the dance floor, making a claim as the companies' best dancer.

Emmanuel is wearing a blue island shirt and a blue flower lei around his neck. His exaggerated moves are smooth and choreographed. Clearly this is another of his many talents.

Mahesh strides out and challenges Emmanuel to a dance-off. The two are in the centre of a large group that surrounds them. After the dance Emmanuel puts his arm around Mahesh, who replies with an enthusiastic high five.

Mahesh then retreats off the dance floor. His work here is now done.

Sunday, 20 November 2022: 9.45 a.m.

Mahesh and wife Usha are being driven by Joe Pato up into the mountains east of Port Moresby. Lunch will be at the Koitaki Country Club on the Sogeri Plateau. But first, a visit has been scheduled to a nearby farm, a new business run by a long-time friend and associate of Mahesh.

Arriving in the Waigani Central shopping centre car park, Joe pulls the white CPL car over and Mahesh winds his window down.

John Wallace is tall and lean. Dressed in white shirt, blue jeans and a cap, he approaches.

'Just follow us,' he smiles. 'If you get bogged, we've got a tow cable … Have you got your gum boots on, Usha?'

The two vehicles set off in convoy. John leads the way in his rugged utility, with his friend Gavin Burgess in the passenger seat. Gavin is the chief operating officer of John's BNG Trading company, the oldest importer and distributor of food products in Papua New Guinea, operating since 1947. In addition, John's Papua Niugini Freezers company operates the largest smallgoods processing facility in PNG.

'John is one of our suppliers,' explains Mahesh. 'I knew his father, Harry Wallace, a great guy. In this town, everybody becomes friends.'

The drive from Port Moresby to the intended farm visit will take approximately one hour via the Sogeri Road. The Koitaki Country Club is located near the Varirata National Park and one end of the Kokoda Track.

As you drive out through the outer suburbs of Port Moresby, you see they are named in line with distance: 7-mile, 8-mile and 9-mile.

'At 9-mile,' recalls Mahesh, 'they used to have Easter showgrounds in the 1980s and 1990s, but that just disappeared.'

Smaller pop-up markets are seen on the roadsides throughout the drive.

'There is no control on them and they just manage themselves,' observes Mahesh. 'The product is very good because it is organic,' adds Usha. 'They grow the produce in their own gardens.'

Dogs roam freely in Port Moresby. They are visible on almost every street. But cats are nowhere to be found.

'I have not seen many cats in Papua New Guinea,' says Mahesh. 'I don't know a single Papua New Guinean who has a cat.'

Sunday, 20 November 2022: 10.50 a.m.

Driving past a security gate at the boundary of the farm property, the security staff on duty wave them through. The vehicles drive along a muddy dirt track that goes past a fenced compound of houses on the right and turns left to go down to a river. Powerlines can still be seen above. The narrow track gets wet and muddy. Joe Pato swerves slowly from side to side, trying to find the best traction.

'Joe is used to this when he takes Ajay out to the farms,' says Mahesh. 'Similar sorts of roads.'

Driving over a small metal bridge, with rich chocolate-coloured water flowing below, the guests finally arrive at the main farmhouse property. Sonny, John Wallace's farming partner, greets everyone warmly.

This is Mahesh and Usha's first visit to this property. The last time they were in this part of Central Province in Papua New Guinea was two years ago.

A number of different crops have been planted near where the vehicles are parked. There are sweet potatoes, ginger and basil. Banana and guava trees are flourishing nearby.

'Pineapples grow like weeds up here,' says Gavin Burgess. 'You plant the head and the pineapple will grow out of it. There is one crop each year.'

John suggests an inspection of a new quarantine station that has been built for sheep. New sheep go into quarantine for two weeks after arriving from overseas. After a short drive across the property, the guests disembark and view a massive tin-roofed steel structure. 'We call this station the dance hall,' laughs John, due to its old, barn-like appearance. It is made to house 120 sheep.

John and Gavin caution to watch out for snakes, as Mahesh and Usha walk around. Death Adders, Papuan black snakes and Coastal Taipans have been seen recently on the farm.

'Snakes need to live in long grass otherwise it is too hot for them,' notes Gavin, suggesting you are safer in the open areas.

Leucaena is a legume fodder crop that grows in tropical and subtropical environments. It provides high-quality feed for farm animals. It is growing around the property as far as the eye can see. Leucaena grows thirty centimetres in a month.

'It is toxic when fresh,' says John, 'but you cut it and feed the sheep the next day when the toxicity is gone.'

John Wallace and Mahesh Patel first met in 2005, soon after the CPL Group purchased the Stop & Shop supermarket chain. They also owned the Gerehu warehouse land site jointly and then later divided it up for individual use. John still has his freezer and logistics business at Gerehu.

'Mahesh has always been our biggest retail customer,' says John, 'and we have always done lots of stuff together. We have had some adventures, with the two big fires. I was there when the supermarket burnt down. Their warehouse fire nearly burnt our freezer down. It was only because the wind went in a different direction. We had a big container wall and that worked like a fire wall for us.'

John speaks highly of Mahesh Patel's business success.

'Mahesh is my inspiration for entrepreneurial stuff,' he gushes. 'Because of what he has achieved starting with one pharmacy. His attitude in having a go at a deal. We all have to deal with lots of challenges, particularly here in Papua New Guinea, but what Mahesh has done is incredible. He has faced major challenges and he just said, "Righto, we'll get it fixed." And he has done it with good faith. When Mahesh says he is going to do a deal, I don't have to worry about it. He is a man of his word.'

Walking around inside the empty quarantine station, which is elevated off the ground, John beckons Mahesh and Usha over.

'We need a photo,' he smiles. 'This is our first royal visit.' A group photo is taken.

'Now, we have had a royal christening,' suggests John.

'Where is the bottle of champagne?' asks Mahesh promptly.

Monday, 21 November 2022: 8.50 a.m.

Sir Mahesh Patel is being driven by Joe Pato. They make their way through the morning traffic north to the suburb of Gerehu, where the newly rebuilt CPL Group warehouse and offices became operational on 21 November 2020. The first warehouse the then-City Pharmacy ever used was 100 sq m in size. This new warehouse is 10,000 sq m.

'We are looking at installing solar panels on the roof of the warehouse,' Mahesh reveals. 'We have just approved it at board level. Once the solar panels are installed, we can finally look at installing a big CPL sign on the roof.'

The new main warehouse is not air conditioned. But all the offices are, along with the pharmaceutical storage area, freezers and chillers.

'The warehouse is taller than the previous one,' says Mahesh. 'But it is about trying not to overbuild or underbuild. You don't want to have a big place with unused capacity.'

A specialist warehouse design consultant was engaged to work with CPL Group management and the board to come up with the best possible modern design, which is functional.

'We had to make sure the new design was best practice,' says Mahesh. 'We have the consultant still working with us. We had to look at the data to see what sort of growth are we going to have in five and ten years' time and to allow for it.'

Previously, CPL had used a DTS (direct to store) delivery process for some of their suppliers. But this created problems with traffic jams at the individual stores' loading docks. Now, all the products come in via the warehouse and are then distributed to each of the CPL stores.

'With this new efficiency,' says Mahesh, 'we are asking, how do we measure that? The previous warehouse cost before the fire was 18 cents per carton pick. It should now be costing 9 cents per carton pick. That is what the consultant is telling us.'

So far, the performance has been encouraging.

'It is working well,' says Mahesh, 'but we are saying to the consultants, "Show us the benefit of us spending 40 million kina [867 million rupees]." You said it will do all these things—show us. We use an advanced warehouse management software, which we haven't used before.'

Gerehu is one of the most populated areas in Port Moresby and is a fifteen-minute drive north from the centre of the city. It is home to approximately 20,000 residents. Driver Joe Pato pulls up at the main entry security gates at the CPL Group warehouse. The access road is unsealed dirt.

The security officer recognizes who is riding in the back of the car and waves them through with a smile. There is a large concreted driveway and loading area outside the main warehouse. CPL-branded trucks are parked in an orderly manner. Others belong to suppliers making deliveries.

CPL leases the heavy trucks and purchases the smaller ones. The company employs a dedicated fleet manager. Nationwide, CPL Group owns or leases over 200 vehicles. Management cars are leased on a monthly basis and CPL provides each of their store managers with a company vehicle for use.

Dressed in a light-blue short-sleeved business shirt, long tan business pants, and black shoes, Mahesh Patel exits the vehicle and immediately spots a gathering of CPL employees outside one of the warehouse driveways.

'I'll go and say hello to these guys,' he smiles. The workers are on their morning tea break.

Mahesh strides upbeat across the wide truck loading driveway to the main warehouse entry section. With forklifts beeping in the background, he speaks personally to the thirty men and women, shaking hands and smiling.

After a few minutes of chatting, Mahesh turns and heads back towards the large office section, located close to the main entry security gates. He continues to wave to other people in the compound as he walks. One young man in blue CPL uniform catches up to Mahesh and asks to shake his hand. His name is Dodong Elavo and he joined the CPL Group in December 2021.

'I wanted to shake hands with the great man Sir Mahesh,' he says, in awe. 'I have heard so much about you.'

'Thank you,' replies Mahesh, warmly. 'What do you do here?'

'I'm a driver,' says Dodong. 'I do the pick-ups and drop-offs. It is very special for me to meet you.'

Mahesh smiles, thanks the man again, and gives him a well-done pat on the back. Dodong walks back to work, filled with pride.

There is a separate driveway entry area where the local farmers bring in their produce. It is checked for quality, counted and received. The section has its own entry gate just for the farmers for safety reasons. While they are on the CPL Group site, they do not enter the warehouse section.

'There is no large-scale commercial farming here,' Mahesh explains. 'It is all individual farmers. In Mount Hagan, we've got a company that we deal with. They collect the produce there.'

Mahesh walks into the receiving area and greets staff and farmers.

'Good morning!' he says, enthusiastically. He fist-bumps one of the farmers he recognizes.

'He is a long-time supplier of ours,' Mahesh says.

There are large mesh bags containing sweet potato. A lot of the fresh green produce, such as broccoli, grows here in cooler climates.

'They are virtually organic,' says Mahesh. Staff have large scales to weigh the produce. The farmers are told in advance how much produce to bring in.

'Initially we didn't know what volumes to ask for,' recalls Mahesh, 'but now we tell them how much we want.'

Produce supply and delivery is coordinated by the CPL staff via telephone. Most of the farmers are regular suppliers, so a routine of produce levels has been established. There are large green crates of turmeric and paw paw stacked on top of each other. The produce when received is crated for storage and then put into the nearby cool room. Another staff member sorts bushels of local aibika. It is a garden vegetable commonly grown in Papua New Guinea. It contains twice as much iron as cabbage, is great for nursing mothers and babies, and can be eaten raw or cooked.

After the CPL staff have sorted and weighed the produce, the farmers are paid. Some farmers make drop-offs two or three times per week. Some drive for over an hour to get to the Gerehu depot.

'It is such a task to manage all of this,' notes Mahesh.

He walks into the adjacent produce office and encourages the supervisor to make changes.

'With these greens,' he says, pointing at the many crates of aibika, 'We need to fast-track the movement. It is sitting in the heat for too long. We need more people on the greens than the other produce and put it in the cool room quickly.'

Staff immediately act on Mahesh's guidance, which brings a satisfied smile to his face.

'Otherwise, the life of the vegetables is wasted,' he says, stepping back. 'You can lose 30 per cent because of the heat. The farmers don't have chiller trucks when making their deliveries.'

The warehouse site has been divided into separate building sections. The main warehouse is in the centre. At the end closest to the main entry gates is the bakery. The meat production area is in another building at the other end of the site.

Mahesh walks over to the main warehouse entry door. Male and female security guards, dressed in all-black uniforms, supervise entry into the warehouse.

'Welcome to CPL,' says one, looking very professional.

Multiple managers have responsibility for the warehouse site and operations. CPL Group staff wear blue uniforms. Management wear orange uniforms.

Rajendra Tiruwa is manager, Supply Chain, and meets Mahesh at the warehouse entry. He joined CPL in 2019. They walk up a set of stairs to the internal office area.

The warehouse is in use seven days per week. There is a small team of staff which commences work at 5.30 a.m. The usual warehouse worker's shift is 8 a.m. to 5 p.m. If overtime is required to complete urgent orders on any day, they will work no later than 7 p.m. On Saturdays, they only work until 5 p.m. Sunday work is done by a skeleton staff. Including all aspects of operation, there are 210 staff currently employed on site. Walking into the operations office, Mahesh says hello as he moves around. Down another set of stairs to a secondary office area, Mahesh finds one of the staff he specifically wanted to see today.

Tuana Kamo started work with the then City Pharmacy on 12 February 1993. She is one of the companies longest-serving employees. She currently works in the pharmacy wholesale division.

'Tua, are you hiding here?'
'Yes.'
'My wife has been looking for you at the other office.'
'Oh, I'm sorry.'
'Tuana, we missed you on Saturday night at the staff dinner. Why were you not there?'

Tuana looks embarrassed.

'I wanted to do a big speech about you,' Mahesh continues.

Tuana hugs Mahesh. She has tears in her eyes and doesn't answer his question.

She first started working for CPL in their small warehouse.

'I did pick and pack and dispatch,' she says. 'Then I went into sales and then I got transferred here.' Tuana now works in a team of two, getting the orders for the warehouse printed.

'Yes, I like it here,' she says, when asked why she has remained at the company for over thirty years. 'We have Sir Mahesh. He is probably the reason I am still here.'

'She is the girl who got me crying,' says Mahesh, 'when I came back to Port Moresby after the warehouse fire. I'm getting tears in my eyes again. A town hall meeting at the supermarket and the staff were all seated down. I was there to say, listen, we are going to survive this. And Tuana is sitting there in the front, bawling her eyes out. I started choking up. I started crying.'

'Mahesh said he would fix it and he did,' says Tuana, hugging Mahesh again.

'It is so good to have people like this with you on the journey,' says Mahesh. 'Usha was going to go to the other office to see you,' Mahesh tells Tuana, 'Then I realized you are working here. I think she is coming here on Wednesday to see Kapi. Usha is a very keen gardener, so she wants to see the gardens here.'

Mahesh says goodbye and continues his warehouse tour. Seeing Tuana prompts memories of past years to come flooding back.

'More than half my life I have been here in Papua New Guinea,' he says, wistfully.

The bakery is a large white single-level building. A gas tank is located nearby, which fuels the bakery ovens. Bakery Operations Manager Ciolen Gurat, dapper in her CPL baking staff shirt of yellow with red trim, welcomes Mahesh at the entrance.

The alluring smell of freshly baked bread wafts through the air.

Bakery staff commence work at 6 a.m. At busy times there will be three eight-hour shifts, twenty-four hours a day. The night shift is 7 p.m. to 3 a.m.—or 4:00 a.m. if overtime is required.

All packaging is done within the bakery. The first delivery truck leaves at 5.30 a.m. Mahesh inspects the bread-making section. Doughnuts and cakes are made in a different area.

The bread dough is prepared and moulded and then put onto large metal racks on one side of the area. It is then put into storage, which is accessed when needed via the baking side. The racks are wheeled into four commercial-sized ovens and turn around inside while baking. The oven temperature is 233 degrees Celsius.

Staff can bake 162 loaves of bread in each oven in 35 minutes. On average they make 5,000 loaves per day. All the different types of bread are baked in the same ovens, as needed. The staff do their own taste-testing.

Ciolen Gurat has worked in various roles for the CPL Group, two years of which have been in the bakery. She also manages the retail side of the bakeries and is driving sales to hotels.

Albert Kuyo is the production manager. He has worked for CPL for eleven years.

'The old bakery was at another site with one of their stores,' he says. 'We only had two ovens back then.'

Mario Babaran Jr. ran a bakery in the Philippines for twenty years and has now worked for CPL for ten years. He went to work for another company and then returned eighteen months ago.

'We brought him back,' smiles Mahesh.

'A lot of our visitors are amazed with our bakery,' says Mario, proudly. 'We can produce at much higher capacity now. The Port Moresby City Council inspectors were very impressed with our set-up and hygiene.'

John Wallace's company supplies a lot of baking ingredients, so CPL used his consultants to work with their team to design the new bakery.

Walking into the slicing and packing room, Mahesh observes the manual process still used. They slice the bread using a dedicated machine and then insert the bread by hand into plastic packaging.

In another room there are two pie-making machines. There is a kitchen in an adjoining room where the meat is cooked. They chill the pie filling prior to cooking.

'You can see the smiles on their faces with all the machines here,' notes Mahesh. Moving into the cake-decorating room, cakes, doughnuts and cream buns dazzle the senses.

'The best cream buns in town,' declares Ciolen, proudly.

'These are a huge seller,' says Mahesh. 'People love them. And interestingly, in the demographics, it is from the high down to the grass roots.'

Cream buns made now will be in the stores later this afternoon. Two or three truck delivery runs are made each day.

When the bakery first opened, there were problems with logistics and deliveries, so one Christmas, Mahesh loaded up one of the CPL cars with driver Joe and took supplies to the Stop & Shop supermarkets.

'There were customers lined up, waiting for bread,' laughs Mahesh.

The doughnuts are made in a mould with a hole in the middle and the ones with intricate designs are produced with a hand pipe.

'It is very challenging,' admits Ciolen, 'but this is a very happy and exciting environment to work in.'

Lamingtons with cream and jam are also very popular.

'They make the Lamingtons in a six pack,' notes Mahesh, 'Which shows you that people like them.'

The bakery inspection finishes and Mahesh poses with his staff in a group photo.

'When are the Christmas cakes out?' asks Mahesh.

'This week,' replies Ciolen. 'We have already received the ingredients and are ready for production.'

Staff work on Christmas Day and the Stop & Shop supermarkets are also open. Staff are paid penalty rates (the Australian term for especially high overtime rates) for working on the public holiday.

'With communal living, people are out of food for the next day,' says Mahesh. 'Christmas Day is as busy as Christmas Eve or any other day. Christmas Day is a big day for us.'

Ciolen Gurat has worked for a number of different employers, but sees something at the CPL Group that she has not experienced anywhere else before.

'Here at CPL,' she says, out of earshot from Sir Mahesh, 'I can see a different culture to anywhere else I have worked before. It's a family. CPL really looks after local people. They give great opportunities to the local people. I have managers and supervisors here who are locals. In previous jobs, all of the managers were expatriates.'

Asked what it means to have the company founder visit the bakery, Ciolen answers enthusiastically.

'When Sir Mahesh visits,' she says, 'we are honoured and happy that he is giving us time. In other companies, they are only giving us 1 per cent of their time. Sir Mahesh, the CEO and COO, they always make time to come and see us and talk to us. They talk to all the staff, even the ones in the lower positions.'

'The staff see Sir Mahesh as a hero,' she continues. 'A friend and part of their family. We have a lot of older staff who have been working with CPL for a long time. Because of Sir Mahesh, they have their employment and they are happy here. We are all very happy here and very proud of our bakery.'

Around the entire perimeter of the warehouse site, an exquisite display of trees, shrubs and fruiting plants have been introduced.

'This is all Usha's gardener's doing,' smiles Mahesh.

Joe drives slowly along the fence line as Mahesh looks at the greenery.

'I said when we planned the new warehouse,' recalls Mahesh, 'let's do some landscaping, so Kapi has planted all of these trees. We let the staff take the produce home. When Kapi finds out Usha is in town, he bags it all up for her and it is too much. We give it away to the staff and friends. My manager was also saying there are arguments amongst the staff as to who takes what. I said, what you should do is to get Kapi to have a market day and sell everything for a kina each, and he can keep the money for his work.'

Kapi Fuali started working as a gardener for CPL in 2007.

'He was always our gardener at the old warehouse and all the shop areas,' recalls Mahesh. 'He was doing gardening at the previous CEO's house. The gardens at the old warehouse were not as big as what we have now. It is more elaborate. It's funny, Kapi only listens to Usha. If anyone else gives him instructions, he says, "no, we have to ask the boss lady." He has done a brilliant job.'

Mahesh observes Kapi's work, as the car slowly continues.

'You have got basil there,' he points out. 'Usha always wanted greenery. A curry leaf tree there ... Joe, wait, wait, wait. What is this one here? I just want to get out quick and see this.'

Joe stops the vehicle and Mahesh gets out and walks over to a section of the vegetation. He inspects one of the trees closely.

'Usha brought some seeds to give to Kapi,' explains Mahesh. 'I'm just trying to see what type of bean this is ... Joe!'

Driver Joe also gets out of the car and walks over to where Mahesh is standing. They inspect the leaves of the plant carefully. By now, gardener Kapi has spotted Mahesh and walks over to see him.

Kapi confirms Mahesh's keen eye, the plant they are looking at has come from the seeds supplied by Usha last Christmas.

'Oh, the beans have not come out yet,' says Mahesh, after listening to Kapi explain in his local dialect. 'They may come out during the rainy season.' Mahesh puts his arm around Kapi's shoulders warmly.

'He is gardener number one,' declares a smiling Mahesh. 'This is all his doing. There was nothing here before. It looks good, Kapi. Well done.'

Monday, 21 November 2022: 2.02 p.m.

Sir Mahesh Patel arrives at the CPL Group buying office in Waigani Central Precinct. He wants to see one of the companies longest-serving employees, Tracey Gotele.

Tracey did not attend Saturday night's staff dinner, where she was to receive a long service award. Mahesh walks up the stairs to the office and startles some of the CPL staff, who are surprised to see him. He walks along a corridor and sees Tracey Gotele.

'Tracey, I want to talk to you,' he says, smiling.

Mahesh walks briskly into a darkened meeting room and looks for the light switch. Another staff member turns on the lights. Mahesh turns on the air-con.

'Send Tracey in,' he requests.

Tracey Gotele has worked for the CPL Group for thirty-two years. She was only seventeen when she was first employed at one of the City Pharmacy stores.

Tracey walks in, looking embarrassed.

'What happened to you on Saturday?' asks Mahesh. 'We were going to give you a big award and you didn't turn up.'

'I didn't have transport,' she replies, sheepishly.

'You should have called us,' replies Mahesh.

He gives her a hug and leaves the room to talk to some other staff members. Away from Mahesh, Tracey explains the real reason she was not at the dinner.

'I knew I was going to be very emotional if I went to the conference,' she admits. 'That's how I felt. I couldn't go because I couldn't find the right words to speak.' Tracey explains how far Mahesh and Usha Patel went to help her when she needed employment the most.

'When my children were born,' she says, 'I brought them to work. Even on weekends. Because I love my job and I couldn't stay away. I had no babysitter, so I had to bring the little ones.'

Monday, 21 November 2022: 2.43 p.m.

Sir Mahesh Patel walks into the CPL head office in the city suburb of Hohola North. A large dark-blue CPL banner on the wall reads: Stay Fit. Mahesh opens a door and sticks his head into a meeting that is already in progress. CEO Navin Raju and other staff are seated with supplier representatives.

'They've come here to take money from us?' Mahesh asks. 'That's no good.' Everyone in the meeting room laughs. He continues, 'Are they going to produce that Pride of PNG Awards video?'

'Yes.'

'All right, see you.' Mahesh starts to close the door, then opens it ajar again. 'Hey Navin, be hard on them. Get a sharp razor blade.' Everyone in the meeting room laughs once more.

Mahesh tours around the two-storey office building. CPL staff are busy at their work desks, all wearing their blue company shirts. A staff member shows Mahesh today's newspaper story on the Pride of PNG Awards. A full page is headlined: 'CPL champions PNG Women'. There are three photos of the award winners being presented by Mahesh and the Governor-General. Mahesh holds up the newspaper for a few seconds and a proud smile washes across his face. A simple idea he had, which benefits so many, has become reality.

Mahesh walks to the rear of the upstairs area where all the tech server rooms are located.

'You can see how crushed we are,' he remarks. 'This is literally the nerve centre here.' He then heads down a separate wooden staircase to the rear warehouse area.

'The plan is to clear all this up and start the renovation from here,' he explains. 'We are going to make it an open-plan office area. Bring the new wall back here.'

Walking out to the loading dock area, four staff are putting together the Christmas signage displays for Stop & Shop stores. There is a narrow driveway to get trucks in for loading and unloading. Mahesh recalls this smaller warehouse area was overflowing after the 2017 warehouse fire.

'It was crazy,' he says. 'We had stuff everywhere. We had to rent four or five other places to house everything.'

He then has another memory from his early days in this building, which they first used as an office-warehouse in 1989.

'I remember telling Usha,' he says, 'when we were much smaller. I used to work late at night in the office by myself, and it felt a bit creepy because it was all pitch-dark here.'

Tuesday, 22 November 2022: 8.15 a.m.

The morning traffic in Port Moresby is busier than usual. Sir Mahesh Patel urges his driver Joe Pato to find another route.

'There must be an accident,' notes Mahesh. 'Everyone is trying to turn.'

The attentive driver finds a way out of the mess and the white CPL car finds a moving lane.

'I have got a bit of catching up planned on emails,' says Mahesh, sitting in the back seat. 'After last week, there is a backlog.' Mahesh laughs to himself and adds, 'Well, I am retired, right?'

Anyone who sees what he accomplishes each day would not think so.

'The thing is,' explains Mahesh, 'I can make as much work as I like or as little as I like. You have to find that balance. Today, I am just trying to stay at home as much as I can and not do anything.'

Mahesh's thoughts are distracted when his mobile phone rings. Usha is calling, asking him to buy some food ingredients while he is driving around.

A friend of Mahesh and Usha's is doing a food preparation drive to help those in need.

'She feeds the poorer folks,' explains Mahesh. 'There is a religious connotation, but instead of spending their time in prayers, they go out and feed the needy. They are preparing food for 150 people. What she does is divide it among people who want to participate, who each prepare about forty packs of fried rice and other food. We also have two cartons of apples from Ajay to give away.'

Usha has asked Mahesh to get the local spinach aibika and also pumpkin.

'She also wants moringa leaves for later,' he says.

Tuesday, 22 November 2022: 9.14 a.m.

Driver Joe Pato parks the CPL vehicle outside Gordons Market. It is a busy produce market spread over two levels. The open concrete structure was rebuilt and then reopened in November 2019, with financial support from the Papua New Guinea and New Zealand governments. Many of the vendors are women, who were consulted on the new design of the market.

'This market was here in the 1980s,' recalls Mahesh, as he walks inside, 'We used to come shopping here. It was notorious for minor pickpocketing and a lot of expatriates would not come. Usha and I used to visit all the time on Saturdays.'

The market was originally a basic table-stalls markets, all one level, with no infrastructure. The local council runs the market. The stallholders pay a small fee to sell their products. Mahesh walks along the aisles and looks happy to be mingling amongst the traders and buyers.

'Look at this papaya, it is so nice,' he says. 'Virtually all of this is organic. It smells so fresh. It will never look as good visually as what's in the stores, but it is much better tasting. It is naturally sun-grown. Look at the quality of the ginger here.'

Mahesh says Usha feels comfortable coming here to shop, even by herself, 'because she has been here at the roughest times'. He stops and chats with the stall holders. There are pineapples, potatoes, cucumbers and sweet potatoes in plentiful supply.

'Look at the quality here,' says Mahesh, admiring bananas. 'Super ripe and super sweet.' Mahesh's favourite is the yellow corn.

'I'm like a kid in a candy store,' he admits. 'This corn tastes completely different to the one in Australia. Very soft. This is beautiful corn.'

Tuesday, 22 November 2022: 9:58 a.m.

Hanuabada is a coastal village on the outskirts of Port Moresby, one of the two stilt villages extant in Papua New Guinea. It is the biggest village of the indigenous Motuan tribe, and is known by its locals as HB. Sir Mahesh Patel looks out of the window intently, as driver Joe Pato drives carefully along the busy streets with many people walking in different directions.

Hanuabada means 'big village'. It has a population of over 15,000. There is also important history here. It was the site of the declaration of the Papua New Guinea protectorate by the British in 1884.

'These are the traditional landowners of this Port Moresby area,' explains Mahesh. 'Quite a few of our staff live here. A lot of people here have cars too. So, they are not all *poor* poor.'

Permanent wooden market stalls are set up on some of the streets. There are long walkways, which lead back into the village of stilt houses over the sea. The people have built a large church too.

Mahesh had a staff member with an accommodation crisis who was sleeping on the balcony of a relative's home in Hanuabada.

'But when he came to work,' recalls Mahesh, 'he was so well turned out, ready for duty.'

Home affordability in Papua New Guinea is a problem and Mahesh does not hold back in blaming the governments over the years.

'We have so many natural resources here and so much money,' he says. 'Yet, it is like the Aboriginal communities in Australia's rural areas. Australia is so mineral rich. But both the governments just cannot get their acts together to sort it out.'

Mahesh longs for the days when governments can help the people who most need it by acting effectively and quickly.

'I wish,' he says, 'that the government would stop talking big and start delivering. Work with the private sector, rather than running conferences and workshops, and writing reports that have little outcome. There are some positive sides to what they have done, but the government needs to play a bigger part in fixing the problems here.'

It is a direct hit at elected officials, but Mahesh does not care whom he offends. He just wants the best for all Papua New Guineans.

'I'm a citizen now, so they can't kick me out,' he points out.

Chapter 21

Fate and Karma

When you analyse the lives of most people from anywhere in the world, it is usually possible to pinpoint a specific event which changed the course of their life. These changes can be controlled by the person themselves or by the actions of others. But sometimes, whether by the greater design of a higher power, sheer coincidence, or just good or bad luck, the course of a life can be changed dramatically by a single event.

The film *Sliding Doors* by writer–director Peter Howitt popularized the term in reference to how a choice or happening can have a profound, lasting impact. The film analyses the alternate possibilities of either catching or missing a train – the sliding doors reference.

Sir Mahesh Patel seems to have a number of these sliding door moments in his life. They started before he was even born.

- His parents Maganbhai and Savitaben making the decision to travel from India to Fiji to live.
- His split-second decision to answer 'pharmacy', when his father asked him what he was going to study at university in New Zealand.
- Failing his pharmacy exams in 1980, meaning he had to repeat a year and thus delay his graduation.

- The head pharmacist at his internship in New Zealand showing him the newspaper advertisement for a pharmacy position in Papua New Guinea.
- Pursuing the possibility of opening his own pharmacy in Port Moresby rather than just working out his contract and returning to Fiji.
- Mahesh's sister Taru's random meeting with Mahesh's future wife Usha Patel in Gujarat.
- The decision to move from Australia to India to start a new business.
- The last-minute decision from a chance meeting, to make an offer to purchase the Stop & Shop supermarket chain.

Were these all just random events?

By changing any one of these, the life of Sir Mahesh Patel would not be the same.

'I always say, there is fate and there is karma,' he says. 'It was probably meant to happen.'

What was it that compelled Usha to decide to go and live in Papua New Guinea with a man who she had only met in person for a few weeks?

'A very complex question to answer,' she says. 'But in this situation, I just followed my inner guidance with my mum's help. The decision was made easier for the fact that Mahesh was, and still is, a kind, charismatic and very easy person to love. We just clicked. I had a bit of control in that I didn't have to go to PNG. My dad didn't want me to go. Mum has always been the brave one. Mum had a comfort level about it, as my aunt had told my mum that Mahesh was from a good family. I wasn't going to marry him blindly without checking out PNG, as I have explained before. It was really on my terms. Then the responsibility is purely mine.'

After spending four weeks in Port Moresby, Usha went back home to the United Kingdom for Christmas and then decided to return to marry Mahesh.

Mahesh must have made quite a first impression to engender such a decision?

'Yeah, he did,' Usha smiles.

'Well, I did have hair and a moustache back then,' laughs Mahesh.

Even sons Nikhil and Ajay find it hard to comprehend the enormity of the decision their mother made.

'That is definitely a question which I have asked Mum,' says Ajay. 'There were times where she has had a glass of wine, and I have asked, hey Mum, what's the real reason? What was actually happening? She gives you the same answer.'

'Usha thought we were living in grass huts,' smiles Mahesh.

'I went there to see what it was like,' Usha admits. 'It was curiosity. Why would somebody go out there? I have since learned that Papua New Guinea is a unique country, complex and multifaceted. But like anywhere else in the world, all people want is a secure roof over their heads and food on their table. Throw in good education and healthcare systems, then everyone truly thrives. I am grateful to PNG for the opportunity to learn and grow to be a better person.'

Usha also says that meeting Mahesh's sister Taru beforehand, also gave her confidence in his upbringing.

One of the business decisions Mahesh Patel made which significantly altered the direction and growth of the City Pharmacy business, was the acquisition of the Stop & Shop supermarket chain from Steamships Trading Company in 2005. But that also came from a random event.

The meeting between Mahesh and John Dunlop in an airport lounge in Fiji was not planned.

'It is all about fate,' agrees Mahesh. 'If I had not run into John at the airport in Fiji, Stop & Shop would not have been part of the CPL Group today.'

The change was not just about the future growth of CPL. Another company, also had interest in purchasing Stop & Shop.

'They were quite disappointed that Steamships did not go ahead with them,' explains Mahesh. 'But if they had taken over instead, all of the CPL pharmacies in Stop & Shop would have been removed. They would have installed their own pharmacies. I am not sure how we would have succeeded and got where we are today, if that had happened. That was the bulk of our business at that time.'

Asked to explain the fortunate timing of his meeting with John Dunlop, Mahesh simply replies, 'It is always about being in the right place at the right time.'

Prior to 2005, Mahesh had not given any thought to the purchase of Stop & Shop, mainly because he never considered Steamships would ever sell it. But covering the potential loss of their pharmacy sites inside the supermarkets was a huge strategic masterstroke.

'It was partly defensive as well,' agrees Mahesh. 'It wasn't just to say, let's go into supermarkets. At that point in time, we didn't have many pharmacies outside of Port Moresby. We had a sprinkling of them. The bulk of the turnover came from Port Moresby and the bulk of that came from pharmacies within the supermarkets. Today it is diversified, because we have a lot of shops outside the main city. But at that point of time, in 2005, it was a huge risk for us. We would have really shrunk down to one or two shops.'

Even the actual decision by Mahesh to make an offer for Stop & Shop was an immediate impulsive decision without prior research.

'It was a risk,' he says, 'because I had put in a bid, albeit a non-binding one. Then I had to ring the bank and explain why they should support us. It was just that it's my nature; I believe in myself. I'm going to dive in. A lot of people would have said, let's do a feasibility study, let's check this. I just said, let's *do* it.'

The other major business event which changed the course of his life was the warehouse fire in Gerehu in 2017. At the time, Mahesh was thinking about pulling back from his active role in Papua New Guinea, perhaps even retiring.

Looking back at it all now, their second major company fire was a significant turning point in the life of Sir Mahesh Patel. As devastating as it was at the time, the long-term outcome has been his reconnection with Papua New Guinea, its people and his great love of helping others.

'It's interesting, like fate,' Mahesh concedes. 'In 2016, I was close to retiring. Then we had the fire in 2017, which forced me back. That's what really got me back, involved deeply with the business again. I was wondering, if that fire had not happened, maybe my life would be different today? It was life-changing for me, because we went more into local farming, more into the local people, and revamped the whole of our community service. Maybe it was a job half done when I was thinking of retiring. If you believe in fate and karma, somebody up there said, your job's not done, and there's going to be a life-changing moment to bring you back. Because I wouldn't have gone back for the length of time I did. Then COVID-19 hit, so we were there for two years straight. Those years, as Usha has reminded me, in the thirty years we have been married, is the longest non-stop time we have spent together. It has given us a different perspective on life and companionship.'

Despite the hardship for many at the time, the fire led to a new warehouse. It kept Mahesh in Papua New Guinea and resulted in him expanding his charity works via the CPL Foundation. This ultimately led to his knighthood nomination.

'The nomination was done in 2019,' says Mahesh, 'so if I had not been there in Papua New Guinea doing all this new work with the CPL Foundation, people would not have seen me and what we have been doing for the community.'

It is therefore appropriate to ask: if Mahesh's sliding doors had closed and he had retired in 2017, what would he have been doing instead. Would he have simply been spending more time on the golf course?

'No, that wouldn't have been it,' he smiles. 'I was searching for ideas and I spoke to a lot of people—psychologists, consultants, people in family businesses. I was talking to as many people as I could, and then I finally said to myself, if I keep thinking about what I am going to do when I retire, I'll never retire. So, I was going to retire and then figure out what I am going to do. I was on the verge of that, and then the fire ocurred.'

Even the timing of the knighting of Sir Mahesh Patel by then-Prince Charles was fortunate. While he received the honour notification from Queen Elizabeth II in 2020, the actual ceremony itself was delayed due to the COVID-19 pandemic. This allowed Mahesh and Usha to travel to England and experience the investiture during the Queen's Golden Jubilee celebrations.

'The weather wasn't too bad where we were,' said Usha. 'It was very pleasant. The kids were out playing, cycling. It was such a good atmosphere.'

Being amongst the English people as they celebrated their beloved monarch is an experience Usha and Mahesh will never forget.

'It was great to see the camaraderie amongst all of the English people,' says Usha. 'It's quite jovial and good to see. After COVID-19 and all the problems, so much gloom and doom, it was so nice to see the happy atmosphere during the Queen's Golden jubilee celebrations.'

No matter what happens in the life of Sir Mahesh Patel, he finds a way to make things better. Perhaps it is just the way he thinks about life.

'There have been people,' he says, 'who have written books about the power of positive thinking. When you are doing it, I don't suppose you are thinking about it. It is just the challenge. I actually work better in a crisis situation. Which is good, but it is not great, because you need a crisis to excel. It seems to suit me.'

Maybe Mahesh Patel's life has been scripted by a higher power. When you consider all the amazing events, it really does seem more like a movie than real life. Perhaps in an alternative reality, he could have been a Hollywood actor with his own *Sliding Doors* movie.

'Papua New Guinea. It is the country which gave him a break,' says Mahesh's friend, Gareth Joseph. 'He came from a family which had established a business in Ba. He was being cavalier, I suppose. He was going out to find his own way and do his own thing. He wanted to be the vanguard in the new chapter of his life. PNG gave him that opportunity. A lot of people went to PNG looking for something. Actor Errol Flynn went to PNG in the 1920s looking for a gold mine. Mahesh could be a swashbuckler like Errol Flynn. He is not a pirate, but a swashbuckler. Errol Flynn was looking for a gold mine and he left. Mahesh found a gold mine and he stayed. He added some gold mines to his belt and made sure many people benefitted from it.'

Chapter 22

Tomorrow

There is an old saying that tomorrow never comes. But for Sir Mahesh Patel, it has already arrived. When you have achieved all your life goals, what exactly do you do with your time? How do you reset and have something to get up for in the morning each day, to work passionately towards? For someone who has always had so much energy for life, it is not easy.

'People say, live for the day,' he says, 'because you don't know what is going to happen tomorrow. I'm saying, *well you should actually believe in it or you don't*. If it is there to be done, and you can afford to do it and have the time to do it, and if it's not going to hurt anybody, then do it. Obviously, when you are married, you have to factor in your family. Now the kids have gone, so only Usha is around. She has been the most understanding. Ninety-nine per cent of other women would have walked away. She gets frustrated, but she's very tolerant. Because she recognizes the fact that we are ying and yang. She would rather stay home and read a book.'

Further, age and physical limitations are important considerations for Sir Mahesh as he continues his path in life. He has always pushed himself to the extremes in terms of extracting the most from every minute of the day. How will he handle not being able to maintain the same pace?

'Yes, that is where I start getting into a bit of an issue with Usha,' he concedes. 'I'm always doing something. I arrive in the country and I'm already saying, *We'll do lunch here*. I think I constantly want to do things. Apart from the business side, I love travelling, going out, doing things. I'm already thinking, *What can we do*. I'm already planning to go to the next rugby World Cup. When you have itchy feet, you've got to do things. I'm enjoying it, absolutely. But the concern is as you get older, you're thinking, what happens when you can't do it physically or mentally?'

Whatever Mahesh does do in the future, it will be less and less about business and more about charity support and the CPL Foundation.

'I've got to keep stopping myself from trying to do new things,' he says. 'I've been coming to a natural conclusion that I don't really want to do new business. That's the focus. Now the challenge is on the community service side: *Can we make an impact?* I have been working on a new programme about family planning that we are looking at launching in Papua New Guinea. I am again diving into it. I try to come up with ideas and then get a team together to work on it.'

Sir Mahesh is still on the board of directors for the CPL Group and there is no timetable currently for his resignation. But as the company founder, whenever he is in the office, the CEO and senior management consult him on things, so it will be hard for him to ever fully extract himself from the business.

'When he gets in the room, he just can't help himself,' says Caleb Jarvis. 'He has got no official title, but he is literally in there, still directing traffic. He has got all that experience, and he is not alone. This is a well-worn path for very successful entrepreneurs. Struggling to step right out of the business because they are so expert. They built it.'

Perhaps there is a compromise for Mahesh between business and the Foundation, which seems to be currently in place.

'The first thing you do when you ring Mahesh is ask him where the hell he is,' says Neville Barrett. 'He could be anywhere in the world. He said, "I've had enough on the business end. I've appointed a new CEO and I'm going to retire." Get stuffed! He will never retire. What his ambition is to do now, and I can see his perfect world, he wants a CEO he can trust. The CEO has to be really intelligent and has to take on making those decisions which are just second nature to Mahesh. He wants to get someone to run the business to his standards. He wants that to happen so he can still be in Papua New Guinea and do whatever he has got the inspiration for, to do things with his Foundation and charity work. I am so impressed how he has gone more and more into that.'

But outwardly, Sir Mahesh seems to be purely focused on his charity work.

'The next journey of my life is the Foundation,' he reassures, 'and ramping up all the social work I am doing. It is just again starting now. A new leaf in life after the pandemic. We have been doing all these bits and pieces. Now we are taking on some big projects. That is what was planned. *How do we save the world? How do we empower girls and women in Papua New Guinea?* Now, that is the biggest challenge in life. As somebody said, it is not about making, it is about giving now.'

Those closest to Mahesh do not see him ever fully retiring in the normal sense of the word.

'Bullshit!' laughs CPL Group chair, Stanley Joyce. 'Mahesh has always had a vision, and I think the last thing he wanted to do was die as a frustrated store manager. But he wants to create the Foundation which goes on and does more of that work. He has always had a belief in that. Now he can do anything he wants to. Before, he had to do things. He wants to help people and if you walk around this place, there are a lot of people to help.'

'Mahesh will just get more involved in his Foundation and charity work,' agrees Jagdish Patel. 'It shows his commitment. He will spend time and provide the leadership. He will do community service and other things to help the people. That, and he will keep travelling around.'

'I think he will always be doing something,' says Nikhil Patel. 'We have always known that his version of retiring is redefining what retirement is. Create a new word for it. When we say retirement with regard to him, we need to redefine what that word means. So, retirement on his terms, I guess. Always working, but working with a little bit more relaxed and chilled-out nature.'

'Retirement? No. It would drive him nuts,' asserts Antoinette Amputch. 'I think the moment you stop, that is when you get old.

I don't think he has that fear of getting old. His attitude to life is very different. He has a good one and it is unconditional—apart from these little negative things that come out of him, and then you have to shove him along. It is usually when he is stressed. His idea of retiring is not that you are going to stop work; to him it just means you are not going to be in the office every day, working nine to five. For him, retiring doesn't mean stop everything. No. His idea of retiring, I would imagine, is very different. He will still be doing many things.'

'He talks about retiring, but I say, what's retirement?' says Vani Nades. 'Mahesh is still driving change and doing all these things he loves doing, and that's keeping him going. It's fun, so he is not going to retire. He talks about retirement and I tell him he is not going to step away from something that he loves. He will still find something that he will continue to do. Especially the work at his Foundation, which he enjoys all the time. He enjoys mentoring and he enjoys travelling.'

Daksesh Patel suggests that Mahesh has slowly been evolving as a person, which has affected what he will do in his later years.

'I think he is becoming more spiritual,' he observes. 'He is also becoming far more conscious of his extravagance. He is less extravagant nowadays. He will take public transport. He has got that edge off driving the sportscar. Maybe that is because he had the hard landing again with the warehouse fire. There is a bit more respect for his resources. I think he is determined to make a difference. It will become his way of life. He is devoted to his charity work and he will continue doing that.'

Asked about his wife's future goals, Mahesh knows exactly what Usha wants.

'It's about her own personal development,' he replies. 'She is very spiritual about life and finding things internally. To her credit, Usha is somewhat of a healer. She solves a lot of people's problems. She helps people. People like talking to her amongst her group of friends and community. She's got that foresight and a much more deeper and sensitive thought process. Whereas they come to me and I say, "Go and have a glass of Scotch and move on with life." That's the complete ying and yang of us.'

'I don't have a to-do list,' reveals Usha, 'but if something opens up for me, I'll go there.' Which prompts the question of where Mahesh and Usha will have their primary residence.

'Usha's reply would be, *Wherever the boys are*,' says Mahesh. 'She would love to spend more time together living close by as a family. But the million-dollar question I ask is, *Where do you find us all finally settling down?*'

For Usha, becoming a grandmother one day is something she would welcome.

'Obviously, it would be great,' she admits. 'But I want Nikhil and Ajay to be happy first and have a stable environment to bring kids into.'

There is some hope in Mahesh's mind that both his sons will live close to him and Usha again one day.

'If Nikhil and Ajay came back to Sydney to live,' says Usha, 'I'd be quite happy. But let it go with the flow, I say. They have to find their own path.'

For now, Nikhil Patel seems entrenched in New York with his work, but he does not rule out a return to Sydney one day in the future.

'I've bounced around between cities and work,' he says, 'and New York is the one city that's really stuck with me. It feels like home, honestly. I've become very comfortable here— definitely, the next four or five years. I think when I have kids, that [return to Sydney] will always be in the back of my mind. That would be the trigger point. When kids start school at a serious level. As a child especially, I think you can't beat Australia. Once I'm settling down a bit more. At least in my late thirties to forty. Yeah, I'll consider it. Sydney is always the real home. But for now, this is better.'

For Ajay Patel, his career and life paths do seem unclear at present.

'I have dreams,' he says. 'I have certain things that I think could be, depending on how you look at them. Some could be childish. Some could be pie in the sky sorts of things. There is still a fair bit of work I know I need to do here in PNG and I think I have got a reasonable idea of how I want my life to run over the next few decades. Because I know I have got enough to start a few businesses here and there and get them flowing, like I have done here. I think I might try and do that in a few other countries.'

It seems for the time being at least, the four-member Patel family will be separated around the globe and have to be content with short visits.

Mahesh Patel enjoys having people around him and is never the sort to sit alone for too long. It is another reason he is constantly on the move, seeking new adventures.

'When I'm home alone, I'm a miserable guy,' he reveals. 'I'm a people person. I always want people around me. But it doesn't quite suit everybody all the time. Usha wants her own space and is happy with it. I suppose that is why we work out well as a team. We're not at loggerheads all the time.'

It was suggested to Mahesh that his life today is regularly spent flying around the world simply holding meetings with people.

'Yeah, I don't mind it at all,' he laughs. 'I think it has become a permanent thing.'

Sons Nikhil and Ajay can see the changes their father has made in his life, slowly removing himself from the day-to-day functioning of the CPL Group.

'He has always got something going on,' says Nikhil. 'He's not ever going to change. But he's toned it down now that he is not running the business full time. He's never yelled and screamed, but there used to be a lot more phone calls. He would say to me, *You have to have a different mindset for each task*. That energy has always been within him. But he has slowed down a bit now, compared to the earlier years. So long as he is happy and not pushing himself too much.'

'There are corners that used to be razor-sharp,' observes Ajay, 'which will slowly soften over time. Rounder edges, I guess, which would be a nice way to put it. Which would be good. It needs to happen. The Decelerate Course he did was quite an impactful time for him. I think that, and a couple of things that Mum introduced him to, around yoga and breathing. Because he has that manic energy.'

Antoinette Amputch says Mahesh's life is not about making money now, 'He has been there and done that,' she says. 'He has put himself in that position absolutely, everything is unconditional and now he has the privilege to be able to give back, and it is always an honour to give back.'

Public success has given Sir Mahesh Patel another tool in his kit to further help the people who need it the most.

'I have always leveraged my success to tap into other people,' Mahesh explains. 'If it helps the CPL Foundation, I am not afraid to ask. If you don't ask, you'll never know. In my experience, there are people wanting to help, if there are reputable organizations and people behind it.'

Mahesh will continue to enjoy each day in the future and respond to things that he comes across in his travels.

'I just live for the day,' he says. 'I don't feel that if I drop off tomorrow, I have anything that I have not done. My main worry is, *have this fixed, have that done*, with the current projects. In a business sense, there are things I keep reminding myself not to do, because that will distract me.'

Mahesh sees no change to this routine. There is no retirement date. No cutoff point where he will step back and simply do nothing.

'I can't see it,' he says. 'Because there will always be somebody out there who needs help. We can contribute back. Because, as they say, *you are not going to take it to the grave*. So, if you can make a change to help others, why not?'

Chapter 23

The Ganges

Sir Mahesh Patel wanted to do something special to celebrate his thirty-fifth wedding anniversary with his wife, Lady Usha Patel. A trip to India was an easy sell to his bride.

'India is part of who we are,' says Usha.

Ten years ago, in 2013, Mahesh and Usha Patel had celebrated their twenty-fifth wedding anniversary in Rishikesh.

'We did not have a proper ceremony when we got married,' Mahesh explains. 'Not a proper traditional Indian wedding. In 2013, we had a proper traditional Indian wedding where you take your seven vows around the fire.'

The seven vows are taken together by the bride and the groom as they do the 'Saat Pherey' (seven circuits) around the sacred fire representing Agni Dev (the god of fire), taking him as a witness to their marriage. This is called Agni Sakshi (fire witness). The groom leads his bride while doing the first four pheras, while the bride leads her husband during the remaining three pheras.

These seven vows include praying for material and spiritual care and support for each other, protection and fidelity, prosperity, strength of family and dutiful progeny, cherishing and honouring each other, health and peace, and love and friendship forever.

'Our beginnings are so humble that we still value the little things,' says Mahesh.

'I always like going to the Ganges,' says Usha. 'It is very, very peaceful there.'

Rishikesh is a town on the banks of the Ganges in the Himalayan foothills in India's northern state of Uttarakhand. The river is considered holy by Hindus, and the town is renowned as a centre for studying yoga and meditation. Temples and ashrams line the eastern bank of the Ganges. This town gained worldwide notoriety between February and April in 1968, when the iconic English rock band the Beatles studied meditation at one of those ashrams.

The couple would stay at the magnificent property owned by close friend Mira Kulkarni, on the banks of the sacred Ganges River.

Mahesh Patel had everything arranged from Sydney. Samrath Bedi and his wife Karishma had helped with the celebration plans in Rishikesh.

'They would organize something special for dinner,' says Mahesh. 'Rishikesh is quite a spiritual place. It is a beautiful location. Usha really likes going there. It is serene. When you are there, you hear the river rushing. When you go to sleep at night, you can hear it. She is probably expecting that we will do something, but she hasn't mentioned it or asked about it.'

While Usha Patel is not materialistic in any way, Mahesh wanted something special to give to her as a gift to highlight the importance of the day. Karishma sourced three pairs of earrings from a family jeweller for Mahesh to select from. He chose a stunning red pair.

'Through all our travels,' explains Karishma, 'I have had the chance to observe what Usha likes. Things that are beautiful but understated, classic and yet unusual. Nothing too flashy but discreet. It's a lot like what I like too, so this was very easy.'

On Valentine's Day, 14 February 2023, Mahesh and Usha boarded a flight in Sydney heading to India.

'Usha said to me,' Mahesh says, smiling, 'I am going to take you to India for Valentine's Day. I said, I'll buy you lunch on the aircraft.'

On arrival, the couple spent two days in Delhi with Samrath and Karishma. They then travelled to Gujarat to visit Mahesh's niece,

Dr Shetal Desai and her husband Dr Tushar Desai, arriving in Rishikesh on 19 February.

Samrath and Karishma gave Mahesh and Usha a gift of replicas of the sandals that Gandhi used to wear. Mira Kulkarni gave them a statue of Ganesha, the widely beloved, plump, elephant-headed god of auspicious beginnings, good fortune and well-being.

On the day of the wedding anniversary, at 11.30 a.m., Mahesh and Usha visited the small temple on the property with Samrath and Karishma. It was decorated beautifully with flowers.

A local Hindu priest who visits for daily prayers, conducted the ceremony.

'It was an old traditional ceremony,' says Usha, 'to do with the marriage, the continuation of it and blessings.'

'It went for over an hour,' notes Mahesh.

'They go through the ancient sacred rituals to do with the blessings,' continues Usha. 'The priest does them in Hindi or Sanskrit. I didn't understand a lot of it. But the energy behind it—you feel it. It is hard to explain.'

The priest put red-and-white hand-spun cotton threads around everyone's wrists as a blessing—left hand for women and right for men. Traditionally, you do not remove them and they fall off over time.

The final part of the ceremony involved just the priest, Mahesh, and Usha.

'They light a fire and as the priest says the shlokas,' explains Usha, 'we put some samagri in the fire as part of a cleansing ceremony. We repeat the final word at the end as if we have said the whole thing.'

Shloka, meaning song, is a poetic form used in Sanskrit.

While they had a traditional wedding ceremony thirty-five years ago, this time it was more of a blessing ceremony.

'It is about continuity of the marriage,' says Usha. 'I felt cleansed. I always do. There are no short cuts to these things. They are ancient traditions.'

'It was very special and went off very well,' says Samrath. 'It was our local priest and just the four of us. The priest remarried them again in a shorter ceremony and it was just a lovely way of reiterating their relationship. Both Karishma and I felt blessed to be a part of it. This kind of event perfectly encapsulates Mahesh and Usha, and who they are.'

Mahesh gifted the earrings to Usha when they went back to their room after the ceremony. She wore them during dinner later that night.

'I like them very much,' says Usha. 'I wasn't expecting anything. But that was a nice surprise. I did appreciate it. Mahesh always has good taste. For me, it was nice just being out in a place like that. It is pretty special. Not many people get to do what we do. Our gratitude is in that, actually.'

'Usha knew we would be doing a prayer,' said Mahesh. 'After thirty-five years, she's probably worked me out by now.'

The next day, they did some trekking in the nearby mountains and valleys.

'It was beautiful weather,' reports Mahesh. 'Cool in the evenings and mornings—down to around 16 degrees Celsius, then during the day, rising up to 24 degrees.' The day after, they did some white-water rafting on the Ganges.

'The water was fast,' enthuses Mahesh, 'but the level wasn't too high. When the snow starts melting up in the Himalayas, the water level starts rising, and when the monsoon comes, it goes really high—it's dangerous. They don't do rafting during the monsoon.'

Usha put her feet in the river.

'We all felt pretty blessed and purified,' says Usha. 'Belief is a powerful thing. You believe the water is cleansing and it becomes so.'

'Going to Rishikesh is always calming,' says Mahesh. 'You can hear the Ganges River any time of the day. Going up into the mountains, the air is so clean. You can see the stars and blue skies. That is relaxing and we enjoyed great trekking.'

Mahesh and Usha enjoyed their short trip. More importantly, it made them both appreciate what they had in life, in each other, and a reminder of how far they had come.

'India is my motherland after all,' says Usha. 'I always think about my ancestors and how they lived before and how we got to be where we are. When I go there, it makes me think how blessed I am. We must be receiving their blessings in one way or another. It is something which is part of you. Wherever I am, I am Indian at heart. I may think in a different way, but India is always in my heart.'

'When we went back to my dad's village one time,' recalls Mahesh, 'I thought, if he hadn't made the move, we would have been living there as farmers. Then, when my family had a dispute in Fiji, my dad was going to send us all back to Gujarat with Mum, but she stood her ground and said, unless we all go, I am not going. Life could have been a lot different.'

'In Gujarat,' adds Usha, 'I think about my great great grandfather's sacrifice in moving out to Africa and what they went through. They were the brave ones. Mahesh's mum at the age of seventeen, got married, still a child, and went to Fiji. How did they do all that? You have got to admire their bravery.'

Thinking of their marriage, Usha seems happy that everything has worked out so well with Mahesh.

'There have been pluses and minuses along the way,' she says. 'But more pluses, so you plod on. No life is perfect, right? No life is perfect no matter what anyone tells me, and money isn't everything.'

Usha only had one minor complaint about this visit.

'Next time,' she says, 'I'd like to extend the trip to India, so we can sit down and smell the roses.'

Epilogue

Australian Prime Minister Anthony Albanese undertook a two-day visit to Papua New Guinea on 12 and 13 January 2023. He joined Prime Minister James Marape for their first Papua New Guinea–Australia Annual Leaders' Dialogue in Port Moresby. The visit was an opportunity to strengthen the close partnership between the two countries, based on high levels of economic and security cooperation, shared interests and strong cultural, sporting, church and labour mobility links.

The prime ministers agreed to a Joint Statement of Commitment to negotiate a Bilateral Security Treaty, which will expand the existing defence relationship and intensify bilateral cooperation on policing, law and justice. The leaders also discussed boosting business ties, trade and investment between the two countries, and agreed to work together on developing potential new trade arrangements and expanding PNG's agricultural production.

Of most interest to Sir Mahesh Patel was: Australia reaffirmed its commitment to support Papua New Guinea to expand women's leadership and equality with the announcement of a new five-year programme, PNG Women Lead.

Sir Mahesh had the opportunity to meet Prime Minister Albanese at a state dinner at Federal Parliament, and was encouraged by what he heard.

'I think his body language,' observes Mahesh, 'and mannerism were probably the most positive and genuine I have seen of many Australian PMs, over the years. I feel positive, but time will tell.'

During the visit, Mahesh also raised some of his concerns, about the appropriation of Australian support funding, with diplomats visiting with the prime minister.

'Something must have stuck,' he notes, 'as at the end of the dinner, one of the protocol officers enquired if I would be available in March, when a high-powered delegation will be visiting.'

Ajay Patel was also invited to the state dinner and enjoyed seeing the two countries' political leaders up close.

'An incredible experience,' he says. 'Most people do not have these sorts of opportunities. I was introduced to Prime Minister Albanese and shook his hand. Those sorts of things are amazing.'

'I think there will be a better connection between Australia and Papua New Guinea,' Mahesh continues. 'Albanese's character, he is more of a humble, down-to-earth person. There was a warm and fuzzy feeling for me. It sounded genuine. Now what happens is the next thing. They'll have to walk the talk.'

The strategic location of Papua New Guinea in the Pacific makes it an appealing ally for Australia, China and India.

On 22 May 2023, Indian Prime Minister Narendra Modi travelled to Papua New Guinea for the Forum for India–Pacific Islands Cooperation summit. It brought together fourteen Pacific Islands—Cook Islands, Fiji, Kiribati, Marshall Islands, Micronesia, Nauru, Niue, Samoa, Solomon Islands, Palau, Papua New Guinea, Tonga, Tuvalu and Vanuatu along with India.

'There is a keen interest in Papua New Guinea developing among political leaders, including those from India,' observes Mahesh.

In April 2023, Mahesh and Usha travelled to India again, visiting Delhi and Rishikesh. They then travelled to the north of India and explored Ladakh for nine days.

Ladakh, earlier a part of Jammu and Kashmir, became a union territory of India in 2019. Since 1947, the area has been the subject of dispute between India, Pakistan and China. Ladakh is bordered by Tibet to the east, the Indian state of Himachal Pradesh to the south, both the Indian-administered union territory of Jammu and Kashmir and the Pakistan-administered Gilgit-Baltistan to the west, and the southwest corner of Xinjiang across the Karakoram Pass in the far north. The high-altitude area extends from the Siachen Glacier in the Karakoram range to the north to the main Great Himalayas in the south. Leh is the largest city and the joint capital of Ladakh, along with Kargil, which was made winter capital in 2019.

'It is very taxing on your lungs,' reports Mahesh. 'Even though the air temperatures were negative, that became a secondary concern. Oxygen became the primary issue.'

'Also, being there in winter,' observes Usha, 'there is no greenery and that is where we get our oxygen from. So, the oxygen levels were even lower. It is amazing how the people get used to it. It is a harsh land to live in.'

The region is home to around 300,000 civilians and a large deployment of military personnel.

'It was quite enlightening to see people's humbleness,' says Mahesh. 'The remoteness and the happiness they have got. It touched us.'

'There were a lot of monasteries,' continues Mahesh. 'We went to two of them. It was so calming.'

'Buddhism is a way of life and they actually live that,' notes Usha. 'Even though you have that strong military presence there, you don't feel it as being ominous. I hope that India looks after the people there, because they are such a special group of people. I just loved being there.'

The couple had flown from Delhi to Leh. It was then a five-hour drive to the camp where they stayed for two nights. There were six families living nearby, who were beginning to farm their land for new crops of potatoes, barley and mustard.

'The best part for me,' says Usha, 'was they have their animals to till the land and they sing to them, so they don't get tired. It was so nice. I was mesmerized. How nice it is that they treat their animals like that.'

Mahesh and Usha love to visit new areas far away from the glitz and glamour.

'Wherever I go,' explains Usha, 'it is always what the people are about. People make any place; let's face it. That's what I tap into. Food isn't a big thing for me because I am a vegetarian. People are what I hone in on. I like going to places where people don't usually get to go. I don't want to see the touristy part.'

During the second day of their time in Ladakh, they had been driven one hour from their camp and then trekked for two hours into the mountains where they met a nomadic woman.

'This lady was really struggling, walking along,' says Mahesh, 'so we stopped her to say, hello. Our guide said she was seventy-seven years of age.'

'She looked so beautiful,' observes Usha, 'and she reminded me of my mum, so we asked could we take a photo with her.'

The couple noticed her eyes were watering in the glare of the sun and were told that she had undergone a cataract operation. Usha was wearing an expensive pair of sunglasses and immediately gestured for the woman to try them on.

'We told her to keep the glasses,' says Mahesh, 'but she didn't want to take them. We asked the guide to talk to her in the local language, asking that she promise to wear the sunglasses every day when she is walking in the sunny areas. She reluctantly kept them.'

When asked why she was so insistent in giving her sunglasses away, Usha replies, 'When you rely on your materialism, you disconnect from your humanness.'

In May 2023, Sir Mahesh Patel and his sons Nikhil and Ajay travelled to Necker Island in the British Virgin Islands, just north of Virgin Gorda. The 30-hectare island is a private paradise owned by British billionaire Sir Richard Branson, chairman of the Virgin Group.

Through an opportunity afforded by *The CEO Magazine*, in collaboration with Virgin Unite, the non-profit foundation of the Virgin Group, Mahesh was invited to attend a four-day gathering of a diverse group of speakers from 11 to 15 May 2023.

Sir Richard Branson was knighted at Buckingham Palace in March 2000, for his services to entrepreneurship. In 2007, he was placed in *Time*'s 100 Most Influential People in the World list. In June 2023, Forbes listed Branson's estimated net worth at 3 billion USD (250 billion rupees).

While the Briton's business success has been astounding, with his Virgin brand known the world over headlining many businesses, Mahesh was more interested in hearing about his substantial humanitarian work.

'It was incredible,' Mahesh says of the experience. 'It was quite awesome. Just the calibre of the people. You start your day talking about artificial intelligence and robots and end up with social networking and gender-based violence and women's rights. The visit was absolutely worth it. What you gain from there, it broadens your mind to what is happening around the world. The wide variety of people who were there was so impressive.'

To reach Necker Island, Mahesh flew from Sydney to Auckland, Auckland to Houston and then Houston to San Juan in Puerto Rico. Ajay had been visiting Nikhil in New York, and the brothers flew direct to San Juan to link up with their father.

The three stayed overnight in San Juan and then flew to Tortola, which is the largest island of the British Virgin Islands in the Caribbean. It was then a twenty-five-minute boat ride to Necker Island.

'The island is fantastic, really,' gushes Mahesh. 'It is well thought out. Sir Richard Branson has done a fantastic job. Everything is to detail. The chefs were great. The bar staff and support staff were great. The service levels were just world-class. The way they planned it all out was just very professional.'

It may have been a short visit, but just spending quality time with his sons in a unique environment made the experience even more memorable for Mahesh.

'A lot of people go there to brainstorm and get ideas,' he says. 'But it was very casual and laid back. I think Nikhil and Ajay gained a lot from it. It is now a matter of them leveraging a couple of the networks they have built, and to think about what they want to do in life as well. They heard from a whole cross-section of people who have different views on the world.'

The contrast over a matter of days between the technology of Necker Island and the basics of life in Ladakh was not lost on Mahesh.

'You start questioning your first-world material values,' he muses.

Looting and rioting broke out in Port Moresby on 10 January 2024. A protest march of approximately 200 police, military and corrections officers, irate about a reduction of 50 per cent of their weekly pay, began at Ungi Oval and proceeded to the National Parliament. After an unsatisfactory meeting with government officials, the workers immediately withdrew their services.

With the absence of police on normal duties, rioting and looting soon began in Port Moresby at around 2 p.m., before spreading to Lae, Kokopo, Goroka, Madang, Bulolo, Kavieng and Rabaul. Shops and businesses were looted and set on fire. Shots were fired and twenty-two people were later confirmed killed—fifteen in Port Moresby and seven in Lae.

Prime Minister James Marape declared a state of emergency, and the Papua New Guinea Defence Force was subsequently deployed on the streets to restore order.

In response to the police strike, the country's Internal Revenue Commission attributed the pay deductions to a computer error and denied rumours of new taxes being introduced by the government. The Prime Minister stated that the pay errors would be corrected in the next payment run.

Sir Mahesh Patel had just returned to Sydney, from a funeral in Fiji. He took the first available flight to Port Moresby. What he saw angered him greatly, telling the media it was Papua New Guinea's 'darkest day'.

The Stop & Shop supermarkets in North Waigani, Rainbow and parts of Badili were burnt to the ground. The Stop & Shop supermarket in Harbour City was looted. The Hardware Haus in North Waigani was also looted and set ablaze.

'It is disgraceful, disheartening, and shameful, and brings tears to my eyes,' lamented Mahesh.

The new CPL warehouse was undamaged, after its security team stood firm.

Mahesh's driver Joe Pato even took many of his family and friends to the CPL stores, armed with bush knives, successfully protecting some of them.

The immediate concern for Mahesh was the future of his CPL employees, a lot of whom are basic wage staff. With a timeline of many months and potentially years to reopen damaged stores, the prospect of 300 layoffs was eminent.

'I don't want to lose them,' he says, emotionally. 'We want to retain them.'

As a public company, CPL has a responsibility first to its shareholders. The business cannot be run as a charity. Further, the CPL Foundation has so many projects running, but if the main company is not making money, there will be no financial contributions to the Foundation.

'The most vulnerable people will be hurt the most,' observes Mahesh.

The day after the riots, CPL was the only retailer to reopen their undamaged stores.

'A ten-year-old boy came up to me and hugged me, thanking me,' gushes Mahesh. 'People were under pressure. They needed food. It brought me to tears. To receive thanks from a ten-year-old boy was just so heartening. That's what drives me.'

Of further concern was the immediate effect on local farmers. With the forced reduction in Stop & Shop supermarket operations, less produce would be needed.

'We just cannot keep buying the same quantities,' said Mahesh.

In the following days, Mahesh spent many hours touring around the CPL stores, surveying the damage and speaking to staff.

'One of our staff with origins from the Highlands, was at the front line,' he says, 'relaying information to the head office on what damage was being done. When I went and saw him, he broke down and started crying. He told me he needed help after what he had been through, so we organized counselling for him. For people to say they need help is admirable. We set up support sessions for all of the staff who needed them. It was traumatic for many. One of the women had called her daughter to say she was trapped inside the store and might not ever be coming home.'

But as Mahesh Patel spent more time on the ground, an uprising of positivity flowed from the community.

'The public outcry of support for CPL was amazing,' he says. 'The women's groups, the church groups and concerned citizens all came to help with the stores, clean-up. The PNG Hunters rugby league team offered to fly over to help out however they could. The many decent Papua New Guineans were just so embarrassed by what had happened.'

The insurance company is denying claims from CPL, stating that riots and civil unrest are not covered under their policy. But after past experiences, this time around, CPL debt levels were very low, putting them in a stronger position to ride out the latest storm.

Mahesh has little interest in going through the how and why of the riot, 'We can keep going on and on, but my position is to look forward,' he says.

Putting on his well-worn crisis management hat, Mahesh Patel liaised with the government to obtain funding to keep CPL staff employed and helped with licensing issues for potential new store locations.

The damage allowed CPL to do some remodelling for their business regarding the best locations to move forward with.

'The whole dynamics have changed in Port Moresby compared to how it was ten years ago,' observed Mahesh. 'It would be silly to just keep doing the same old thing.'

The riots damaged the reputation of Papua New Guinea worldwide. But Sir Mahesh Patel was heartened by the many positive outcomes, and points out that the rest of the world has its own similar problems.

'There are so many good people in Papua New Guinea,' he says, 'and yet, like other countries, a small group ruins the reputation. It gives people the opportunity to put forward misinformation that the country is not safe. We received so many positive endorsements from average Papua New Guineans.

'The problems in the Middle East and even in the USA, where so many people are shot and killed daily, are much worse than any problems we have in Papua New Guinea. There is always a criminal element in every society. You cannot brand the entire country just because of that. It was a one-day affair which became world news. Other conflicts around the world are ongoing.

'I have always been so pro-PNG. You have to weigh the positives and the negatives. Twenty-four hours after the riots, everything was back to normal. From all of my experience over the last forty years, I know the real Papua New Guinea. There are just so many more positives here, starting with its people.'

Though Sir Mahesh Patel's family origins are from Gujarat in India, he is not Mahatma Gandhi or Vallabhbhai Patel. But he channels some of the same spirit with his own devoted community service. His is a unique life. There have been faults, of course, but the overriding theme has been one of perseverance. A drive to achieve and a desire to help those less fortunate, no matter the obstacles that have been placed in front of him.

'Mahesh is a global citizen,' says Greg Wisbey. 'He had a mountain to climb to get to where he has got to. When you look at his life holistically, he has regrets about a lot of things, but it is a magical ride with a great ending.'

'Mahesh is one of a kind,' observes Daksesh Patel. 'If you take Mahesh as a package, his goodness far outweighs his weaknesses, and he has passion and vision. Any way you look at it, he is just a larger-than-life character. A man determined to take a course and finish it, always. He doesn't do anything half-heartedly when he puts his mind to it. He likes to complete it, and gives it a damn good shot. He doesn't give up easily and has strength. You have got to give it to him.'

'I got more of an education because of Mahesh and PNG,' declares Neville Barrett, 'than any university or anyone else could have given me. He is one of the most inspirational guys I have ever met. I got so much out of him and I was happy to suck it in like a sponge. He was prepared to give it and give it and give it and never stop giving it. I'm now in a different environment in Australia, where there are so many regulations. You just sit there and ask yourself, what would Mahesh do?'

'I feel very fortunate,' says Robyn Jarvis, 'that because of a vague meeting between Mahesh and Les Moore, Mahesh, Usha, Nikhil and Ajay have been part of our journey in this life, and will be into the future.'

'He is a high-energy person,' observes Ajay Patel. 'He does not sit back and relax. Go with him to an airport where there are flight delays, when it is just havoc. You will see him with a very specific energy. He absolutely hates it. He will be onto every single person trying to get things fixed. It's a control thing. He is intent on maximizing the use of every minute he has, not to waste a second.'

'A message that was told to us throughout our childhood,' recalls Nikhil Patel, 'was selfless giving. Don't expect anything back if you help someone. Even around the house, just help out. I think that was always the message. To the point that he is a man of the people, I'll tell you about this: There was a pharmaceutical distribution company, a family business in Sydney. I was talking to the founder of that business, and he said, your dad has one quality that very few people have, which is the ability to talk to anyone. No matter what level they're at. He can talk to anyone and build that connection with them.'

'Mahesh's story is one for the generations,' says Usha Patel. 'Because we are in it, we do not see the full impact of his achievements through sheer hard work and good determination. Future generations will be able to look back and see what his life was like, and it will be an inspiration. To live a life fearlessly, with courage, despite all the obstacles, it was always about doing the right thing. That power of perseverance with good intentions is a very potent combination.'

Sir Mahesh Patel sits down in his home and gives thought to his life, everything he has done and all that he has achieved.

'The journey has been amazing,' he says, emotionally. 'You sit back and think, how did we do all that? People ask me, would you do it again and I say, no. I would not do it exactly the same way because it was all spur-of-the-moment. I lived for each day and it just simply happened.'

Acknowledgments

My sincere thanks to Sir Mahesh Patel, Lady Usha Patel and their sons Nikhil and Ajay, for welcoming me into their lives and homes and trusting me to put their family history into print. Special thanks to Anil Patel, who was especially helpful with all things related to the Patel family and also Fijian history.

This book is the result of hundreds of hours of interviews, research and writing, since its beginning in January 2022. Many kind and talented people assisted along the way.

To Sachin Sharma, Rakesh Chander and Amrita Mukerji at HarperCollins *Publishers* India, thank you for this unique opportunity. I also thank company chief executive officer Ananth Padmanabhan and his dedicated team.

The invaluable manuscript editing and consultation of Hina Khajuria and Padmini Smetacek can never be truly measured. My enduring appreciation for their work.

The careful proofreading by Shreya Gupta is greatly appreciated. Typesetting was performed perfectly by Sushanta Gayen and Rajan Yadav.

Thank you to art director Mugdha Sadhwani and cover designer Rashmi Gupta for the eye-catching cover design.

Photographer John Laham (www.johnlaham.com) once again demonstrated his genius with these lovely photos of Sir Mahesh and Lady Usha on the book cover.

Greg Wisbey, Daksesh Patel, Caleb Jarvis and Jagdish Patel were always extremely helpful with information about the world of

Sir Mahesh Patel. My eternal thanks to the extraordinary Alija Dangi, who assisted with information and research on Nepal and India.

All of the CPL Group staff I came in contact with during this writing journey, both in person and via email, were especially helpful, thank you.

Samrath Bedi and Neha Gadi at Forest Essentials assisted in ensuring this book reached its best audience.

To Lamana Hotel general manager Yiannis Nicolaou and his wonderful staff in Port Moresby, thank you for taking care of me.

To everyone I interviewed for this book—over one hundred people—thank you for your time and willingness to share facts and stories. All of the information received from each one of you was invaluable in honing this story, even if some direct quotes did not make the final edit for brevity.

Writing professionally has been a cherished gift afforded to me. I value everyone who has engaged my services since I began in 1999. I have been privileged to work with and learn from esteemed American author, Thomas Hauser—boxing great Muhammad Ali's biographer—who has always been extremely generous with his time and tips. Patrick Kehoe in Canada has been an ongoing source of inspiration.

I thank my closest friends Andrew J. McGlinn and Patrick Harmer, who have always encouraged my love of writing.

I extend special thanks to: Harold Kerr, Maryann Knight, Peter Fletcher, Jenny Abraham, Andrew Goodman, Dr Judy Hyde, Grant Ovens, Eric Francis, Mario Sardelich, Jim McDonald, Neha Modi, Sandra Rossi and Catherine Tawali.

To all of my friends at Highgate in Millers Point, Sydney, thank you for your kindness and support.

To my parents, John and Ronda Upham, sister Terese Upham, brother Peter Upham (*Shire Speed and Strength* gym at Caringbah, Sydney), sister-in-law Su Upham and nephews and nieces Tiago, Sequoia, Hazlitt, Zoe, Kirk and Clare, I hope I continue to reward your faith in me.

Most importantly, to my amazing wife Angelina, our children, Giselle, Joshua, Celeste, son-in-law Jarrod, grandson Kyro and pugs Cesar and Lenny, your love and support are cherished and appreciated. None of my life's achievements would have been possible without you. Sending my everlasting love.

List of People Interviewed

Ajay Patel: second son of Mahesh Patel
Alan Jarvis: co-founder of City Pharmacy Ltd and CPL Group
Amit Patel: nephew of Mahesh Patel
Anil Patel: younger brother of Mahesh Patel
Andrew Petrie: former Lord Mayor of Woollahra and friend of Mahesh Patel
Antoinette Amputch: friend and insurance broker for CPL Group whom Mahesh Patel met in India
Betha Somare: daughter of former Papua New Guinea Prime Minister Sir Michael Somare
Bhupendra Patel: elder brother of Mahesh Patel
Bipin Patel: elder brother of Mahesh Patel
Caleb Jarvis: son of Alan and Robyn Jarvis; former City Pharmacy Ltd CEO
Daksesh Patel: cousin of Mahesh Patel
Dan Ansbaugh: American friend of Mahesh Patel
Gareth Joseph: friend of Mahesh Patel whom he met in Port Moresby
Greg Wisbey: friend of Mahesh Patel whom he met in Port Moresby
Jaive Smare: mentee of Mahesh Patel and business partner of Ajay Patel
Jagdish Patel: friend of Mahesh Patel whom he met at university in New Zealand
Jiten Patel: friend of Mahesh Patel whom he met at school in Fiji

Karishma Bedi: former Forest Essentials executive director Samrath Bedi's wife

Kusum Patel: elder sister of Mahesh Patel

Magan Patel: friend of Mahesh Patel whom he met at university in New Zealand

Manisha Patel: wife of Anil Patel; Mahesh Patel's sister-in-law

Mel Donald: friend of Mahesh Patel whom he met in Port Moresby, first customer of City Pharmacy

Mira Kulkarni: founder, chairman and managing director (CMD) of Forest Essentials

Navin Raju: former CPL Group CEO

Neville Barrett: City Pharmacy executive, born in New Zealand

Nikhil Patel: first son of Mahesh Patel

Pravin Patel: eldest brother of Mahesh Patel

Ragini Shah: younger sister of Usha Patel

Ramesh Mahtani: business associate of Mahesh Patel whom he met in Port Moresby

Ravi Singh: former CPL Group CEO

Robyn Jarvis: wife of the late Alan Jarvis and mother of Caleb Jarvis

Samrath Bedi: son of Mira Kulkarni and Forest Essentials executive director

Shefali Mehta: friend of Mahesh Patel whom he met in Port Moresby

Shetal Desai: daughter of Taraben, eldest sister of Mahesh Patel, who sadly passed away

Stephanie Copus-Campbell: on the CPL Group and CPL Foundation board of directors

Taru Patel: elder sister of Mahesh Patel, also known as Taraben

Tracey Gotele: long-serving CPL Group employee

Udhay: friend of Mahesh Patel whom he met in Singapore

Usha Patel: wife of Mahesh Patel

Vani Nades: mentoring associate of Mahesh Patel

Vasant Bhuta: friend of Mahesh Patel whom he met at university in New Zealand

Notes

Information, facts and quotes for this book have been compiled from a number of sources by the author, between January 2022 and October 2024. The majority of the quotes used have been obtained by the author, in person, during exclusive interviews.

Information and quotes have also been obtained from telephonic interviews, letters, emails, SMS texts, social media, press conferences, media press releases, public company financial reports and television broadcasts.

Other information from third parties has been referenced as follows in these chapters:

Prologue

- 'Fiji: Queen Elizabeth visits Suva 2087/70 60' 16mm LIB (1970)', Reuters' historical collection, www.britishpathe.com/asset/206003/.

Chapter 1

- G.S.P. Freeman-Grenville and Stuart C. Munro-Hay, *Historical Atlas of Islam* (Continuum International Publishing Group, 2002).
- Rajesh Rai and Peter Reeves, *The South Asian Diaspora: Transnational Networks and Changing Identities* (Routledge, 2008).

- Adrija Roychowdhury, 'How Sardar Vallabhbhai Patel, V.P. Menon and Mountbatten Unified India', *Indian Express*, 31 October 2017, www.indianexpress.com/article/research/how-vallabhbhai-patel-v-p-menon-and-mountbatten-unified-india-4915468/.
- Lyn Norvell, 'Gandhi and the Indian Women's Movement', *The British Library Journal*, vol. 23, no. 1, 1997, pp. 12–27.
- Suresh Raval, *Renunciation, Reform and Women in Swaminarayan Hinduism* (Swaminarayan Aksharpith, 2012).
- Kantilal Jinna, Anita Tanna and Sunanda Bhave, *Savita Ba: Power Personified, Devotion Incarnate* (published by the Patel family, 2018).
- Paul Knaplund, 'Sir Arthur Gordon and Fiji: Some Gordon-Gladstone Letters', *Historical Studies*: Australia and New Zealand, vol. 8, no. 31, 1958, pp. 281–296.

Chapter 2

- Kantilal, et al., *Savita Ba*, 2018.
- Meaning of Mahesh's name, www.wikipedia.org/wiki/Mahesh

Chapter 4

- The Steamships Trading Company, www.steamships.com.pg

Chapter 7

- B. Spiegelberg, T. Parratt, S.K. Dheerendra, W.S. Khan, R. Jennings and D.R. Marsh, 'Ilizarov Principles of Deformity Correction', Annals of the Royal College of Surgeons of England, 2010, pp. 101-5.
- Sinclair Dinnen, Ron May and Anthony J. Regan, *Challenging the State: The Sandline Affair in Papua New Guinea,* National Centre for Development Studies and Department of Political and Social Change, Research School of Pacific Studies, Australian National University, 1997.

- The Sandline Affair—describing a conflict in Bougainville, now officially the Autonomous Region of Bougainville—was a defining moment in the history of Papua New Guinea. The conflict over the Bougainville island's independence from Papua New Guinea, ended the government of Prime Minister Sir Julius Chan, and brought Papua New Guinea to the verge of a military revolt. The event was named after Sandline International, a United Kingdom-based private military company, who was involved in the crisis.

Chapter 8

- Forest Essentials, www.forestessentialsindia.com

Chapter 9

- CPL Group listed on the Port Moresby Stock Exchange (20 February 2002), becoming a publicly traded and owned entity. Once a privately held company is ready to become a new public entity, the formal process typically takes six months or more. The process involves investment bankers, attorneys, and accountants, who work with company management to navigate the initial public offering (IPO), www.investopedia.com.
- Post PNG is the government-owned postal service.
- IGA, Inc. is a franchised chain of grocery stores that operates in more than 41 countries. Unlike chain stores, IGA franchises are independently owned and operated.

Chapter 10

- Kokoda Track campaign, www.wikipedia.org/wiki/Kokoda_Track_campaign

Chapter 11

- Order of the British Empire, www.gov.uk/honours/types-of-honours-and-awards

- OBE Official Announcement, 16 June 2012. Issued from St James's Palace, London, *The London Gazette*.
- Queen Elizabeth II's quote, Sir Mahesh Patel Investiture, 8 June 2022, British Ceremonial Arts Limited.

Chapter 12

- CPL Foundation, www.cplfoundation.com.pg
- 'Programme encourages women in business', *The National*, 9 March 2015, www.thenational.com.pg/programme-encourages-women-in-business/.
- Oprah Winfrey Leadership Academy for Girls, www.owlag.co.za
- Arnold Schwarzenegger, *Be Useful: Seven Tools for Life* (Penguin Press, 2023).
- Mother Teresa of Calcutta, *A Gift for God* (Harper & Row, 1975).

Chapter 13

- 'CPL gets K10 million fire insurance settlement', 31 July 2017, *The National*, www.thenational.com.pg/cpl-gets-k10mil-insurance/.

Chapter 14

- Knight description, www.wikipedia.org/wiki/Knight & www.gov.uk/honours/types-of-honours-and-awards
- Officer of the Most Excellent Order of the British Empire, www.wikipedia.org/wiki/Order_of_the_British_Empire
- Behind the scenes: Investitures, www.royal.uk/behind-the-scenes-investitures
- Knight Bachelor official announcement (10 October 2020) was issued from St James's Palace, London, *The London Gazette*
- Kava ceremony, www.royaldavuifiji.com/the-traditional-fijian-kava-ceremony

NOTES

- Windsor Castle, www.rct.uk/visit/windsor-castle
- Rob Harris, 'Queen withdraws from speech to parliament for first time in 59 years', *The Sydney Morning Herald*, 10 May 2022, www.smh.com.au/world/europe/queen-withdraws-from-speech-to-parliament-for-first-time-in-59-years-20220510-p5ajw0.html.
- Prince Charles quote, Sir Mahesh Patel Investiture (8 June 2022), British Ceremonial Arts Limited
- Knights Bachelor Insignia, www.wikipedia.org/wiki/File:Knights_Bachelor_Insignia.png
- Knight Bachelor celebration speech quotes obtained from video supplied by Patel family
- George Bowden, Marie Jackson and Sean Coughlan, 'Queen Elizabeth II has died', BBC, 9 September 2022, www.bbc.com/news/uk-61585886.

Chapter 15

- CPL Group, www.cpl.com.pg
- Warren Buffet quote, www.intelligentim.com/from-the-desk-of-warren-buffet
- Newworld Limited, www.newworld.com.fj

Chapter 16

- Adeshola Ore, 'Meet the business woman behind Papua New Guinea's first co-working space', *BusinessAdvantagePNG*, 3 June 2019, www.businessadvantagepng.com/meet-the-business-woman-behind-papua-new-guineas-first-co-working-space/.

Chapter 17

- Sandra Diaz-Twine quotes from exclusive interview (online) with author
- Telikom Limited, www.telikom.com.pg

Chapter 18

- Abbir Dib, 'Is There a Right Way to Ask "Where Are You From"?', 31 May 2022, *Sydney Morning Herald*, www.smh.com.au/lifestyle/life-and-relationships/is-there-a-right-way-to-ask-where-are-you-from-20220526-p5aou3.html.
- Ganges, www.wikipedia.org/wiki/Ganges

Chapter 19

- 'Video: Steve Jobs one-on-one, the '95 interview', Computerworld Information Technology Awards Foundation, www.computerworld.com/article/1534762/video-steve-jobs-one-on-one-the-95-interview.html

Chapter 20

- National Parliament House, Papua New Guinea, www.parliament.gov.pg/about/parliament
- Pride of PNG Awards speeches transcribed in person by the author
- Sir Bob Bofeng Dadae, governor-general of Papua New Guinea, www.wikipedia.org/wiki/Bob_Dadae
- CPL Group management convention speeches transcribed in person by the author
- CPL Group annual staff dinner speeches transcribed in person by the author
- BNG Trading Company Group, www.bngtrading.com.pg
- Hanuabada, www.wikipedia.org/wiki/Hanuabada

Chapter 21

- *Sliding Doors,* directed by Peter Howitt (Los Angeles: Miramax, 1998), www.imdb.com/title/tt0120148/

- 'Errol Flynn: The Rabaul Years', Rabaul Historical Society, www.pngattitude.com/2020/04/errol-flynn-the-rabaul-years.html.

Epilogue

- Australia-Papua New Guinea Annual Leaders' Dialogue, 8 February 2024, www.pm.gov.au/media/australia-papua-new-guinea-annual-leaders-dialogue
- Forum for India, Pacific Islands Cooperation, www.fipic.ficci.in
- Ladakh, www.wikipedia.org/wiki/Ladakh
- Sir Richard Branson, www.virgin.com/branson-family/richard-branson
- Necker Island, www.virginlimitededition.com/necker-island
- 'Sir Mahesh: Our Darkest Day', 11 January 2024, *The National*, www.thenational.com.pg/sir-mahesh-our-darkest-day
- Papua New Guinean unrest (2024), www.wikipedia.org/wiki/2024_Papua_New_Guinean_unrest

HarperCollins *Publishers* India

At HarperCollins India, we believe in telling the best stories and finding the widest readership for our books in every format possible. We started publishing in 1992; a great deal has changed since then, but what has remained constant is the passion with which our authors write their books, the love with which readers receive them, and the sheer joy and excitement that we as publishers feel in being a part of the publishing process.

Over the years, we've had the pleasure of publishing some of the finest writing from the subcontinent and around the world, including several award-winning titles and some of the biggest bestsellers in India's publishing history. But nothing has meant more to us than the fact that millions of people have read the books we published, and that somewhere, a book of ours might have made a difference.

As we look to the future, we go back to that one word— a word which has been a driving force for us all these years.

Read.